AF583074

Dancing in Their Light

Dancing in Their Light

A Daughter's Unfinished Memoir

Debbie Chinn

Strange Fate Publications
2022

www.debbiechinn.com

Published by Strange Fate Publishing
San Francisco, CA

ISBN: 978-0-578-35599-3

Book designed and produced by Lucky Valley Press
Jacksonville, Oregon www.luckyvalleypress.com

Photos of the author on the front cover and page 272: Ben Krantz Studios

Map of China, page 1: based on darios/123rf.com

Tsingtao image, page 6: arcor/123rf.com

Long Island map, page 55: based on Rainer Lesniewski/shutterstock.com

Printed on acid-free paper

CONTENTS

Part Four: Growing Up

Part Five: Seismic Shift

Part Six: The Sunset Years

Epilogue: Moving Into the Light

INTRODUCTION

Growing up in a restaurant and nightclub, selling cigarettes at the age of three, working as a bartender's helper at the age of six, and spending my weekends performing as a hula dancer during my teenage years are naturally good fodder for a memoir. There aren't many people whose childhood included learning how to walk on fire and dancing with sharp knives.

I was reminded of all this when I rediscovered Dad's eight-page memoir about the history of our family business, the House of Mah Jong Restaurant, which rose to great acclaim during its lifespan in Syosset, New York in the 1960s and 70s. I scanned through his memoir many times after he finished it in 2002 and thought nothing of it until, on a whim, I shared some old photos of Mah Jong on social media; specifically on various Facebook affinity group pages associated with my hometown. Over 400 posts and conversations poured in, mostly from people I never knew, with stories and remembrances of Mah Jong. As I read through the comments and conversations, I was stunned that people could recall specific details about their Mah Jong experience, including sensory memories of what they ate, what it was like to celebrate a special occasion there, the names of the bartender and waiters, my young restaurant-worker outfits, and Mah Jong's sui generis decor. They remembered the toys purchased at the gift shop saved and passed along to their grandchildren, the nostalgia of life before the onslaught of technology, and they fondly remembered my parents' warm hospitality.

I responded by offering some behind-the-scenes personal stories of growing up at Mah Jong. I received requests to send more stories and to keep uploading photos. It was nearly insatiable. Then someone posted, "Debbie, PLEASE, you have to write a book about your life and include all of this!" More comments followed in full agreement: this needed to move into a different medium.

Encouraged by these responses, I set forth to someday write a book on Mah Jong's distinct personality and a bygone era, when dining out together as a family was a weekly tradition, when restaurants had private phone booths and coat check rooms, when men wore hats, women wore gloves, and children had manners, as well as a golden age of Polynesian floor shows ubiquitous in the 1960s and 70s.

How did a simple Chinese restaurant like ours grow to be so ingrained in people's memories throughout all these years? What was it about Mah Jong that engendered decades of customer loyalty? What was unique about our family's business approach that is missing in today's workplace?

A book about our family restaurant is incomplete without the story of my parents and our family elders, whose lives were uniquely chiseled by the effects of war, starvation, diseases, tragic loss, mystery, luck, and divine opportunities. Considering these circumstances, it is remarkable that my parents persevered, and that Mah Jong ever got off the ground in the first place.

After the deaths of my mother and father, both joyful storytellers and always eager to launch into a tale about the "old days," I began to seek ways to document their stories and those of my family elders, which I envisioned would be a preamble in my book about Mah Jong.

I embarked on an oral history project with Mom's younger sister, Daisy, who had an illustrious 17-year career as a Chinese language and history teacher at Yale University. From 2009–2019, I met with Daisy at her home in Irvine, California for our semi-annual storytelling weekends. As a teacher, Daisy encouraged me to study maps of China and to read books by some of her favorite authors, including historian Jonathan Spence, journalist Richard Bernstein, and my Uncle Paul Chih-Meng, whose book *A Sixty-Year Search* is considered by Daisy to be an exceptional historical resource. Sitting at her small kitchen table, I took notes as she told stories about our family elders and her childhood memories. We looked through dog-eared copies of our family tree and faded photographs. With each return visit, I brought a stack of old family photos from Mom's collection so Daisy could help identify them. We'd take a break for a simple lunch of boiled dumplings or leftover Chinese food from the night before and play a couple of rounds of Rummikub before resuming our conversations about family members and Daisy's remembrances. Even though she eventually struggled with short-term memory, her ability to recall details from her childhood and adult years were astonishingly acute.

My weekends with Daisy piqued my curiosity to dig into my parents' steamer trunk, used when they left China to come to the United States in 1947. I was sentimentally attached to that trunk which represented an escape from their homeland with their most-prized possessions. I repurposed it to store items *I* valued, including family memorabilia and letters Mom and her siblings wrote to me throughout my life. I re-read the letters and, with the temperance of my middle age, grasped a clearer understanding of the meaning of their words in context with Daisy's information.

Then, a resurgence of anti-immigration vitriol surfaced in 2017. National discourse accelerated towards the building of walls and the deportation and detention of immigrant families and children. The COVID-19 pandemic, referred to as the "Kung Flu Virus" and "the Chinese Virus" by Donald Trump, fueled the rise of vulgar racial slurs and dangerous stereotypes of the Chinese. I watched news reports of Asians—particularly the elderly, women, and the young—systematically targeted, beaten, and killed on the streets of America with alarming frequency.

I began to believe we were on the precipice of another dangerous chapter in U.S. history and the possible return of the Chinese Exclusion Act or new congressional acts designed to ban immigrants, especially those of color, from coming into the United States.

With a sense of urgency, I was jolted into action on this book. I shifted the balance to highlight more of the stories of my own family of Chinese immigrants who emigrated to the United States, bringing with them specialized skills, connections, and a spirit of invention, all of which greatly contributed to this country's economic growth and reputation in the fields of science, engineering, medicine, nursing, research, aerospace, higher education, cultural diplomacy, artistic heritage, and culinary hospitality during the 20th century.

My family played a sizable role in advancing humanitarian endeavors. I want to tell their stories so we remember an era not that long ago when the United States and China enjoyed a cordial bicultural relationship. The Chinese people weren't the enemy then and we are not the enemy now.

My research unearthed stories of unimaginable horror and tragedy that befell our family, much of which I never knew. In equal measure, I discovered how good fortune and chance opportunities softened the coarse edges of misfortune and smoothed the way for better chapters.

This is by no means an authoritative history about China and the United States. This memoir is a compilation of inspiring and unfathomable stories woven together with archival family letters and papers, interviews with family, friends, and colleagues, my 10-year research work with my Aunt Daisy, and the assistance of many experts who provided key divining rods to additional layers of my family's broad impact. I have focused on just one slender portion of my family tree. Omission of other family members is certainly not intentional.

And so, I give you my memoir which encompasses the influences of my elders, all the tasty morsels of my restaurant days, and how my own life was shaped by strange confluences of fate.

Successes, struggles, and failures at survival are a strong family theme—and that includes my own experiences. Therefore, for the first time, I am publicly disclosing details of a significant episode that punctured my childhood innocence and altered the course of my life, but not without a persistent intent to end it when I was a young teenager. Suicide was also a family theme. Steadily finding the conviction to move through my trauma, which continues into my adulthood, underscores my inheritance of a resolve to survive and thrive.

The guiding hands of my ancestors and elders have escorted us through the fires of fate, and me towards progressive learning voyages for which I am deeply grateful. It is an honor to illuminate their legacy and to share some of our adventures with you.

Note: I often indicate two spelling versions when referencing Chinese cities. The Wade-Giles spelling is used for episodes which occurred prior to the Communist takeover of China. After 1949, I refer to the Pinyin spelling. For example, Peking/Beijing is to denote both the Wade-Giles and Pinyin reference to that city.

Any factual errors you might find throughout this memoir are mine.

PROLOGUE

The Huilan Pagoda at the end of Zhanqiao Pier, Tsingtao China, recognizable on the labels of Tsingtao Beer

THE BACKDROP OF DISCOVERY

Throughout much of history, attempts to develop and spread Christianity in China were unsuccessful. From the 7th Century (Persian Nestorian monks) to the 12th Century (Catholic Franciscans) to the 16th Century (Jesuits), Christianity failed to take root in China due to anti-foreign sentiment.[a]

However, a successful Christian development was attributable to Robert Morrison, who arrived in China in the 19th century to introduce a Protestant missionary presence.[b]

The number of Protestant missionaries in China increased after the First and Second Opium Wars when China was defeated twice: by Great Britain in the First Opium War (1839-1842) and by Great Britain and France in the Second Opium War (1856-1860). These defeats resulted in the Treaty of Nanking in 1842, granting Protestant missionaries the right to establish residencies and businesses in key coastal cities of China.

It is against this backdrop that I learned how important the missionaries were for the creation and survival of my family.

Plus, I discovered that my maternal family surname is Hartwell.

DEDICATION

"Always look for a sign.
When there is a coincidence, that is me."

Dedicated with love to my mother, Nellie Kwoh Chinn,
who encouraged me to step into my own light and
who continues to guide me towards confluences of fate.
This is her story, as well as mine.

– PART ONE –

Beginnings

Map of China

Jesse Boardman Hartwell, Jr. (Southern Baptist Historical Library and Archives)

Mary Hartwell (seated, second from right), Yu Jung Kwoh (seated 2nd from left), with their three sons behind them, l-r Big Center, my grandfather Frank, Paul Ernest, circa 1906 (Author's collection)

CHAPTER 1

IT BEGAN WITH THE BAPTIST MISSIONARIES

My maternal great grandmother, born around 1850, was a young child when she was discovered in a church lying next to her deceased mother. They were fleeing the Taiping Rebellion (1851–1864) in Peking, China, making their way to Shanghai.

The child was very much alive and strong enough to make a sound, catching the attention of an American missionary stationed near the church. The missionary, Jesse Boardman Hartwell, Jr., rescued my great-grandmother and brought her to his local missionary. He adopted her and named her Mary Hartwell. Mary learned to speak English while adapting to the ways of the Baptist missionary lifestyle. Growing up with Jesse Hartwell, his wife, Eliza, and their family—traveling between Shanghai and the United States—Mary was steeped in the influences of the Western world, undeniably more "Western" than "Eastern" during her formative years.

Jesse Boardman Hartwell, Jr. (1835–1912) graduated from Furman University, Greenville, S.C. in 1855 at the age of 20, then completed a year of instruction in Furman's Theological Institution. His primary desire: to travel to China to share the message of Salvation with the people. However, he needed to earn funds and relieve his father of the debt for his education, so he served as professor of Mathematics and Natural Sciences at Mt. Lebanon University for one year. During this time, Secretary Taylor of the Board of Foreign Missions of the Southern Baptist Convention learned of Jesse's wish to enlighten the Chinese and wrote to encourage him to send an application to the Board. He eventually invited him to Richmond, Virginia to be appointed as a missionary. Upon his official ordination on May 2, 1858, Jesse Boardman Hartwell, Jr. was formally appointed by the Board for China.

After his appointment, Jesse traveled to Macon, Georgia to raise funds for foreign missions. There he met 21-year-old, Eliza Holzendorf Jewett, also called by God to become a missionary to foreign lands. They married September 29, 1858 and shortly thereafter proceeded to China where they welcomed their first son in 1860.[1]

In October of 1862, Jesse helped organize the first Protestant church in China north of Shanghai. In Henan, China, he and Eliza established Dengzhou's North Street Baptist Church in 1869. Within the same year, Eliza started a school for girls and a second Baptist church was formed. While the mission grew, so did their family. The couple welcomed four more children, Carrie (1861–1864), Ellen Edwards "Nellie" (September 1863), and twins, John Holzendorf and Anna B (March 1870). After Eliza died in June of 1870, Jesse married Eliza's sister, Julia, in 1871; they had no children together. Julia died December 3, 1879 in San Francisco, California.[2]

In 1881, Jesse married Charlotte E. Norris while working among the Chinese in San Francisco, California. He and Charlotte had three children—Charlotte, Charles, and Janie. Four of Hartwell's children, Nellie, Anna, Lottie, and Charles, also worked in China missions. After living in China for ten years, Charlotte died in 1903.

During the Taiping Rebellion Jesse Hartwell devoted himself to the Chinese people: "At one time for nearly six weeks he had on his premises one hundred refugees, to whom he acted as surgeon, nurse, and preacher. Dangers beset him and his; more than once he was forced to put himself under the protection of the United States Consul, and on one occasion he and his family were forced to flee on horseback to save their lives."[3]

Jesse Boardman Hartwell, Jr., the man who started my family, died in 1912 in Chefoo (now known as Yantai), China.

In China, circa the late 1870s, Mary Hartwell married Yu Jung Kwoh. They had three sons: Feng Han, born in 1881, also known as "Big Center." The second oldest son, Feng Chow, was born in 1883 and given the English name of Paul Ernest. Paul became a successful businessman for Shell Oil in Tsingtao.

The youngest son was born in 1889. His name was Feng Shu, or Frank, my grandfather. Growing up, the three Kwoh sons spoke fluent English due to their mother's upbringing. Uncle "Big Center" became an executive for the Chinese railroad company. He had one son (Harry) and three daughters (Flora, Huan You, and Naomi).

Paul Ernest's wife, Lillian Chao, could not bear children. At the time of his marriage to Lillian, he had a concubine with whom he had one son.

Frank married Kate Li Cheng (born in 1890). Kate came of age just after foot binding was banned in 1912 and was among the first generation of young girls not forced to bind their feet. Frank was born in the Year of the Ox and Kate in the Year of the Tiger. According to the Chinese horoscope, the Ox and the Tiger are not particularly compatible. In general, someone born in the Year of the Ox is steady and dependable. Born in the Year of the Tiger, one is considered to be intense and prone to outbursts. Upon learning more about my grandparents and how they moved through their lives, I find these animal signs for Frank and Kate just the opposite. Frank seemed intent on playing by his own rules and Kate was the sturdy ballast to the Kwoh family.

Over 13 years, Frank and Kate had eight children, all given both English and Chinese names: twins Norris (unknown) and Mamie (Huan Wei, 1914), Bertha (Huan Shou, 1916), Teddy (Huan Tsing, 1918), Grace (Huan Jung, 1920), my mother, Nellie (Huan Ying, 1923), Daisy (Huan Hsing, 1925), and Edie (Huan Chun, 1927). Norris died in childbirth, leaving Teddy the only boy among the remaining seven siblings.

After Grace was born, Frank and Kate had four children with a fifth on the way. Frank made a deal with Paul Ernest to give him the next newborn, since Frank and Kate already had a large brood. It is said that when the fifth child (my mother Nellie) was born, she was "so cute and pretty"—lore accentuated and embellished by my mother throughout her life, verifying that she was, indeed, an adorable baby. How could Frank possibly give up that irresistible child? Even though the prevailing attitude in China was that boys were more valuable than girls, Frank considered his girls of equal stature. And so it was that Frank changed his mind and called off the deal, adding my mother to his growing family.

Paul Ernest and Lillian eventually adopted a daughter, Dora, born in 1922, a year older than my mother. Dora and Mom were inseparable playmates and remained close into their adult senior years.

Frank, Kate, and the children moved from Peking to Tsingtao around 1932. Tsingtao, situated on the Yellow Sea coast of Shandong Province, was a prime naval defense base. In 1897 Germany took control of Tsingtao in response to the murder of two German missionaries and demanded a 99-year lease on the Yellow Seaport.[4] The Germans used Tsingtao as a base for their Far East Squadron during 1898–1914 to control operations throughout the Pacific. It was here that the Germans built a city infrastructure, including shipyards and railroads. Homesick for their beer, Germans established a brewery in 1903, the origins of Tsingtao beer.

When Frank was in his 40s he managed the personnel for the Jiao Ji Railroad in Tsingtao. He, Kate, and the children had settled in a six-unit apartment building owned by Germans on Hunan Road, a block from the train station.

To accommodate their growing family, Frank and Kate moved into a modest two-story house with a small yard on 65 Gwangxi Road, with four rooms on each floor; a combination of bedrooms, storage, and eating areas.

The backyard was seldom used except by the neighbors who situated their outdoor toilet there. Frank and Kate's house was considered upscale, with indoor toilets and a family bathroom.

"Big Center" lived on the first floor with his family. Frank and Kate lived on the second floor. There were so many young girls in Frank and Kate's family that their male servant lived with "Big Center" and his family on the first floor. Kate and the servant prepared each day's menu for the children and the servant handled all the cooking and cleaning.

Kate worked for the nearby Protestant church making hand cream which was sold to the locals. Kate donated all proceeds back to the church. The Kwoh siblings attest that their mother was a devoutly religious woman who believed we all have the same god to honor and serve with humility. She found comfort and strength in quietly reading her Bible every day. She maintained her fealty to Frank, keeping the household running while he was at work and traveling. This deep sense of piety was instilled in the Kwoh siblings who kept prayer at the center of their lives and relied on their faith as adults.

The Kwoh household was filled with music, singing, poetry recitation, storytelling, dancing, and laughter. The Kwoh children and their parents sang church hymns and American folk songs. Bertha, Grace, and Daisy played the piano. Mom played the violin.

Tsingtao bottle label

Their home on Gwangxi Road was less than a five-minute walk to the Yellow Sea; the younger Kwoh siblings spent their time playing by the Pier and the iconic landmark, the Huilan Pagoda, built in the 1800s. (*See page xi.*) The image of this Pagoda is featured on the cans and bottles of Tsingtao beer as an homage to the German and British brewers who founded the brewery.

My mother had a natural talent for acting and was cast in many of the school plays in elementary school. Daisy recalls that Mom was extremely personable, had natural stage presence, and got all the good parts. Mom was also a tomboy and loved to roughhouse with brother Teddy. Her tough scrappiness was a hallmark characteristic throughout her life. The Kwoh siblings remember their early childhood years with fondness. Unfortunately, those years were brief.

Kate and Frank Kwoh flanked by their children (l-r) my mother Nellie, Bertha, Mamie, Teddy, Grace, Daisy. In the middle is Edie.

Back row, center, Frank Kwoh. His wife, Kate Li, is in front of him. And in front of Kate is her mother (my other great-grandmother). The others are Kate's brother (back row, left) and his wife, and Kate's sister and her husband. This picture was taken in China before the Japanese occupation of 1937 when the Kwoh and Li families were still intact. circa late 1920s/1930.

CHAPTER 2

1937 ANNUS HORRIBILIS

Frank and Kate's children all remember exactly where they were on July 7, 1937, when tensions between China and Japan intensified at the Marco Polo Bridge near Peking. The Chinese—fortified by a growing sense of nationalism against Japanese domination of their country—refused to yield. The Japanese, in turn, hastened efforts to bring China to submission.

In 1937, Nanjing (today Nanking), located 300 miles north of Tsingtao, was the capital of China. Chiang Kai-Shek, head of the Nationalist government, moved the capital inland to Sichuan to establish the war capital of Chungking/Chongqing, thus evading the growing Japanese invasion from the coast.

On December 13, 1937, the Japanese invaded China in what is known as the Nanjing Massacre or the Rape of Nanjing.[5] The invasion lasted six weeks but the emotional, psychological, and physical impact on Frank and Kate was felt during their entire lifetimes, especially among their children.

GRACE

Frank and Kate's fourth child, Grace, in a high school operated by American nuns, was the first to be affected by the Japanese occupation of China. One day a nun asked her to run to the local store for a spool of thread for the classroom. While Grace was off the high school grounds, she witnessed a Japanese soldier shoot a Chinese civilian point blank. She ran back to the school to tell the nuns.

The nuns contacted the local United States Consulate office to find a way for Grace to escape to America. The Consulate, in turn, contacted Frank to say it was not safe for Grace to remain in China; the Japanese would surely track her down as the sole witness to the murder and kill her before she could identify the soldier. Grace needed to leave China immediately. But how and where?

The nuns and divine intervention provided solutions. Through a connection with one of the nuns, they identified a sister organization in the United States that accepted Grace immediately: the St. Joseph Mercy Hospital School of Nursing in Aurora, Illinois. The nuns wanted to place

Grace on a ship headed to America from the port of Tsingtao. The ship was completely full, but at the last minute a young girl failed to show up to claim her spot. The nuns spoke to the captain, described the dire circumstances, and Grace was accepted into that last spot.

Daisy recalls the sadness and sorrow when the Kwoh family gathered in Tsingtao to say goodbye to Grace. When she headed to Hong Kong to board the *SS President McKinley* bound for Seattle, Washington, no one knew when or if they would see each other again. Grace arrived in the United States on November 10, 1937. She was 17 years old.

FAMILY FRAGMENTATION

The following year, Frank borrowed money from eldest brother "Big Center" to send Mamie and Bertha, the two eldest sisters, to America to finish their studies.

Mamie was engaged to Shih-Chun Wang (known as S.C.). Born in Tientsen/Tianjin, China he received his Bachelor of Science degree from Yenching University, a post-graduate college of Peking University. He also received his graduate degree from Peking Union Medical College and in 1937 was awarded a Fellowship from the Rockefeller Foundation to pursue graduate studies at the Institute of Neurology at Northwestern University in Illinois. This afforded a way for Mamie to leave China. Mamie boarded the *SS Empress,* Nov 15, 1938, bound for Seattle, Washington.

At the age of 22, Bertha concluded her studies at Yenching University and departed Shanghai on Aug 20, 1938. She arrived in the Port of Seattle on September 6, 1938, destination: Sioux City, Iowa where she enrolled at Briar Cliff College, a Catholic School for women.

By the fall of 1938, the Japanese were advancing towards Changsha. Chiang Kai-Shek ordered his Nationalist army to follow a scorched-earth policy; burn Changsha to the ground if the Japanese succeeded in capturing the city. The Japanese had already invaded Shanghai on the east, Hankou to the north, and Canton to the south. Along the way they slaughtered civilians, pillaged the food supplies, raped women and girls, and captured Chinese soldiers and old men to use for bayonet practice.[6]

Teddy was 18 years old and attending Shandong University in Tsingtao. Many university students, including Teddy, were moving expensive laboratory and scientific equipment inland to prevent it from falling into Japanese hands. The family feared the Japanese might capture Teddy and other young Chinese boys to use for medical experiments. Frank knew Teddy should escape from Tsingtao, a major seaport and vulnerable to occupation.

Frank didn't tell his children that Teddy would be sent inland. It needed to be kept a secret. As Daisy recalls, "We were told to burn anything that could be perceived as anti-Japanese in case the Japanese soldiers arrived at our house." Mom, Edie, and Daisy used their bathtub (with a stove to warm the water) to burn all their books, periodicals, family letters, photographs, poems, and music. The fire purge was so relentless, the chimney broke down.

Teddy was unable to communicate with his family for eight long years and they feared that attempts to write or wire him would be intercepted by the Japanese, putting him in danger.

This left Mom, Daisy, Edie, and their mother, Kate, at their home in Tsingtao. However, their home was not safe; Frank and his brothers were prominent businessmen and easy targets for the Japanese. St. Joseph High School in Tsingtao, where Mom, Daisy, and Edie attended, served as a sanctuary for Kate and the girls during the Japanese invasion. The nuns allowed them to temporarily live there for protection.

Frank was no longer living with his wife and children. Several years earlier, he began an affair with a young high school classmate of my mother's named Mary. The affair was a shock and an embarrassment to Frank's children, especially to Mom, who adored her father. Frank chose to live with Mary, with whom he had a son. Frank was unable to find work in Tsingtao; the Japanese, who occupied most of the area by this point, only hired Chinese who declared their allegiance to the Japanese. Refusing to do so, Frank and his concubine Mary moved to Peking where he found a job teaching high school students.

The Sino-Japanese War lasted from 1937–1945. During those eight years, Mom, Daisy, Edie and their mother Kate subsisted on a diet of potatoes and cabbage, all they could afford. Cooking oil was rationed and expensive, so Mom learned how to stir fry potatoes using water. Daisy might make a meal of boiled potatoes the following week. When it was Edie's turn, she stir-fried cabbage in water. The sisters tried to grow vegetables but the ground was tough and yielded little growth. Daisy recalled the sisters searching for seeds to plant and after much coaxing of the hard soil, early signs of turnips gave them hope. However, nearly everyone in their region was starving. It was common for people to steal from visible gardens. The sisters eventually gave up.

The sisters were well-educated and among the few lucky ones to find jobs. Mom and Edie worked at a bank while Daisy taught first grade reading and gave singing lessons at a school. The money they earned was still not enough to buy food. The most they could afford was sub-standard rice or millet deliberately mixed with sand.

This was a time of profound despair for the Kwoh sisters. The family had been torn apart. The routine of going to school was deemed dangerous, and the childhood joys of playing with classmates came to a swift end. Venturing out of the school confines was extremely perilous; they felt like refugees at St. Joseph's High School, not knowing how long the school could safely harbor them.

Adding to the misery, in the 5th grade Daisy developed tuberculosis (TB) for which there was no known cure. TB was a deadly and highly contagious disease and noted for its easily transmitted bacterial infection of the lungs. Daisy was merely advised by the doctors to avoid strenuous activity. Kate suffered from hypoglycemia (low blood sugar) and hypocalcemia, a calcium deficiency. The latter caused her muscles to suddenly and frequently spasm and tense up. There was no available medication or treatment. She was in constant pain and could barely walk alone.

In 1938, St. Joseph's High School became a possible target for Japanese; there were concerns that young girls in the school might be captured and raped. Frank's middle brother Paul Ernest took Kate, Mom, Daisy, and Edie into his home, a risky move. Daisy recalls constant anxiety and worry, wondering if their home would be invaded. Paul Ernest removed all listings of the Kwoh name from the outside of their homes. Everything came to a standstill and to survive, they had to hide and keep a low profile. Nothing could be delivered, anyway. There was no reason to announce the Kwoh name on the front door.

Daisy wrote to me in 2003, revealing how the nightmares of the Japanese occupation continued to torment her. I had sent her a recording of one of her favorite piano pieces: Chopin's "Fantaisie-Impromptu" (op. 66). She wrote, "This piece always gives me the blues and yet I always die [sic] to listen to it whenever I can. You see, Debbie, because of the Japanese invasion of China, our family broke up. When a nun in our school was visiting the United States, she saw Auntie Bertha who was attending college in Iowa. Auntie Bertha's college was kind enough to let her make a recording of this Chopin piece to bring back to us. When the nun returned to China, she gave us this 78-rpm record. We tried to play it on an old gramophone (winding by hand), but we couldn't afford to buy a steel needle. Finally, we played it with a needle made of bamboo splinters. Toward the end of the recording, we heard Auntie Bertha's sad voice saying, 'Dear Papa and Mama and little sisters, I miss you very much and I hope to see you soon.' Our family was living on two sides of the ocean with no way to communicate. Debbie, sometimes I wish I had no memory because that period is too sad to remember."

Mom often spoke about the hardships and sadness during this period of her life. When the Japanese began their occupation of China, she was 14, the oldest child left behind when the other siblings left the country and Teddy escaped inland. She felt responsible to care for Daisy and Edie (then 12 and 10 years old) as well as her fragile mother. When recounting this era, I asked Mom how she managed to get through each day. She said the sisters found solace in singing to each other and recalling memories of their earlier and happier years. They found strength in their prayers, their imaginations, and the encouragement of the nuns and each other.

CHAPTER 3

JAPANESE SURRENDER

With the formal surrender by Emperor Hirohito to General Douglas MacArthur in 1945, all Japanese residents had to leave China. In Manchuko (Manchuria), the Japanese army evacuated the area, cutting telephone lines and blowing up the bridges to sever the delivery of provisions.[7] When it appeared safe for Teddy to return to Tsingtao, he made his way back home, still apprehensive about the possible interception of cables or letters.

As Daisy recalls, when Teddy showed up at the house unannounced he did not see his family's name on the gate. Frank and his concubine Mary had since gone to Peking. Teddy's first thought was that his father was dead. Teddy went to call on "Big Center," creating jubilant pandemonium since no one ever expected to see Teddy alive.

Teddy left China for the United States in April 1947 with a scholarship to Lehigh University in Pennsylvania where he eventually received his master's degree in engineering.

Upon his graduation Teddy was hired by the China Institute in New York—a job secured for him by his brother-in-law, Paul Meng (Bertha's husband)—and began to raise a family in New York City.

By now, Mom had concluded six years of study at St. Joseph High School and left Tsingtao to continue at Fu Jen Catholic University in Peking.[8] She studied Home Economics, developing her lifelong passion for sewing, cooking, and crafts.

CHAPTER 4

DAD - PAPER SON

Peter Chinn was born in Canton (now Guangzhou) just as the final dynasty of China came to an end. There are no birth records for him, but he believed he was born on October 15, 1915.

The Qing Dynasty, established by the Manchus in 1636, ended with the Chinese Revolution of 1911 and the birth of the Republic of China under the leadership of Sun Yat Sen, who served as the Republic's first President. This forced the abdication of China's last emperor, six-year-old Puyi, in 1912.

In 1930, the political instability of a fledgling Chinese government convinced Dad's mother to send him to the United States. Dad was put on a boat heading for the Port of Seattle with instructions to get to his brother, Eddie in Buffalo, New York. Dad was alone. He was 15 years old.

Entrance into the United States was not guaranteed due to the passage of the Chinese Exclusion Act of 1882, legislation enacted by Congress and signed into law by President Chester A. Arthur. This was in response to the backlash against Chinese immigrants accused of taking jobs away from white workers in United States during the Gold Rush era. At present, it is the only congressional act of the United States that specifically mentions the exclusion of a race by name.

The Pacific Railway Act of 1862 created initiatives to build the first transcontinental railroad which established the Central Pacific Railroad Company. The railroad barons known as the "Big Four"—Leland Stanford, Mark Hopkins, Collis Huntington, and Charles Crocker—were awarded an exclusive contract to extend the railroads eastward from Sacramento, California. The Union Pacific Railroad was offered the contract to build westward from Omaha, Nebraska. Chinese workers provided cheap and plentiful labor, especially to blast through the Sierra Nevada mountains, the range along the eastern edge of California, made of nearly impenetrable granite. Crocker theorized that if Chinese ingenuity could build the Great Wall of China, they were the people to build a railroad infrastructure.[9]

Chinese workers proved to be more efficient and cheaper than Irish, English, German, and Italian laborers. The more Chinese workers were hired, the more jobs taken from their white counterparts. The anti-Chinese sentiment grew after the Transcontinental Railroad was finished in 1869, when the Chinese workers were no longer needed and employment opportunities dried up. In California, a 1879 ballot reflected that 99% of voters were against Chinese migration into the United States.[10] Within three years, the Chinese Exclusion Act of 1882 prevented Chinese from entering the United States and from becoming naturalized citizens. A subsequent law in 1888, the Scott Act, ensured that any Chinese living in America who traveled outside the U.S. was banned from re-entering. Approximately 20,000 Chinese were stranded after being promised an exemption from the Exclusion Act.

By the time Dad left China, the Chinese Exclusion Act had been made permanent by yet another law, the 1902 Geary Act, which affirmed that Chinese immigration into the United States was illegal. Chinese now had to produce more documentation of their reasons for living in this country, such as a Certificate of Residence. Chinese who could not substantiate their documentation were subjected to deportation or detention.

Meanwhile, many Chinese workers brought to the United States by the railroad barons began to raise families in the U.S and further claimed citizenship for "offspring" in China. The "Paper Son" underground system was born; numerous false paper documents were created, alleging that boys entering the United States from China were the sons of Chinese workers living in the United States, using brokers as middlemen.

Dad knowingly entered the U.S. illegally and at great risk. His brother, Eddie, arranged for intermediaries to meet Dad when he arrived in Seattle, Washington. As arranged, Dad was Eddie's registered "Paper Son." Before he disembarked from the boat at Seattle, he was instructed to listen for Chinese men on the dock shouting out the names of the Chinese villages of their "sons." When he heard his village of Canton shouted out, Dad made his way to the man, who gave him the name of Peter on his "Paper Son" document, to replace his Chinese name Bao Ming.

We are not sure if Chinn was Eddie and Dad's original name since the translation from Chinese to English sounds more like "Chun." The Americans interpreted Chun as *Chin*. We believe the extra "n" was added by the Seattle authorities.

Dad said it was to differentiate the Chinese who entered the U.S. via Seattle (Chinn) vs. San Francisco (Chin). Eddie and Dad played it loose with the spelling; sometimes using Chinn, other times, Chin.

Once disembarked in Seattle, Dad made his way by train to Buffalo, New York, to reunite with Eddie. He traveled on the Trans-continental Railroad from Seattle to the end of that line, somewhere in the midwest. He connected to the New York Central line to his final destination: the Buffalo Central Terminal in upstate New York.

Chicago businessman George Pullman had created the "Pullman Porters:" former black slaves who had left the South after the Civil War and during the Reconstruction Era (1865–1877). Pullman hired them to serve the white customers on luxury railcars. By the early 1920s, the Pullman Company was the largest employer of black men in the United States.[11]

The rising anti-Chinese sentiment in the U.S. found a resonant chord with the Pullman Porters, who understood the Chinese plight of racism and persecution. Taken under the porters' wings, Dad was kept hidden from sight and allowed to ride the train across the country. His "job" was sweeping up cigarette butts at the end of the night; he unraveled the butts, took out the small bits of unused tobacco and re-rolled them in new cigarette papers which he and the Porters smoked before going to bed. Through the kindness of the porters, who sheltered and fed him and other young Chinese boys, Dad was able to get from Seattle to Buffalo for free.

Buffalo's early Chinese population immigrated from Southern China. There were just over 100 Chinese living in Buffalo in the 1930s and a small Chinatown formed on Michigan Avenue near Broadway and Williams.[12] Eddie operated a restaurant called Chinn's Chinese Restaurant, at 888 Main Street, likely part of this small quadrant of other Chinese businesses.

Eddie taught Dad the fundamentals of the restaurant business. Despite not knowing English, and possessing only a 5th grade education, Dad attended Buffalo High School. Dad was scrappy and scrawny and one of the smallest boys in his class, determined to get a good education, and he was popular—all traits that carried him into his adult life. His interest in chemistry eventually got him elected President of the high school chemistry club.

By 1933, Dad had saved enough money to enroll at New York University where he majored and received his undergraduate degree in chemistry. News of the Japanese invasion of Nanking reached the students of NYU during his senior year in 1937. Dad, who played the erhu (a Chinese two-stringed fiddle), organized street concert performances by fellow classmates and passed the hat to raise money for a China Relief Fund.

After NYU, Dad enrolled at Harvard Business School as Peter Bao Ming Chin. One of his professors of accounting was Robert S. McNamara, later the Secretary of Defense during the John F. Kennedy and Lyndon Baines Johnson administrations. According to the 1940 Federal Census, Dad was listed as 26 years old; his occupation, waiter at a Chinese restaurant for 26 weeks during the year, with a total earnings of $450.

Dad received his MBA degree from Harvard Business School in 1941.

Dad was one of four Chinese students chosen from American universities to participate in Goodyear Tire and Rubber Company's international training course in Akron, Ohio in 1944.[13] In cooperation with the U.S. State Department, the Committee on Wartime Planning, and financed by the Chinese government, Goodyear had established a training program for young men to learn about hands-on factory production and corporate business as well as broadening their educational opportunities in engineering, research, and management.

The May 24, 1944 edition of Goodyear's employee newspaper, *The Wingfoot Clan*, noted that:

"The Chinese group is especially interesting. Four of these citizens of China are hard at it in many phases of the company's business.... Two South China boys from Canton, Kwantung province—Harvard graduate Peter Chinn and Frank Chan from Baldwin-Wallace College—are acquiring practical knowledge of purchasing and factory cost accounting respectively."[14]

Before graduating from Harvard, Dad became a U.S. citizen, allowing him to enlist in the military to serve his adopted country. He chose the U.S. Marines, was eventually promoted to Captain and was assigned to the World War II Intelligence Corps in the 6th Marine Division to probe the whereabouts of secret supplies of Japanese ammunition. After Japan surrendered to the Allies on Sept 2, 1945, signaling the end of WWII, the 6th Marine Division was sent to Tsingtao to assist with the surrender of Japanese troops occupying parts of China and to help stabilize Chiang Kai-Shek's government.

MOM MEETS DAD

By 1945, Mom had graduated from Fu Jen University in Peking and returned to Tsingtao to reunite with Kate, Daisy, and Edie. She again found work in a bank and life resumed with a short, guarded sense of normalcy.

Dad's close friend in the 6th Division was Choh-Yi Ang (known as Ang) who joined the U.S. Marines in 1946 as a language specialist and

Dad (right) with brother Eddie, circa mid-late 1930s (Author's collection)

Dad (right) with his U.S. Marine buddies. Choh-Yi Ang is in the middle. (Author's collection)

The four Chinese students chosen to participate in Goodyear Tire and Rubber Company's international training course in 1944. Dad is kneeling, lower left.

(Goodyear's employee newspaper, The Wingfoot Clan, *May 24, 1944)*

civilian interpreter. They had occasion to run into the Kwoh sisters in Tsingtao. Their social interactions led to courtships: Dad and Mom, and Ang and Edie.

Dad and Mom were married in Peking on October 27, 1946. Dad wore his Marine dress uniform and Mom was dressed in a white wedding gown. Some of Mom's classmates from Tsingtao reunited in Peking for the occasion. It was wartime and money was scarce, so several of her instrument-playing classmates performed a few pieces during the wedding ceremony.

Because of growing tensions between the Nationalist government (Kuomintang Party), led by Chiang Kai-Shek and the emerging power of the Communist Party, led by Mao Tse-Tung, peace was tenuous. By 1946, a civil war began. The Communist Party's armed forces (the People's Liberation Army) gained power. The Nationalist government was beset with corruption and weak management, eventually eroding public confidence. Mao capitalized on the growing dissension and galvanized a strong grassroots movement.

Wartime prevented Mom and Dad from enjoying a honeymoon. Instead, they returned to Tsingtao where Dad resumed his assignments for the U.S. Marines. Mom returned to work at the bank. On August 18, 1947, their first child was born: Katherine (named after my grandmother, Kate).

Mom and Dad's courtship, China (Author's collection)

Nellie Kwoh in her early 20s in Tsingtao, China (Author's collection)

U.S. Marines Choh-Yi Ang (2nd from left) and Dad with Kwoh sisters Edie and Mom in Tsingtao China (Author's collection)

Mom and Dad's wedding photo, October 27, 1946, Peking (Author's collection)

CHAPTER 5

THE RISE OF COMMUNISM IN CHINA

In a report to the Chinese Communist Party's Central Committee in December 1947, an optimistic Mao observed, "The Chinese people's revolutionary war has now reached a turning point.... The main forces of the People's Liberation Army have carried the fight into the Kuomintang Area....This is a turning point in history."[15]

As a Captain in the U.S. Marines Intelligence Corps, Dad saw the Nationalists losing influence and knew Mao's Communist regime would soon seal the borders. Through his influence and connections within the U.S. Marines, he made arrangements to take Mom, Kathy, Frank, and Kate out of China.

Frank made the choice to stay behind in China with Mary and their young son. This was a tremendous blow to Kate and the Kwoh children, most of whom were in the United States waiting and hoping to reunite. Mom pleaded with him to leave China, but Frank's allegiance had shifted to his new family. In recounting their goodbyes, Mom said Frank's last words to Kate were, "I'll see you in Heaven."

ESCAPE

With little time to spare, Dad arranged immigration and visa paperwork for Mom and Kate in Tsingtao. At the end of 1947, Kate, Dad, Mom, and 3-month-old Kathy departed for Shanghai to board the *SS Marine Adder*, one of the last naval ships leaving China.

The ship's Manifest of Alien Passengers for the United States listed 16 passengers in First Class. Passenger #3 was Katherine Chin, 3 ½ months, occupation: baby. Passenger #4 was Nellie Chin, listed as 25 years of age, occupation: housewife. Passenger #10 was E-Way Kwoh (Kate), age 57, occupation: housewife. The *SS Marine Adder* left Shanghai on December 15, 1947, bound for San Francisco.

On January 8, 1948, the *SS Marine Adder* arrived. The immigration officer admitted everyone except Passengers #3, #4, and #10. The ship manifest indicated they were to be held for questioning.

1	2	3		4		5	6	7	8			
No. on List	HEAD-TAX STATUS (This column for use of Government officials only)	NAME IN FULL		Age		Sex	Married or single	Calling or occupation	Able to—			
		Family name	Given name	Yrs.	Mos.				Read	Read what language [or if exemption claimed, on what ground]	Write	
1	✓105.1	1900-73744-9-404 for E+D. 7/11/48 CHAN	WAH	41		F	S	AMAH	Y	ENGLISH	N	C
2	✓105.1	1300-73743 for E+D. CHAN 9-404 - 7/11/48	YOU	43		F	S	AMAH	Y	ENGLISH	N	C
3	USC	CHIN	KATHARINE dtr.		3½	F	S	BABY				U
4	✓105.1	~~CHIN~~ KWOH	NELLIE moth. wife of CHIN BOW MING	25		F	M	HOUSEWIFE	Y	ENGLISH CHINESE	Y	C
5	U.S.C.	CLEMENTS	EDISON HOWARD	32		M	M					U
6	✓105.1	CLEMENTS Wei	MON LAN	25		F	M	HOUSEWIFE	Y	ENGLISH	Y	C
7	✓105.1	HUANG	MIN SHAN	34		F	S	STUDENT	Y	ENGLISH	Y	C
8	USC	KAO	YORK M.	38		M	M					U
9	✓105.1	~~KAO~~ KWO	ANNA	23		F	M	HOUSEWIFE	Y	ENGLISH	Y	C
10	✓105.1	KWOH	E-WAY moth. of	57		F	M	HOUSEWIFE	Y	CHINESE	Y	C

Detail of the ship manifest, Dec 15, 1947, listing the Kwoh passengers, Kate, Mom, baby Katharine, among those aboard the SS Marine Adder as they escaped Communist China (Author's collection)

Once those entries were clarified, the second immigration officer wrote "permitted as indicated." Dad, Mom, Kate, and baby Kathy disembarked the SS *Marine Adder* to begin a new life in the United States.

Daisy and Edie were left behind in Tsingtao just as the Chinese civil war intensified. They stayed at home and sold everything to survive. In 1948, Edie's husband, Ang, made arrangements with his family in the Philippines for his eventual arrival with Edie and Daisy.

Daisy remembered facing the dilemma: stay in China on her own or, flee? She could not bear the thought of living with her father who had so crudely betrayed the family, nor could she imagine how she'd survive if left in Tsingtao or Peking with her cousins, many of whom faced uncertain futures. Separation was unfathomable.

In early 1949, Ang, Edie, and Daisy left Tsingtao and moved to the Philippines. Daisy felt like a refugee—separated from most of her siblings settled in the United States. She was dependent on Ang and Edie and they were selflessly devoted to taking care of her. Through Ang's connections, Daisy secured a job teaching Chinese to Filipino students. She recalls that it was not a "safe haven;" the Filipinos were jealous of Chinese migrating into the country to take local jobs.

Daisy filed a request on October 7th, 1949, to enter the United States under the Ninth Proviso, a section of the Immigration Act regulating the admission or refusal of persons entering the United States. In Daisy's application it was noted that she disclosed diagnoses of tuberculosis as reasons to come to the United States to seek medical treatment. Her application was approved on October 21, 1949. She arrived in the United States on January 3, 1950.

Edie and Ang left the Philippines on August 28, 1950 aboard the *SS President Cleveland* bound for San Francisco. Ang was 30 years old, Edie was 23. They arrived in San Francisco on September 17, 1950.

Now, with Edie and Ang's immigration to the U.S., all seven Kwoh siblings (Mamie, Bertha, Teddy, Grace, Nellie, Daisy, and Edie) along with their mother, Kate, were on U.S. soil. All were immigrants. Their children, with the exception of my sister Kathy born in China, would become first generation Chinese in the United States.

Young Daisy Kwoh (Author's collection)

Daisy, Ang, and Edie taking refuge in the Philippines, 1949 (Author's collection)

Kwoh women: Standing L-R: Emily Kwoh (Teddy's wife), Grace. Seated l-r: Edie, Bertha, Daisy.

– PART TWO –

MIGRATION

Dad, Mom, Kate, and Kathy as they prepare to board the SS Marine Adder, leaving Shanghai to come to America, December 15, 1947 (Author's collection)

Dad, Mom, and Kathy as they settle into their new life in the United States, San Francisco, 1948 (Author's collection)

Mom, Dad, Kathy and Lowell, San Francisco, California, 1949 (Author's collection)

CHAPTER 6

Peter, Nellie, Kathy and Kate Arrive in San Francisco

When Mom, Dad, Kathy and Kate arrived in San Francisco, they settled in an apartment in Chinatown. Through his connections Dad secured a job managing a Goodyear Tire dealership in San Francisco.

On April 26, 1949, Mom and Dad welcomed a son, Lowell, named after the Massachusetts town Dad grew fond of while a student at Harvard University.

Mom tended to two young toddlers, Kathy and Lowell, at their apartment on Jackson Street, one of the steepest streets in the City. To get their provisions, Mom pushed Lowell in a stroller and walked with Kathy up and down the Chinatown hills. This was an arduous task since Mom's health was compromised by starvation and other hardships during the Japanese occupation of China.

As she negotiated those hills of San Francisco in 1950, she didn't realize her persistent cough and difficulty breathing would be diagnosed as TB.

She unwittingly passed the disease on to Lowell, who died on August 8, 1950 at the age of 15 months.

Lowell was laid to rest in the children's graveyard section at Holy Cross Catholic Cemetery in Colma, California. Mom and Dad could not afford to buy a headstone but they scraped up enough money for a few toys to put into Lowell's casket. The scent of carnations, the most affordable flowers for the memorial service, repelled Mom for the rest of her life.

Mom's TB was treated immediately. The first step was collapsing the infected lung, thereby depriving it of oxygen, and further weighing down the lung with beads to push out all the air, leaving the bacteria with nothing on which to survive.

Then the pneumonectomy could begin. Mom's left lung was removed, leaving her with a deformed, caved-in chest. Because that side of her chest was hollow, she couldn't sleep on her left side for the rest of her life.

Mom was sent to recuperate at a sanatorium[16] located in Redwood City, 30 miles south of San Francisco. Dad balanced work at the Goodyear Tire dealership and taking care of Kathy. He was unable to visit Mom in isolation and was struggling as a single parent when Daisy and Edie passed through San Francisco for a visit. Dad asked them to take Kathy to New York where she could stay with Kate.

Five of Kate's children had settled in the greater New York City area and had set her up in a shared two-bedroom apartment in Manhattan, to be near them all. The second bedroom was occupied by a young couple, therefore the living room became little Kathy's bedroom. On weekends, Kathy and Kate visited with Mamie, Bertha, Grace, Teddy, Daisy, and their young families.

Kathy remembers being with her cousins as a wonderful time. Kate, a doting grandmother, gave Kathy her first taste of coffee. She cleaned out an eggshell and put in two small drops of coffee with a tablespoon of sugar and gave it to Kathy in the mornings. Kathy proudly credits Kate, "Granny got me hooked on caffeine!"

Three-year old Kathy was settling into a routine with Kate and the East Coast family members when she developed symptoms including stiff joints and rigidity in her neck. Daisy immediately contacted Teddy who took Kathy to Bellevue Hospital in New York City. As the oldest public hospital in the United States (established in 1736), it was highly respected for its innovative patient care and medical education.

Kathy was diagnosed with tuberculosis meningitis (TBM), an inflammation of the membranes surrounding the central nervous system, notably the brain and spinal cord. Fortunately, the doctor in charge of the children's "chest clinic" at Bellevue Hospital was Dr. Edith M. Lincoln, one of the most influential American pediatricians who pioneered the use of drugs for treating TB in children. She was one of the first women physicians to be accepted as an intern at Bellevue Hospital in 1917 and by 1922 she led the children's chest clinic until her retirement in 1956.

Kathy was treated at Bellevue for nine months with massive doses of streptomycin. Mamie and S.C., with their experience in nursing and neurology, were astounded that three-year-old Kathy survived the treatment. Even if you survived, the high dosage often left you blind or deaf.

Kathy had no residual effect. She had received a lot of love and care, tended to by Nurse Ruth Hayward with whom she remained friends until Nurse Hayward passed away when Kathy was 30 years old.

Mom, age 28, recuperating from her pneumonectomy (removal of her lung) at a TB sanatorium in Redwood City, California in 1951 (Author's collection)

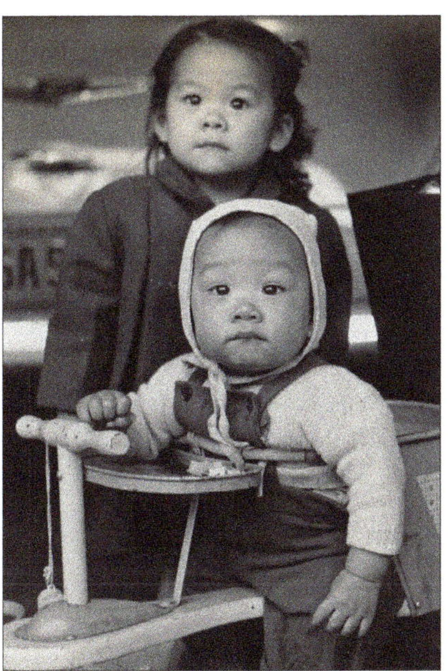

Siblings Kathy and Lowell Chinn, San Francisco, California 1949 (Author's collection)

Three-year-old Kathy recuperating from tuberculosis meningitis at Bellevue Hospital. Note the large pillow. (Kathy Chinn Slazak collection)

Mom was in the middle of her own slow recovery so no one mentioned that Kathy was at Bellevue undergoing acute treatment. Mom kept asking for pictures and Mamie and Daisy took a picture of Kathy sitting up in her hospital bed. She was in her pajamas propped up against a big pillow, smiling broadly for the camera.

Mom noticed something amiss the minute she saw the picture. The large white pillow was just wrong. The only place to find a pillow like that was in a hospital. Mom insisted on the truth and Daisy reluctantly broke the news. All Mom could do was remain isolated with her worries 3,000 miles away.

Kathy, however—once out of Bellevue—was having the time of her life. She was surrounded by her grandmother, cousins, aunts and uncles. This tight-knit family convened with matriarch Kate for regular family gatherings.

CHAPTER 7

DAD ARRIVES IN NEW YORK

Dad always said he never wanted to work for anyone else; his intention was to always be his own boss. Having learned about the restaurant business from his brother Eddie in Buffalo, Dad was determined to start his own restaurant. His fascination with chemistry, he claimed, is what drew him to the laboratory environment of a restaurant kitchen.

Now that Dad held a MBA from Harvard Business School, he was poised to apply his management education and start his own business. Leaving Mom behind, he ventured to New York City to be closer to Kathy and to look for work by networking with Chinese restaurant owners in Chinatown. On his days off, he took Kathy for walks in Chinatown to study the patterns of the food business.

Mom arrived in New York in 1954.* She lived with Dad and Kathy in Glen Oaks, a neighborhood in Queens, about 25 miles east of Manhattan.

As Kathy remembers, "That was the beginning of a sad part of my life. I lived with two people who didn't know each other and who had just lost a son. Mom was inwardly oriented and alone since I was at school. Dad couldn't stay with her because he was always working. She perked up for Daisy's visits on weekends, but otherwise she was withdrawn. She got a job at a sewing factory in Chinatown to which she took a bus an hour and a half each way. She left me little notebooks with math problems inside to work on when I got home from school."

Mom was happier with something productive to do. She had people to talk to other than Dad and Kathy and earned her own money, which gave her a sense of independence. The sewing factory specialized in clothes for fine department stores in New York City; B. Altman, Saks Fifth Avenue, and Bonwit Teller. These boutique stores had their labels sewn onto the clothing by factory workers like Mom. It was a verification of coveted prestige and highest quality.

Mom brought some of those labels home to sew onto Kathy's clothes. There was no money to buy fancy clothes so the Kwoh sisters simply faked it. For instance, they scouted out dresses at the major luxury stores. When they found a dress they liked, they bought it, took it home, carefully removed the seams, taking care not to cut off the price tag, and made a pattern of it.

With cheaper fabric, they made imitation dresses. They sewed the original dress back together and returned it to the store for a refund. Immigrant ingenuity at its finest and no one was the wiser.

*There was a two-year period when Mom and Dad lived in Akron, Ohio in 1952 and '53. Not much is known about their time in Akron other than Dad had the opportunity to work at the Goodyear Tire & Rubber Company headquarters and Mom was able to travel with him after her discharge from the sanatorium. They lived in an apartment above the Tea House Inn and Mom took comfort by worshipping daily at St. Bernard's Catholic Church.

CHAPTER 8

THE KWOH SIBLINGS IN AMERICA

GRACE (HUAN JUNG) was one of 18 student nurses who graduated from St. Joseph Mercy Hospital School of Nursing in June 12, 1940. She moved from Aurora, Illinois to New York City to attend Teachers College at Columbia University for her nursing graduate work. Founded in 1887, Teachers College is the oldest graduate school of education in the United States,[17] as highly esteemed then as it remains today. Grace's conduit to Columbia was through her older sister Mamie, who was attending Columbia University to secure her master's degree in Nursing (achieved in 1943).

The nursing program was established in 1892 as the Presbyterian Training School for Nurses, later renamed Columbia University School of Nursing; one of the first nursing schools in the United States.[18] In addition to its nursing program, Columbia University had a new program in the field of nutrition education—the first in the nation—founded in 1909 by Mary Swartz Rose PhD.

Nutrition education was a component of a new home economics focus in the U.S. when activists advocated for the teaching of modernized domestic activities, such as sewing, cooking, laundry—all aligned with the advent of new technology available to consumers (the electric sewing machines by 1905, electric washing machine in 1907, electric stoves by the 1930s).[19]

The American Home Economics Association,[20] formed in 1908, lobbied for federal and state grants to bolster home economics programs in schools and universities. With this wave of interest, Grace remained at Columbia University but switched her studies from nursing to Home Economics. This sparked her artistic interests in gardening, cooking, and domestic entertainment, which became the focal point of her life after she met the man who would become her husband.

In New York City, there were organized social activities for young Chinese college students. Grace and her fellow students were encouraged to attend these activities sponsored by Columbia University's Chinese Students Club.

Grace with daughter Vivian, 1949 (Author's collection)

Shih-Chun Wang (S.C.) (Phyllis Wang Wise collection)

Below: Mamie Kwoh (3rd row, right) as a nursing student (Phyllis Wang Wise collection)

These get-togethers also drew the attention of a young engineering student at Purdue University in Indiana, as well as his five Chinese classmates. These college undergrads, who dubbed themselves the "Six Brothers," were inseparable during school years and remained in touch throughout their lives.

One of the "brothers" was Yang-Hu Tong, the son of Chinese immigrants Sally and Hollington Tong. Hollington (1887–1971) studied journalism at Park College in Parkville, Missouri, attended the University of Missouri where he received his B.A. in 1912 and was in the first graduating class of the Columbia Graduate School of Journalism.

Hollington eventually became Chiang Kai-Shek's English teacher and his biographer. He served as a journalist for the *Peking Daily News* and *The China Press.* After the Communists seized control of China in 1949, Chiang and his forces fled to Taiwan where they set up their own nationalist government. Hollington was appointed by Chiang to serve as the Ambassador to Japan in 1952 and as Ambassador of the Republic of China to the United States during 1956–1958.

Yang-Hu originally wanted to be a doctor but his mother decided engineering was a better career for him. Dutifully, he enrolled at Purdue University in Indiana in 1938.

The driving distance from Purdue University to New York City is just under 800 miles, an adventurous distance if one has a car and some close friends. One "brother" owned a typically large (by today's standards) car that easily fit six college boys. They thought it would be a fun weekend getaway to drive to New York to hang out and meet fellow Chinese students, especially girls, at one of the social gatherings.

Yang-Hu and another "brother" spied Grace at the gathering and the competition was on. The next day Yang-Hu borrowed the keys to the gas-guzzling car and drove Grace to the Bronx Zoo just 10 miles north of Columbia University. His hopes to impress her with a fashionable lunch were dashed when he realized most of his money went into filling up the gas tank for the round trip. He could only afford to buy one sandwich to split with Grace on their first date. As a student, Grace had little means of supporting herself and learned at an early age to be careful with her money. She did not mind the half sandwich; in fact, she fell in love with the man who was her instant soulmate. It was a swift courtship.

Grace married Yang-Hu Tong in New York on May 24, 1943. Upon Yang-Hu's graduation from Purdue, they moved to Lexington, Kentucky where he had been offered a teaching position at the Aeronautical Research Library.

In short order, they had a daughter, May, born in Lexington on May 5, 1944. May was the eldest of the first generation of Kwohs born in the United States.

The Tongs moved back to New York City. Daughter Vivian was born in New York on Sept 22, 1948. Yang-Hu and Grace became U.S. citizens and by the 1950s, Yang-Hu was beginning his career as an engineering executive with International Business Machines in Poughkeepsie, New York; he was then transferred to their IBM offices in San Jose, California. According to May, "My father worked for IBM in San Jose where he and Alan Shugart invented the disc drive for the IBM 2321 (first direct-access storage device). When Shugart set up Shugart Associates, my father became his Chief Operating Officer. Subsequently, when Shugart set up Seagate Associates, my father went to Xerox in Dallas, Texas, to manage their operations on the West Coast. He was also consulting with starts-up (for free) and went to China to help them launch a class of tech entrepreneurs.

Grace eased into the life of a corporate wife and the daughter-in-law of U.S. Ambassador Hollington Tong. However, the deep scars of Grace's experiences during the Japanese occupation of China never healed. She believed that Japan did irreparable damage to China, its people, and its future. In the Tong household, she banned Japanese-made products (electronics, pianos, food) and anything made with Japanese components. According to May, their stereo was made in America, Yang-Hu's cameras were manufactured in Germany, and their watches were from Switzerland. Their computer was custom-made at the IBM facilities and avoided the use of Japanese components. When Grace sewed and taught sewing, she forbade the use of Japanese fabrics (at the time, Japanese silks were inexpensive substitutes for Italian silks).

When she and Yang-Hu retired, she relented and allowed a few Japanese electronics into the house. However, when May was assigned to a regional job in Tokyo for seven years, Grace refused to visit. Grace never forgave Democratic President Truman because she believed he allowed the Japanese to dominate China. She switched her party allegiance and voted Republican for the rest of her life.

BERTHA (HUAN SHOU)

After graduating from Briar Cliff College, Bertha made her way to New York City in 1942 to begin graduate studies at The Juilliard School, a private performing arts conservatory founded in 1905 as the Institute of Musical Art by Frank Damrosch, the godson of composer Franz Liszt.

The Juilliard School was located at 49 E. 52nd Street, just under a mile from the China Institute at 125 E. 65th Street.

THE CHINA INSTITUTE

The China Institute gained a prestigious reputation for its impact as a membership-based organization created to foster bicultural understanding between the United States and China.

The Institute was established in 1926 by Chinese educators Hu Shi and K.P. Wen and American scholars Paul Monroe (1869–1947) and John Dewey (1859–1952). John Dewey was regarded as a leading philosopher and educational theorist of his time. In 1911, he went to China at the invitation of his former Chinese students. His experiences in China inspired him to partner with Paul Monroe, a professor of comparative education at Teachers' College in Peking, to address the absence of a reciprocal understanding of China in the United States.

Start-up funding for the China Institute can be traced back to the Boxer Rebellion and the reparations issued to countries whose embassies and missionaries were killed while in China by the Chinese rebels. Although the United States received compensation, American diplomats and educators lobbied to return the funds to China to invest in their Chinese education system. President Theodore Roosevelt authorized the first remission of the funds, which led to the establishment of The National Tsing Hua University.[21] The success of this endeavor led to a second lobbying effort to endow the China Foundation for the Promotion of Education and Culture. This second funding led to the creation of a special bureau in New York which became the China Institute. And this is where my family came into the China Institute picture.

In 1930, Bertha's husband, Paul (known as Chih-Meng) was appointed Director of the China Institute[22] whose goal was to promote a closer relationship between Chinese and American educational institutions through the exchange of professors and students, to assist Chinese students in America in their educational pursuits, and to stimulate interest in America in the study of Chinese culture.

Chih-Meng was a 73rd direct descendent from the Chinese philosopher Mencius (372–289 BCE). Mencius extolled the teachings of Confucius (551–479 BCE): tolerate all religions, keep an open mind, avoid dogmatic conclusions on uncertain beliefs.[23]

Paul was longtime friends with the Henry Luce family, particularly Dr. Henry Winters Luce, an American missionary born in Shantung Province, the province of Paul Meng, my family, and Jesse Boardman Hartwell.

Henry Winters Luce and his wife Elizabeth Middleton had four children. The eldest was Henry R. Luce (known as Harry), the founder of *Time* magazine and the publisher of *Look* and *Fortune* magazines. Harry was also born in Shantung Province.

Paul Chih-Meng recalls, "By the autumn of 1942 I had gathered enough courage to tell (Harry) Luce why I wanted to see him. He invited me to lunch in *Time*'s private dining room in the Time-Life Building in Rockefeller Center. He told me his father and sister had mentioned to him how cramped the Institute was for office space and expressed his willingness to help. We looked at twenty-seven houses for sale on the East Side between 60th and 80th Streets. His first choice was the Arthur Curtiss James house at 68th between Park and Lexington Avenues, his second the Frederick Leigh house at 65th between Park and Lexington Avenues. He was prepared to acquire either one and present it to us as a gift…the trustees accepted the Leigh House."[24]

With this new acquisition, the China Institute reincorporated itself from a membership-based organization into a tax-exempt educational organization. The Leigh House became the China House with a grand dedication celebration which took place on the 2495th anniversary of the birth of Confucius (Aug 27, 1944). At the invitation of Paul Chih-Meng, opera singer Marian Anderson[25] performed two spirituals: *My Soul is Anchored in the Lord* and *Sometimes I Feel Like a Motherless Child*. She donated her time and fees, knowing of Paul Chih-Meng's deep relations with, and commitment to, black educators and colleges.

Bertha and Paul Chih-Meng married on Sept 23, 1944. She was 28, he was 44.

Bertha and Paul were a formidable couple at China Institute. Under President Franklin D. Roosevelt (1933–1945), China was not considered a global enemy nor vilified by the United States. On the contrary, many American sons and daughters of missionaries in China returned to the United States with an interest in raising awareness and appreciation for Chinese history, art, and cultural understanding. Among the noted missionaries who influenced my family during the 1930s and 1940s were Henry R. Luce, John Leighton Stuart, and Pearl S. Buck.[26]

Paul Chih-Meng rose in prominence as an international expert in Chinese-American cultural relations. At the same time, he and Bertha became friends with the noted politicians, sociologists, scholars, and historians who sat on the Board of Trustees for the China Institute. Some of their many colleagues: Sidney D. Gamble (grandson of James Gamble who founded Procter & Gamble), John R. Mott (1946 Nobel Peace Prize Winner and President of the YMCA's World Committee), T.V. Soong (Minister of Finance), John Leighton Stuart (President of Yenching University), and Edwin F. Stanton (first U.S. ambassador to Thailand).

Paul and Bertha purchased a 4-bedroom, 3-bathroom Tudor-style home in White Plains, New York, 30 miles north of Manhattan.

Son Paul Chih-Meng Jr. was born in 1946, daughters Elizabeth and Virginia followed in 1951 and 1952, and son James in 1954. While they were given anglicized names, they were known to family and friends as Ni-Ni, Mei-Mei, Wa-Wa, and Di-Di.

Paul Chih-Meng became an American citizen in 1955. Bertha and Paul instilled rigor and discipline within the household. All four children spoke Chinese at home and all were expected to play a musical instrument. Bertha, through her Juilliard studies, continued to play the piano as part of her association with the China Institute. She and Paul Chih-Meng often presented recitals at their home featuring their own poetry and songs. Three of their works are included in the 1952 archive at the Library of Congress.[27]

By the time the last child was born, Bertha was 38 years old and Paul was 54. This age difference was noted, not always in a positive way, by Mom and some of her siblings on many occasions, about how it might have impacted the children. In the 1960s and 1970s I spent time with the Meng family and felt there was always something strained within their household. I often wondered what it was in the home environment or biological byway that manifested the set of inexplicably cruel fates that befell the Meng family in later years.

MAMIE (HUAN WEI)

When Mamie arrived in the U.S. in 1938 via Seattle, she continued on to Chicago to reunite with Shih-Chun Wang (S.C.), who arrived the year prior to begin his graduate studies at the Institute of Neurology at Northwestern University in Illinois.

They were married in Cook County, Illinois on January 9, 1939. She was 25, he was 29.

S.C.'s thesis at Northwestern was recognized by Sigma Xi, the Scientific Research Honor Society, one of the oldest and largest scientific organizations in the world. Sigma Xi has more than one hundred and twenty-five years of distinguished history of service to science and society. Scientists and engineers, whose research includes the disciplines of science and technology, comprise the membership of the Society. More than 200 Nobel Prize winners have been members.[28]

After S.C. received his Ph.D. from Northwestern in 1940, he and Mamie planned to return to China with medical and scientific knowledge to help rebuild the country after the Japanese occupation. Mamie was getting involved with the American Bureau for Medical Advancement in China (ABMAC), established in 1937 to aid Chinese medical and public health services by working through existing Chinese medical agencies.

Between 1937 and 1945 China received more than ten million dollars in aid from ABMAC. After World War II, ABMAC concentrated on aiding six national medical colleges by administering a fellowship program for their faculty members for a year of study in the United States, and by sending American medical faculty members to the six colleges as visiting professors. They also provided technical assistance such as books for medical libraries, textbooks for the classroom, equipment for laboratories, and other educational materials. [29]

Using the following year to get their travel and paperwork ready, Mamie and S.C. eventually had their affairs in order, planning to set sail for China on December 12, 1941.

However, when the United States was attacked by the Japanese at Pearl Harbor on December 7, 1941, Mamie and S.C. decided to remain in the United States to support the U.S. war efforts. They built a new life together while assimilating and being the best Americans they could be.[30] S.C. was offered a faculty position at Columbia University's College of Physicians and Surgeons in the Department of Physiology at 630 West 168th Street. Mamie pursued graduate studies at Columbia University's School of Nursing.

By 1943, Mamie had received her master's degree in nursing and S.C.'s career and reputation as a neuroscientist, pharmacologist, and physiologist was gaining even greater prestige. Daughters Phyllis and Nancy were born in 1945 and 1948. Mamie and S.C. filed for naturalization papers in 1949, officially becoming United States citizens.

Mamie and S.C. set their distinct imprint on the field of nursing and neuroscience. Mamie became a Professor at the Cornell University New York Hospital School of Nursing where she helped develop comprehensive training for nurse practitioners. Her expertise in the field of nursing and of new approaches towards patient care are cited in publications such as the *American Journal of Public Health* and the *American*

Mamie, S.C. and daughters Nancy and Phyllis, 1948
(Phyllis Wang Wise collection)

The Kwoh siblings, Bertha, Daisy, Edie, Kate, Mamie, Grace with SC, and Yang-Hu with their young families. My sister Kathy is holding Kate's hand. (Author's collection)

Journal of Nursing. Her research papers were published and supported via grants by the U.S. Public Health Service.[31]

Meanwhile, S.C. focused his research on motion sickness and became an expert on the brain's stabilization functions. He was hired by the National Aeronautics and Space Agency (NASA) to study the problem of nausea in astronauts in the battle between acceleration and gravitation.

He was responsible for the invention of the famous "Vomit Comet" of the 1960s space program and improvements in combating motion sickness. According to the *New York Times*, "His research led to a fundamental understanding of motion sickness and the development of drugs to prevent vomiting and other adverse reactions. It also opened windows on other kinds of deviations from normal functions and led to effective countermeasures, like drug therapy for hypertension."[32]

In 1952, with two young girls and the need for a larger home, Mamie and S.C. moved to the Township of Teaneck, New Jersey, a growing suburb of New York City, 12 miles west over the Hudson River. The Wangs briefly moved to Englewood in 1961 before settling into their home at 18 Kent Road, Tenafly in 1963. This was one of our family basecamps where the Kwoh siblings and their families gathered for reunions over happy and sad occasions.

S.C remained at Columbia's Department of Physiology until 1956 when he joined Columbia's Department of Pharmacology—a position he held until he retired in 1978.

TEDDY (HUAN TSING)

After Teddy graduated from Lehigh with his master's degree in engineering he moved to New York and, at the invitation of Paul Chih-Meng, began work at the China Institute.

He married Emily Tzu Ying on June 12, 1950, in New York City. Emily escaped from the Chinese civil war in 1947. She received a graduate degree from Harvard in Psychology and went on to Columbia University to prepare for a career in Early Childhood Education.

Son Theodore Jesse Kwoh (known as Jesse and presumably named after Jesse Boardman Hartwell, Jr.) was born in 1951, followed by daughter Bonny in 1952. They lived at 635 Riverside Drive within close proximity to Mamie and S.C., as well as Bertha and Paul Chih-Meng.

Teddy's career as a civil and structural engineer included projects with architect James Stewart Polshek,[33] then Dean of the Columbia University Graduate School of Architecture, Planning and Preservation and who later served as architect of the William Jefferson Clinton Presidential Center.

Wedding of Teddy Kwoh and Emily Tzu Ying, New York City, 1950. (Author's collection)

Emily established herself as a prominent restaurateur in Manhattan. In 1958, she opened The Mandarin House at 133 W 13th Street to introduce a broader range of Chinese cuisine to the United States. Emily was born in Shanghai and her restaurant menus reflected Northern Chinese cooking, virtually unheard of in the U.S. where Chinese food was primarily known as chop suey and chow mein.

The 400-seat Mandarin House was located on the bottom floor of an old brownstone building Teddy and Emily owned in Greenwich Village. Conveniently, they and their children lived in the apartment units upstairs which led directly into the restaurant. The success of Mandarin House spawned Mandarin East located at 1085 2nd Avenue on the Upper East Side.

In 1966, American journalist and author Emily "Mickey" Hahn was hired by Time Life Books editor Richard Williams to create a new series called "Foods of the World." Emily Hahn was notorious for her life in Shanghai in the 1930s, immersing herself into the lifestyle by taking on a Chinese lover, developing an addiction to opium, and scandalizing Shanghai society.[34] While preparing to write her book, *The Cooking of China* (published in Nov 1968), Hahn was unsure how to accurately describe the regional styles of Chinese cuisine. The book's researchers, Diane Kelly, Marjorie Chester, and Iris Unger Friedlander, approached Teddy and Emily to host a Chinese Food Summit at Mandarin East in March 1967 so Emily Hahn could learn, observe, and take notes.

In Mark McWilliams' report of the Food and Communication Proceedings of the Oxford Symposium on Food 2015, "Marjorie suggested a discussion of the regional breakdown and we might get each person to voice his opinion as to the specialty of his region: Theodore Kwoh on Shantung and Peking; Emily Kwoh on Shanghai and Szechuan…." "Emily Kwoh and her husband owned the hosting restaurant and others in Manhattan…."[35]

According to a 1967 *New York Times* article, the now classic mu shu pork—a staple dish of Northern China—was first introduced by Emily Kwoh to the United States. Emily's further contribution to the culinary field and to home/commercial kitchens was through her invention of a reversible multiple cooking oven, steamer, grill, and griddle.[36]

During the late 1950s while Emily made headlines as a restaurateur in Manhattan, Dad was forging a similar path on Long Island. They greatly respected each other as colleagues, and both played historic roles in introducing authentic Chinese cuisines to Americans.

DAISY (HUAN HSING)

While he worked at the China Institute, Teddy explored sponsorship opportunities to help Daisy emigrate from the Philippines to the United States. By chance, a woman associated with the New Jersey State Teachers College went to the China Institute seeking recommendations for Chinese exchange students. Teddy arranged for the College to issue a six-month scholarship and Daisy boarded the *SS Wilson* on December 15, 1949, departing Manila, Philippines, bound for San Francisco.

Daisy c 1950s at Yale (Author's collection)

When she arrived in San Francisco, she briefly reunited with my parents, Kathy and new son, Lowell, in San Francisco. Their time together was brief because Daisy needed to start her new job in Trenton. She took the train from San Francisco to New York and was met by Teddy, who helped her get settled in New Jersey. Within three months of her arrival at Trenton, Daisy had immersed herself into student life. Towards the end of 1950, Daisy remembers, "I started working for the Chinese delegation to the United Nations. I found this opportunity through the China Institute. I was a secretary for the Economic and Social Council for two and a half years."

Due to the United States' growing global commitments, there was a corresponding need for foreign language education programs and instructors. Through a referral from The China Institute, Daisy was hired by the Army Language School, located at the Presidio in Monterey, California. The most requested foreign language education needs were Russian followed by Chinese, Korean, and German.[37]

Daisy recalls, "I taught Mandarin to U.S. Army students. There were eight students per class. Since each student had other chores to do at the school, they often missed class and were far behind on their assignments. I was very strict with them, otherwise they would not be able to graduate. I lived in one room in a nice house on High Street in Monterey with an American lady, but I was not allowed to use the kitchen so I had to look for a place to eat every day. The other tenants in the house were language teachers, mostly Russian. The Army Language School was the precursor to what is now the Defense Language Institute."

Daisy was a born teacher. Her genteel yet firm approach to discipline endeared her to students, fellow teachers, and administrators. One of those administrators was the Dean of the Army Language School, an alumnus of Yale University, who mentioned that the U.S. Air Force had recently been contracted by Yale University to teach intensive Asian language courses to members of the military for Cold War intelligence operations.

Daisy's experiences and reputation as a Chinese language teacher were precisely what was needed for the new Yale Institute of Far Eastern Languages (IFEL). She was recruited by Yale University and moved to New Haven, CT in 1955 to begin her 17-year career as a Chinese language and history teacher.

One of Daisy's graduate students was Robert (Bob) Oxnam, who had received a financial aid package from the National Defense Education Act supporting studies about "critical countries" (a euphemism for countries such as China). As improbable as it sounded at the time, he felt that China—with its vast history and deep cultural impact—would be a significant global force in the future. He was Daisy's student from 1964–1969, during which he wholeheartedly gravitated towards Chinese art, history, politics, and economics. He credits Daisy for igniting his zest for the Chinese culture which would become the hallmark of his celebrated career.

Grace and Yang-Hu with daughters Vivian and May, Poughkeepsie, New York, c 1950 (Author's collection)

Mamie and SC, Bertha and Paul, Grace and Yang-Hu with their children Phyllis, Ni-Ni, May, 1950s New York (Author's collection)

After receiving his Ph.D. in Chinese history from Yale, Bob joined the Asia Society, a non-profit organization based in New York City, founded by John D. Rockefeller III, to promote greater knowledge of China within the United States. He was in charge of the Asia Society's Washington Center and asked Daisy to join him as his executive assistant. Daisy finished up her teaching semester, gave her notice to Yale University, and moved to Washington, D.C.

In 1981, the Asia Society promoted Bob to President and he again asked her to join him in this next endeavor which involved a relocation to New York City.

In a 2005 interview with ABC-TV, Bob said, "My Yale experience from 1964 to 1969 was an eye-opening voyage into Chinese and Asian art, history, politics, and economics at a time when few graduate students were attracted to the field. The Chinese program was spearheaded by two exceptional scholars, Arthur and Mary Wright (Mary was a pioneer in modern Chinese history and the first female full professor at Yale). The Chinese-language department, created to train Air Force officers in the Second World War, had a great array of linguists. My first Chinese teacher, the talented Daisy Kwoh, eventually became my assistant at the Asia Society and has been a close friend ever since. It was Daisy Kwoh who gave me a lovely Chinese name—An Xilong—rich in meaning and historical allusion, always producing knowing nods from prominent Chinese."[38]

With Daisy's continued influence, Bob was inspired to write his first novel, *Cinnabar*, a mystery thriller which takes place in 20th century China. The dedication in Bob's 1989 novel was *To Daisy Kwoh, Master teacher and incomparable friend.*

Daisy lived her life with modesty. When she worked at the Asia Society, she lived at 347 E. 78th Street on the Upper East Side of Manhattan, considered a posh address. But, Daisy's apartment was a small studio on the top floor of a five-story walk-up. She seldom entertained except when dignitaries from China were curious to know what a typical American apartment looked like. They insisted on visiting Daisy, who loved to tell the story of how the visitors asked, "Where is your bedroom?" to which Daisy replied," You are sitting in it." They asked, "And where is your dining room?" Again Daisy replied, "You are sitting in it." In answer to questions such as, "Where do you hang your clothes?" or "Where is your linen closet?" Daisy simply reached over and opened a small door to a little closet containing 2–3 business suits, a set of towels, her bedding, and 2 pairs of shoes.

EDIE (HUAN CHUN)

Edie was the last Kwoh sibling to come to the United States. After disembarking at the Port of San Francisco in September 1950, she and Ang made their way to Golden, Colorado where Ang had been a student at the Colorado School of Mines, earning his undergraduate degree in Mining in 1943. In February 1944, he continued his studies and earned a master's degree in mining and metallurgy in 1947. He intended to resume his studies to earn a doctorate degree.

However, that year Ang was offered a job as a metallurgical engineer by P.R. Mallory and Co., based in Indianapolis, which specialized in the production of dry cell batteries. (In 1978 the company was purchased by Dart Industries and renamed Duracell after its alkaline battery brand was introduced in 1964). It was a brief employment since Ang chose to pursue a doctorate degree at the University of Illinois at Champaign.

Edie and Ang moved to Illinois in 1951. Their son, Roy, was born December 1952. During this time, under President Dwight Eisenhower, the U.S. Government enacted the Refugee Relief Act of 1953 which allowed the admission of over 214,000 refugees fleeing persecution and seeking asylum in the United States.

In 1955, Ang (hoping to be allowed permanent admission to the U.S. as an immigrant) applied for an adjustment of status under the provisions of the Refugee Relief Act. He was denied on the grounds that he could conceivably return to his place of birth (the Philippines) without fear of persecution. Deportation proceedings were instituted on Jan 23, 1956 and he was found to be subject to deportation for failing to maintain the status in which he was admitted. Voluntary departure in lieu of deportation was authorized.

Fortunately, Ang gained the attention of U.S. Senator Homer Caperhart (R-IN) who wrote a letter of support for Ang as part of the House Judiciary Committee's "Relief of Certain Aliens" report presented to the 84th Congress (June 1956). Senator Caperhart cited Ang's distinguished education, his military service as a language specialist for the U.S. Marine Corps, and his specialized skills as an engineer and materials science.

Ang and Edie were allowed to remain in the United States where Ang's career as a prominent technical engineer flourished. Ang was approached by NASA to serve as a consultant in the field of materials processing in space. This took him to Los Angeles where he became a member of the technical staff at the Aerospace Corporation in Los Angeles. Ang worked at the Ivan A. Getting Laboratories, founded by Ivan Getting, the original pioneer of the Navstar Global Positioning System (GPS). The Angs relocated again, this time to San Diego and eventually in Santa Ana, California.

DORA

On Paul Ernest's side of the family, Dora, who emigrated to the U.S. in 1956, was very much a part of our family. She settled in New York City and lived in close proximity to her cousins Mamie, Bertha, Teddy, Daisy, and Mom. Dora was considered a sister and was included in all of our family reunions. She, too, experienced hardships growing up in China and was taken care of by Mom and her siblings.

Dora lived simply and without pretensions. Mom said Dora always had good luck in that money usually found its way to her. She'd get the winning scratch-off lottery ticket, a surprise discount, or she'd find money on the street. She was a cashier at a Chinese restaurant near her apartment on 135 W. 13th Street and volunteered for nearby St. Vincent's Hospital. Dora spent more money on others than she did on herself. Never one to shop for the latest fashions she, in fact, did most of her clothes shopping at bazaars in Chinatown, street corners, and thrift shops.

It was common to see Dora wearing a mishmash of attire—fashion, color, and patterns all akimbo. In her 60s, she bundled up against the cold with an old wool ski hat, a bright pink and red coat, an orange scarf, ragged mittens, and scuffed up shoes. She sat at the bus stop, fingers wrapped around her Styrofoam cup of coffee. A man, thinking she was homeless, came over to give her loose change; a true money magnet. Dad jokingly told her she should reenact that scene to fluff up her retirement savings.

Dora was a kind and generous woman. At family gossip sessions, she never said a bad word about anyone. She gave everyone a pass, even family members who had insulted or hurt her feelings.

When she came to visit, she never came empty-handed. She had something for everyone and we were the eager recipients of her shopping bargains since she was always able to find obscure and outlandish items. When she sent birthday and Christmas cards, she taped a $20 bill inside.

KATE (MY GRANDMOTHER)

Kate lived alone in her apartment in New York City and the Kwoh siblings took turns visiting her. Not a week went by when Kate was without one of her children visiting and tending to her needs. I recall Dad driving us into the City to visit with Kate on a regular basis. Since it was difficult to find a place to park, Dad double parked for several hours while Mom, Michael, and I were with Kate. Dad was content to sit in the car reading the paper and listening to the sports station, in between cat naps. While one Kwoh sibling was caring for Kate, the others took turns making sure she received phone calls from the other children.

Mom and her mother, Kate

With my brother Michael and our grandmother Kate, New York City c.1963 (Author's collection)

The tender care the Kwoh siblings wrapped around Kate was offered selflessly and with great love. As I and my cousins got older, we were expected to visit with Kate, whom we addressed as Lao-Lao or "Maternal Grandmother." Mom called her every weekend and no matter what I was doing, I was expected to take the phone and say a few words to my Lao-Lao. Kate didn't speak English well but it didn't matter. The important thing, Mom said, was for Kate to hear the sound of my voice and for me to hear hers.

Kate spent a few days with us when I was in grade school. When Lao-Lao and I sat together watching "The Three Stooges," she was at first befuddled at the slapstick debauchery, but she was such a good sport she continued to watch in silence. By the closing credits, she was chuckling and wanting more. Our language and generational chasm were bridged by Moe's eye-poking, Larry's head-bonking, and Curly's antics.

FRANK

When Grandfather Frank's concubine Mary died of TB, the Kwoh siblings tried to get him out of China and into the United States.

My Grandfather Frank Kwoh c.1965 (Author's collection)

Although the borders of China were closed, the Kwoh siblings tapped into their connections and associates of Frank's brothers who had Western business contacts with Shell Oil and the railroads, looking for a way to get Frank from Peking/Beijing in the north to Hong Kong/Macau in the south, where he would be met by an intermediary. Daisy said that even though some of her siblings harbored resentment towards their father for remaining in China with his new family, Kate encouraged unity and forgiveness.

A secret operative was underway, and Frank made his way south to Hong Kong to meet the man who would give him false papers to get on a boat and sail for the Port of San Francisco.

However, Frank went by a different name than what the intermediary was given. Daisy assumed Frank wanted to remain undetected. He and his brothers were well-known and, if caught, the remaining Kwoh family members in China could be executed. He may have used his English name instead of Feng Shu, or a variation of his Chinese and English names. Whatever the case, Frank waited for his connection and finally gave up when the ship left. He returned to Beijing where he died alone in 1965 at the age of 76.

– PART THREE –

THE RESTAURANT BUSINESS

Map of Long Island, New York, showing Huntington and Syosset

Original facade of Chateau Maggi and Raay-Nor's Inn, Huntington
Photo: Tichenor Collection, Boston Public Library,

Architect Poy Gum Lee (New York Times photo from Lee Family archive)

Artist rendering of Poy Gum Lee's new facade for King Wah Restaurant

CHAPTER 9

A RESTAURANT IS BORN

The year was 1954. Dwight Eisenhower was President of the United States. The top-rated show on television was *The $64,000 Question*. The second rated show was *I Love Lucy,*[39] *a*nd it was the year Dad's restaurant dream became a reality.

HOW IT BEGAN

On a chance drive with friends out on Long Island, Dad noticed an architecturally distinctive building for sale at 1000 West Jericho Turnpike at Round Swamp Road in Huntington. Jericho Turnpike is a major corridor running from the western part of Long Island (Queens) to the end of the northeastern tip just off Long Island Sound. 1000 West Jericho Turnpike is near the midpoint of Long Island, where the hamlet of Syosset and the town of Huntington meet.

The building, formerly a restaurant known as Chateau Maggi, was owned by Pat and Lena Maggi. According to the newspaper archives:

> "After the Maggis sold the restaurant to Cliff Fearn in 1940, it was known as Pavillon Henri IV and featured a live orchestra. A year later the owner and the orchestra were the same, but there was a new chef and a new name: The Patio. The original name of Cliff Fearn's restaurant suggests that he served French cuisine. Although the quality of the food is unknown to us, perhaps the bigger attraction was Mr. Fearn's novel idea of a 'television theatre.'"
>
> "Mr. Fearn claimed to have the world's largest television screen—eight feet by ten feet. Weekly bulletins were mailed to patrons advising them of the nightly schedule.
>
> [For example, in July of 1948, one week's schedule included baseball (Monday), *Texaco Star Theatre* (Tuesday), *Kraft Television Theatre* (Wednesday), the Democratic Convention (Thursday), the CBS feature film (Friday), the Brooklyn Handicap (Saturday) and *Author Meets the Critics* on Sunday.]
>
> "The novelty of French cuisine and the world's largest television were not popular enough to sustain The Patio. Within a few

> years, new ownership invited Huntingtonians to 'Dine delightfully in a beautiful Spanish inn'—a Spanish inn serving southern fried chicken, sirloin steaks and sugar-cured ham steaks. Known as Raay-Nor's Inn, it was the North Shore companion to Baldwin's Raay-Nor's Cabin, which opened in 1946. In Baldwin the country cuisine was matched by the building's log cabin architecture, similar to Linck's Log Cabin in Centerport."[40]

Dad was enthusiastic about its prime location, its visibility along Jericho Turnpike, and the fact that it was built for commercial restaurant purposes. Pooling everything they owned, Dad and his friends bought the property and formed the King Wah Corporation, a restaurant serving Chinese fare. Dad was named President. He offered each of the two dozen employees of King Wah an ownership stake in the new restaurant venture.

Dad first changed the exterior of the building to highlight the new Chinese cuisine. He removed the European façade and hired Chinese-American architect Poy Gum Lee (1900–1968) to create a Chinese architectural statement. Poy, who lived in nearby Mineola, was born in New York City's Chinatown and studied design at Brooklyn's Pratt Institute, Massachusetts Institute of Technology, and Columbia University. He was hired as an architect in China, introducing Art Deco elements into YMCA and YWCA buildings throughout the country, particularly in

Kathy, Mom, Dad, Michael and I at King Wah 1959 (Author's collection)

Shanghai. His most notable architectural works are the Sun Yat-sen Mausoleum in Nanjing (Nanking) and the Sun Yat-sen Memorial Hall in Guangzhou (Canton).

During the Japanese occupation, Poy's home in Shanghai was destroyed and other property was confiscated. He returned to New York City at the end of World War II to work as a senior architect for the New York Housing Authority. Poy was asked by Chinese civic leaders to create an identity for Chinatown, blending traditional Chinese styles with modern influences of the post-World War II era.

The Chinese Merchants Association Building, Poy's first major work in New York City's Chinatown, caught Dad's attention. It had a dramatic three-tiered red pagoda roof, the only building of its kind in Chinatown at the time.

According to my email exchange with urban and architectural historian, Kerri Culhane, "The original drawings by Lee were made September 23, 1954, and they are pretty well-developed plans, so your dad must have been in touch with Poy that summer, if not earlier."[41]

Poy replicated the tiered pagoda and situated it atop the front entrance of King Wah. The front entrance windows were replaced with octagons, known as Pa Kua (also Bagua). The eight symbols represent the balance of universal energies. In traditional Feng Shui, a Pa Kua symbol is placed above the front door or by an entrance for good energy.

The striped awnings left from the Chateau Maggi and Raay-Nor and the rest of the building exterior were retained. A large neon sign at the corner of Jericho Turnpike and Round Swamp Road announced, "King Wah - Chinese American Cuisine." The sign and the tall pagoda made King Wah hard to miss.

Dad's interest in chemistry complemented his fascination with testing food ingredients, and to great success. Here is an excerpt from a 1957 article in *The Long Islander* featuring Dad and King Wah. It begins with this headline:

"Former Marine Captain Who Probed Secrets of Jap Ammo Supplies Now Busy with Recipes for Patrons"

"The King Wah kitchen seemed a masterpiece of efficiency and cleanliness. It is divided into two sections, one for American and one for Chinese food and most of the activity is centered around several large Chinese cooking ranges. These are essentially large cauldrons, about three feet in diameter, suspended over the cooking flames. Everything

from Chow Mein and moo-goo-guy-pan to Captain Chinn's own "experiments in Chinese cooking" are mixed and simmer [sic] for hours in these cauldrons. A small but complete bakery prepares all the baked goods served at the restaurant. Nearby is a six-foot high oven designed solely for the barbecuing of spareribs. In a semi-circle to the left, a group of men were diligently slicing fresh celery while two others were placing strips of bacon in freshly cut butterfly shrimp.

"A small spice closet contained such typical Chinese delicacies as dried lotus roots, dried orange peel, truffles, and a large box of "birds nest." This latter, explained the Captain, are very small strips of dried fish, used by birds off the China coast to build nests. Next to the barbecue oven is another Chinese range. When asked why it was so far from the other ranges, Captain Chinn smiled and replied, 'That is where my chef, Lum, and I fool around with meats and vegetables to invent new dishes.' During the slow hours, it seems, they take a 'busman's holiday' and spend hours experimenting over the range.

"'First,' says the Marine Reservist, 'we try the new dishes on our employees. Then, if they approve, we serve it to our special customers who ask for the specialty of the house. We listen to their comments and criticisms and then maybe go back to the range to improve the dish. Sometimes we discover a dish that tastes excellent and is easy to produce at a reasonable cost. That's why we enjoy this hobby so much. We had an awful time getting started here...for a year and a half we were almost ready to close down. But the people of Huntington have accepted us.'"[42]

Dad's 20-mile commute each way from their home in Glen Oaks to King Wah Restaurant in Huntington inspired Mom, Dad, and Kathy to move to Huntington to shorten the commute and be part of the Huntington community. Mom and Dad rented a house on 24 Boulevard in Greenlawn, a hamlet of Huntington, across the street from the Greenlawn Fire Department.

In order to establish business connections, Dad was encouraged to join the Kiwanis Club. He joined the Huntington chapter near our home in Greenlawn, paving the way for a series of networks that guided our family through successes and challenges, as well as forging life-long friendships.

On January 30, 1957, a cold blustery winter afternoon with forecasts of snow and rain, Dad dropped Kathy off at the home of a King Wah customer who offered to look after her while Dad went to work. Mom was home alone when she unexpectedly went into labor later in the afternoon.

She walked across the street to the Greenlawn Fire Department, calmly explained her predicament and asked them to rush her to the hospital. The fire chief and his crew helped her onto their fire truck and off she went with sirens blaring to Huntington Hospital where, after a relatively easy labor, I was born at 6:02 pm. My theatrical escort to the hospital was fate, telling me I was destined to make grand entrances throughout my life. I asked Mom why she named me Debby (the official spelling on my birth certificate). She said it was for the initials of her sisters Daisy, Edie, and Bertha. Praise the naming gods she didn't designate these initials in reverse order.

By comparison, my brother Michael's arrival at Huntington Hospital on December 7, 1958, was routine. Now Mom had three children to raise, mostly alone. Again, as at Glen Oaks, Mom felt isolated, so Daisy drove from New Haven, Connecticut to Greenlawn, New York on weekends to keep her company.

With Mom and Dad in Greenlawn, NY, 1957
(Author's collection)

CHAPTER 10

THE MAH JONG ERA BEGINS

King Wah Restaurant was the dress rehearsal which prepared Dad for the main event in his life: the opportunity to build a new business, literally from the ground up.

Bill Froelich, one of King Wah's customers, owned potato fields on both sides of the county line from Bethpage to Plainview and South Syosset. Most of Bill's land was sold to housing developers in response to the rapid suburbanization of Long Island after World War II.

Soon after I was born, Dad left King Wah to help his friend Stacy Wai open a Chinese restaurant in Yonkers, NY. When Bill learned of Dad's commute (over two hours/day from Greenlawn to Yonkers seven days a week in an old Chevy) and that he had a newborn child at home, he told Dad he was nuts to drive all that way for a job. He mentioned that the Froelich family still held an old potato barn in Syosset just seven miles to the west. It was a large property on Jericho Turnpike with tremendous appeal, and not yet sold to developers.

According to Dad, Froelich said, "Go take a look and if you can use it for a restaurant, you can have it for $60,000. Just give me as much as you can and I'll hold on to the mortgage."

Froelich saw an old potato barn in a bucolic setting but Dad envisioned a restaurant bustling with business. He raised money by showing prospective funders the property, conveying his dream by saying, "That is going to be a restaurant." Dad rustled up a small deposit. A week later, Froelich asked for $4,000 more to help pay the taxes.

Another new friend of Dad's joined our family circle: Nino Loiacono. Uncle Nino, as we called him, with his wife, Aunt Rose, offered a $3,000 investment. Dad and Nino met at a diner where Nino handed over $3,000 in cash. Dad wrote a receipt on a paper napkin and handed it to Uncle Nino who wadded it up and threw it in his coffee cup, signifying no need for documentation. A friendship is a friendship; the cash was Dad's.

While Dad was raising more money, Froelich and his wife were in the process of a divorce. When his wife heard about the property sale, her lawyer instantly put a lien on it. Bill could no longer hold the mortgage.

With big sister Kathy in the backyard of our home in Greenlawn, New York 1957 (Author's collection)

In the backyard of our Greenlawn home with Dad, Easter 1959 (Author's collection)

Froelich suggested Dad approach someone for financial help, otherwise the barn property would be seized. Dad's King Wah networking, as well as his association with the Kiwanis Club came in handy.

Rocco (Rocky) Setaro, a member of the Huntington Kiwanis club, was a frequent customer of King Wah. Rocky was so close with Dad, he became my godfather. Yes, I have an Italian godfather.

Another Kiwanis member from the Hicksville chapter and a friend of Rocky's was William Koutensky, the larger-than-life President of the Long Island National Bank.

Rocky set up a meeting with Dad and Bill Koutensky at the famous Linck's Log Cabin Inn in Centerport, Long Island. Linck's was known as *the* place to do business meetings and deals. Rocky dictated two stipulations to Dad: sit next to Koutensky and, even though it was customary to have a cigarette or cigar after a meal, don't smoke around the banker.

Bill Koutensky liked my dad. Bill was beefy, and at well over 6 feet he towered over my barely 5'4" 120-pound father.

Dad told Koutensky about the Froelich barn, his restaurant dream and his difficulties raising the capital. Closing was postponed twice because Dad couldn't raise the money in time, and it dragged on for months.

After the meeting Koutensky returned to Long Island National Bank and contacted Froelich's lawyer. Was the barn still encumbered by a lien? It was and, due to the speed of the divorce proceedings, "time is of the essence."

Koutensky set up the closing date and asked Judge Lebchoker, a member of the Long Island National Bank's board of directors, to be Dad's lawyer. Judge Lebchoker took out a temporary loan from the bank and closed the purchase. At closing, Dad was presented with a surprise check for $3,000 from the insurance company. Some neighborhood kids had set fire to and partially destroyed a shack behind the barn. The Judge said, "This is your insurance check. You owned the property at the time it burned."

Dad got the barn property but still did not have enough money. Koutensky asked how much more he needed for the restaurant. Without thinking, Dad blurted, "$60,000."

Koutensky asked to meet Dad's friends and proposed business partners: Bill Yee and Arthur H. Jong.[41] They knew nothing about the restaurant business which positioned Dad, with his King Wah managerial experience, as the lead partner. With a handshake at the bank, Koutensky gave Dad the money to buy the barn. All the original partners became the first shareholders of The House of Mah Jong, Inc.

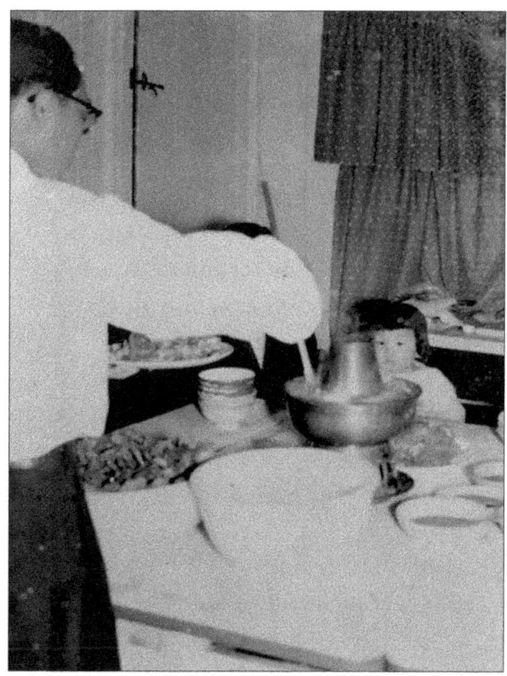

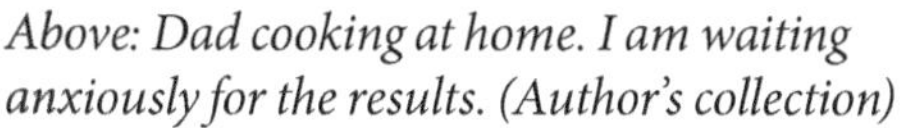

Above: Dad cooking at home. I am waiting anxiously for the results. (Author's collection)

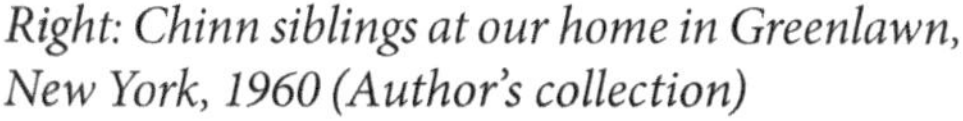

Right: Chinn siblings at our home in Greenlawn, New York, 1960 (Author's collection)

Left: After my baptism, attended by my godfather Rocky Setaro and my godmother Ann Reynolds, Huntington, New York, 1958 (Author's collection)

THE BARN BECOMES A RESTAURANT

Dad, Bill, and Arthur first planned the front entrance, a kitchen in the back of the barn and a full basement. At King Wah, Dad established relationships with the top major restaurant equipment and supply dealers in New York City specializing in Chinese restaurants. He recruited experienced restaurant crew members, mostly from King Wah in Huntington and Mandarin Garden in Yonkers.

The barn was duly converted and The House of Mah Jong opened for business, with a liquor license, on August 4, 1960. Mah Jong's "continental" menu offered broiled steaks, lobsters and shrimp cocktail for the western palate, but the essence of the menu was authentic Cantonese fare created by Chinese cooks from China.

King Wah customers and Kiwanis club friends followed Dad, whom they respected and admired, to Mah Jong. Koutensky spread the word about Mah Jong and, as head of Long Island's major financial institution, his endorsement carried significant clout.

After Mah Jong opened in Syosset, Dad, without consulting Mom, announced we were moving to be closer to the restaurant. He needed to be at Mah Jong to nurture the nascent business. He wanted Kathy, Michael, and me to be in Syosset's excellent school district. And he wanted to buy a house. He purchased our three-bedroom ranch home at 150 Southwood Circle in Syosset for approximately $16,000. Kathy was in the middle of 8th grade and unhappy at the thought of yet another move. Dad allowed her to stay behind in Greenlawn with the family of a classmate for several weeks.

By 1960, the Chinns (Mom, Dad, Kathy, Michael, and I) were all living in the same house at the same time; a new experience. Just ten years earlier, our family had been torn apart due to illnesses, the death of young Lowell, the separation of Kathy from Mom and Dad, and the constant uprooting as our family members migrated at different times from San Francisco to Akron to New York. In addition, the demands of starting a business meant Dad was seldom home.

We learned how to live with each other since there was no separation of work and home. As the years progressed, we spent more hours together as a family at Mah Jong than we did at our home.

This decade was destined to be the start of a different and hopeful chapter. 1960 was the Year of the Mouse (Rat), the first animal of the Chinese zodiac, symbolizing new beginnings and renewals.

MAH JONG OPENS ITS DOORS

Mah Jong grew steadily but was still undercapitalized. I recall my father at home late in the evenings and early mornings scratching out numbers with pencil and paper. He was constantly worried about finances. I would wake up to find the kitchen table littered with Dad's financial scribblings left next to the remnants of his midnight snack: either a slice of cheese-cake from the local diner or pieces of Hostess Sno Balls, a cream-filled chocolate cake covered with marshmallows and coconut sprinkles. He never finished his coffee and I drank whatever was left in his cup. Like my sister, I got hooked on caffeine before kindergarten.

Besides financial worries, Dad's big concern was where to find and how to keep good, authentic Chinese cooks. Long Island was predominantly white so he drove to Chinatown in the mornings—an hour each way—to pick up the cooks. He brought them to Syosset for lunch and dinner service and drove them back to Chinatown at night. Dad purchased two Hudson station wagons—one for each shift—and arranged for his managers to help with driving. Still, the strain of that daily shuttle and commute was not sustainable. He had to think of employee housing.

This reminded Dad of his dilemma at King Wah when he built a house for employees behind the restaurant. To allay neighbors' complaints about those "Chinese guys walking around every weekend," Dad personally visited the King Wah neighbors. A list of violations reported to the city attorney's office, including that the house was all bedrooms and bath-rooms with no kitchen, was corrected.

While securing the zoning permits for the dormitory at The House of Mah Jong, Dad looked for a quick solution to keep his head chefs happy. A King Wah connection, Bob Stedman, who owned the Stedman Oldsmobile dealership in Oyster Bay, heard of Dad's dilemma. Bob's wife, Gladys, offered to transform her antique shop in the back to house two Mah Jong chefs while the dorm was built.

By October of 1960—a mere two months after Mah Jong opened for business—all permits were obtained to extend the kitchen and to add a full basement for storage and the employees' dormitory. I was forbidden to go into the basement; it was deemed too slippery and dangerous. I was a young teenager when I discovered the real reason.

Warren Chang, one of my regular playmates, was the son of the bar-beque cook inexplicably named Chico. Chinese Chico was perhaps 40 years old but looked 80. He wore thick Coke-bottle glasses and I wondered

Right: Kenny the bartender and Charlie Ma (Author's collection)

Below: Michael and I receiving our Easter gifts from Loretta Koutensky at Mah Jong, c 1962 (Author's collection)

Opening Day, House of Mah Jong Restaurant, L-R: Arthur Jong, Bill Yee, Congressman Steven Derounian, William Koutensky, Dad, August 4, 1960 (Author's collection)

Mom giving a take-out order to a waiting customer, 1961 (Author's collection)

One of the head chefs of Mah Jong (Author's collection)

how he made it up and down those basement stairs if they were truly dangerous. He deftly wielded his way with a cleaver at the barbeque station where he was in charge of making the spareribs. While he hoisted his cleaver up and down in a steady cadence to hack the spareribs, he kept watch on the oven, pointed at the kitchen staff to get more supplies, pushed back his thick glasses which slid down his nose due to sweat, and constantly motioned to the waiters to hurry up and pick up their barbeque orders. All with the same cleaver-weaving hand. It was miracle he retained all of his fingers. Chico's masterful Clams Casino were made by leaving the whole clam (not chopped or minced) in the shell, layering a piece of bacon on top, adding some breadcrumbs and putting it under the broiler. I have never known anyone or any place that makes Clams Casinos like Chinese Chico made at Mah Jong.

Some of Mah Jong cooks and chefs, and Kenny the Bartender (back, center) (Author's collection)

My curiosity got the best of me one day and I followed Warren down into the basement. Off to the left I saw rows and rows of white tablecloths hanging from makeshift poles. Behind each tablecloth was an employee alcove. There were mattresses and a common use bathroom/shower. The walls were covered with photos of nude and semi-nude pin-up girls. Several bulbs hung from the ceiling providing stark light. The concrete floors offered cool respite during the summer months. During the winter, the cooks rolled out pieces of carpet for extra warmth.

The basement ran underneath the whole length of the Mah Jong dining room. Sacks of rice, linens, kitchen provisions, waiter uniforms, industrial sized cans of condiments, and catering job paraphernalia (chafing dishes, carts, bins and baskets) occupied every available wall and floor space.

The cooks ate their meals in a communal area, smoked and played cards, watched a small black and white TV with a bent antennae wrapped in tin foil for better reception, and enjoyed a fraternal camaraderie in a mini-Chinatown in the Mah Jong basement. The cooks were clad in nothing but t-shirts and shorts (if that).

Dad was right, young girls didn't belong there. I never ventured back.

MAH JONG HITS ITS STRIDE

At the House of Mah Jong, a set of glass doors welcomed you into a small entryway, offering protection from the elements. Just two steps further and more glass doors opened into the restaurant. On your left was the women's room; next to that, the men's room; and on your right, a phone booth with a folding wooden and glass door. Before reaching the hostess stand, you'd pay a visit to the coat check room. Beyond that was Mom's curated gift shop.

Dining out was a special experience in the sixties; an occasion to dress up. Men wore fedora hats and overcoats. Women were proud of their mink jackets and fine stoles. Mom oversaw the coat check room and used sturdy wooden hangers, each with three red plastic tags. Each tag had the same number. One tag went to the customer, one placed in the band of the hat or on a brief case or satchel, and one tag left on the hanger for identification. The double Dutch door with moveable swing-out top made delivering the heavy coats easier. Mom encouraged tipping and instead of a sign, glued a small plastic tray to the top of the double Dutch door. On top of the tray, she affixed a silver quarter, her not-so-subtle hint to tip. Customers invariably tried to scrape the quarter off the tray but Mom glued it down tight.

The Mah Jong clientele steadily grew because everyone felt part of the Chinn family. Mah Jong was a destination for birthdays, anniversaries, and weekly dinners. Customers' children were often the same age as Michael and me; we played together in the gift shop or in the phone booth while their parents finished their meals.

ON THE JOB TRAINING

Mom and Dad spent all their time at Mah Jong and brought Michael and me to the restaurant where we happily hung out. When it opened in 1960, I had jobs and responsibilities at the age of three. Mom ordered cases of cigarettes each week and my first job was to line up and display the cigarettes in the glass case.

Michael and I behind the cigarette and cigar counter, 1970

The case was roughly 4 feet wide and 3 feet tall, with glass on the top and front so customers could see the cigarettes and cigars for sale. A sliding glass door at the back of the case allowed me to reach in and grab a pack and stand on tiptoe to hand it to the customer on the other side of the counter. I arranged cigarette packs by color. To the left, the white packs: Lucky Strikes and Camels (unfiltered), L&M, Kent, Chesterfield, Viceroy, Tareyton. Then I lined up the red packs: Pall Mall, Winston, Marlboro. Finally the blues and greens: Salem, Newport (my Dad's brand).

Inside the case, next to a small dish with a wet sponge (a little humidity to keep the cigarettes and cigars moist) was a small change box with a coin slot. Usually, I received a dollar bill for a 45-cent pack. I learned quickly how to mentally calculate change from the box.

I loved the exquisite decorations on the cigar boxes—embossed in yellow and gold, some festooned with ribbon—next to my colorfully arranged cigarette packs. It was a beautiful work of art in there and my canvas to maintain.

I felt badly for the cigars (slower sellers than cigarettes) left unspoken for in their boxes. Mom told me to try to sell some cigars, and I learned how to "upsell;" I casually mentioned that the cigars were on sale—even though they weren't—and on a good day, I sold loose cigars for 25 cents each. My change box filled up fast.

Mom taught me how to reconcile my sales. I dutifully counted the contents of the change box—piling the pennies, nickels, dimes and quarters and smoothing out the dollar bills. Mom double-checked my work and put it in the main cash register. I wrote down the tally and stuck it back in the change box.

The display case smelled exotic and earthy. I loved putting my head in the display case to inhale the aroma. Not too many three-year old kids start out in an olfactory playground of tobacco.

When I got a little older (and taller) Mom let me come from behind the counter and escort a few customers to their tables. She either wanted to diversify my skills or was concerned about my fixation with the contents of the cigarette counter, but I loved greeting everyone and working with the captains. A six-year-old hostess was a guaranteed "Awwww" factor. Mom told me I took too long dawdling and daydreaming while seating customers at the far end of the dining room (she wasn't sure I'd come back). She reassigned me to seat customers in the front area where she could keep an eye on me.

The first two rows were the booths and banquettes. The stand-alone tables were at the back where they could be reconfigured easily for larger groups. I eventually learned to pull the banquette table out at a 30° angle so the women could slide in without having to scoot. Today, most booth tables are bolted to the floor. It is rare to find an "old-fashioned" booth with a stand-alone table.

My parents worked all day and into the evening, and I generally spent my after-school hours at Mah Jong during elementary school (grades 1–6). Mom arranged for the bus driver to stop on the street just behind the back entrance of Mah Jong. From there, I climbed a small dirt path and emerged at the far end of the Mah Jong parking lot. School ended after lunch service and before the dinner crowd arrived. I was put to work on restaurant prep.

One of my prep jobs was at the bar helping Kenny the bartender make the garnishes for drinks; impaling toothpicks in olives and onions for martinis, for instance. I used special toothpicks with colorful flags to spear the maraschino cherries for Manhattans and the more exotic drinks like Singapore Slings.

Cartons of fresh lemons were brought to the bar from the kitchen; each lemon-half was freshly squeezed by a manual juice press with a heavy rotating handle. Sometimes Kenny put the lemon-half onto the round plate and let me pull down on the handle with both hands. It was challenging for a six-year old girl but Kenny told me, "It's good for your muscles." The oranges were freshly pressed but too big for me to squeeze and the grapefruits were a formidable challenge.

ON THE JOB TRAINING PART 2

Mah Jong was in a prime location across the street from Syosset Hospital, Lafayette Electronics, and about a mile from a Grumman Corporation plant on Jericho Turnpike.[42] Many nearby office workers came in after their workday, starting about 4:00pm.

As a six-year-old girl on a bar stool sticking toothpicks in cherries, I was a bit of a novelty. My mother said I was, "good for business" since customers stayed at the bar to chat with me...and perhaps have another drink. I was encouraged to keep doing my side work as the cocktail hour crowd poured in. Although I had no intention to grow up as a barfly before I was even old enough to drink, it had educational value; I learned how to engage in small talk and put people at ease.

Another one of my jobs was helping the waiters peel fresh snow peas. We'd sit in the back room around a large square table—enough to seat 10–12 workers—with piles of snow peas waiting to be processed (the large tip and the strings on both sides removed).

Peeling snow peas was not nearly as fun as making fresh wontons. We gathered around the large square table and, instead of snow peas in the middle, a 2-foot-tall mound of seasoned ground pork was plopped on a waiter's tray. The wontons had to be stuffed quickly before the wrappers dried out. We scooped a bit of meat onto the wrapper with a butter knife, sealed the edges with battered egg and then twisted and egg-sealed the tip. My brother and I raced to see who could make the most wontons in an hour. I usually won. The secret to my speed was eventually revealed when waiters received complaints from customers that their wontons were just wads of boiled dough. No meat whatsoever. I was busted and henceforth banished from wonton stuffing duty.

My mother then assigned me the task of refilling the metal sugar packet holders, salt and pepper shakers and the soy sauce dispensers. I worked alone, going from table to table and, to alleviate the boredom, I imagined I was a great scientist discovering an elusive magic potion.

There were more complaints. Some of the customers said the soy sauce was rancid. My soy sauce elixir included a combination of salt, sugar, Tabasco sauce, lots of pepper, and—for the heck of it—a dash of the Coke I sipped while doing my side work. It was a nasty surprise for the unsuspecting customer at the wrong table at the wrong time.

My parents didn't invest in a babysitter, other than Kathy when she wasn't in school; they felt that bringing Michael and me to Mah Jong was the logical thing to do. I spent most of my childhood at Mah Jong. It was my playground and fueled my vigorous sense of imagination.

After school and before customers came in for drinks and/or dinner, I might turn a bar stool on its side with the back of the stool on the floor. I liked to lie down on the stool and pretend I was an astronaut headed for space. The bar stools rocked back and forth, too, adding additional drama as I radioed to NASA, "I'm being hit by asteroids!"

My brother and I built forts with the overturned square dining tables. Using them as ramparts, we finger-pistoled our barrage of imaginary bullets at the enemy.

Mah Jong's pay phones were encased behind a folding wooden door with a full-length window where you could be seen but, for privacy, could not be heard. Making a call required a dime to get a connection and, depending on the length of your call, the operator would tell you how much more to deposit after your call was finished. If a call didn't go through, the dime was returned into a bottom of the phone where it could be retrieved from a silver slot.

I often checked that slot for loose forgotten dimes and it was a lucky day to snag some unclaimed coins. I closed the door and called my make-believe friend, "Dodo." Dodo and I chatted about silly things and gabbed until I saw a customer waiting to use the phone. In the opening credits of the TV series, "Get Smart," featuring Don Adams as Agent 86, Agent 86 moves through a series of doors leading to a phone booth. He dials a number, faces the camera, crosses his arms, and disappears downstairs. I reenacted that scene in the Mah Jong phone booth, often taking Dodo with me. The waiting customers either peered inside the glass to see if I had dramatically fainted or they opened the door and simply asked me to leave.

Credit card payments were rare. Most transactions were cash—and lots of it. I learned early how to handle and count cash. The waiters brought over the bill with the cash and Mom showed me how to count from the right to the left: pennies on the far right, followed by nickels, dimes, quarters, and silver dollars. If a bill came to $10.63, I took 2 pennies to add up to .65 cents, then one dime to get to .75 cents, and then a quarter to get to the next dollar. There were no cash register tapes; everything was done manually.

Recording machines and voicemail had not yet been invented. If we missed a call at Mah Jong, we most likely lost some business. We had to answer the phone by the second ring. There were several phones in the front: by the cashier, by the hostess stand and in Dad's office. If the main number: 516-WA1-0500 [43] was busy, the call rolled over to one of four lines and buttons flashed to signal a call waiting. Sprinting to the phone became a Chinn relay sport.

Original Mah Jong dining room, 1961 (Author's collection)

MAH JONG'S EARLY DECOR

The early color themes of Mah Jong were red and gold, with stately black accents. Red is a lucky color for the Chinese—it signifies happiness, good luck, and success. The Chinese word for gold or yellow is *huang*, which is similar to the word *royal*. The red walls of the converted barn featured large Chinese scrolls. Red, black and gold wooden chairs surrounded the square tables. Gold booths seated parties of four or five, and a long gold banquette along the back wall, with tables put together, accommodated a party of 12. Wait stations in the middle of the dining room held silverware, clean tablecloths and napkins, extra condiments, and ceramic water pitchers. Mirrors in three panels shaped like an open fan filled the space behind the gold-padded bar. The bar seated approximately 15 customers on tall-back stools, and there was a large banquette and several square tables for cocktail seating. The swinging red doors to the kitchen were scuffed in black at the bottom from waiters kicking them open while balancing large trays.

The table setting was always the same for lunch and dinner: pressed white tablecloths, white cloth napkins, teacups and saucers and an array of silverware. After each meal the soiled tablecloths and napkins were gathered by the waiters, brought into the kitchen and tossed down a chute near the dishwashing station, where they slid into a large canvas bin parked in the basement. Each week a linen company picked up the dirty tablecloths and delivered a fresh supply. It might have been economical to use paper placemats over the linen tablecloths as we see today but Dad felt it cheapened the fine dining atmosphere.

A DAY AT MAH JONG

Mah Jong opened for lunch by 11:30am and stayed open through dinner until midnight, Mondays through Thursdays and Sundays. On Fridays and Saturdays, we stayed open until 2:00am. During the 1960s, our family had one car for Dad's use. Mom got ready for work by 9:00am. She plugged in her hot curlers and enjoyed her cup of Taster's Choice freeze-dried instant coffee while setting her hair. She slabbed Jiffy peanut butter onto a piece of white toast. She put on her girdle, nylon stockings and a full-length slip and went into the bathroom to do her make-up (simple foundation, eyebrow pencil, a dab of red lipstick). The curlers came out and she combed her hair, added hairspray and put on her cheomsang and, in later years, a simple blue A-line dress made on her Singer sewing machine. Mom finished up with white imitation pearl clip-on earrings and a white knitted sweater (with a "Made in Hong Kong for the B. Altman department stores" label). She donned simple black pumps and, with her black handbag, walked through our neighborhood to Mah Jong, just over a mile away. This was her routine every day until she bought a Dodge Dart in 1968.

Dad arose just after Mom left and drank his cup of Taster's Choice freeze-dried instant coffee with a leftover dessert from the diner or one of his beloved Hostess pink marshmallow Sno Balls or a Twinkie. He wore the same outfit every day: dark suit with a handkerchief stuffed into his pocket, white shirt, tie, dark socks, laced dress shoes.

Arriving at Mah Jong, Mom opened the gift shop, organized the cash register, arranged the coat check room and checked the reservation book.

The staff was asked to arrive by 10:30. The captains arrived to set up the lunch tables in accordance with the reserved party sizes. Kenny the bartender was on site to bring buckets of ice from the kitchen to the bar tubs and to prep the bar. The waiters not living in the dormitories would arrive by 10:30 to get their station assignments and do their side work (checking the tables for condiments, set up the teacups and saucers, linens, silverware) and receive from Mom a supply of paper order pads, each individually numbered. Mom kept track of waiters and order pads; a bit of control helped with nightly reconciliations. She gave each waiter a fresh laundered and pressed uniform from the coat room.

Before turning on the dining room lights, Mom started Muzak or the record player with our family collection of LPs, from Chopin, Perry Como and Henry Mancini to other soft easy listening background music. The level was set non-intrusively low but subtly detectable for refined ambiance during lunch and dinner.

The kitchen staff emerged from their dormitories early each morning to chop and dice fresh produce, prepare sauces and begin making the large quantities of steamed rice which accompanied every meal. White rice was steamed in large pots, scooped into a smaller hot food pan and placed in the central warming station atop hot water, right next to the egg drop and wonton soup pots.

Chefs were divided into kitchen stations: barbeque and appetizers, seafood, meat dishes, and the head chef, who stepped in during busy times. The kitchen's large barbeque station hummed with constant preparations: lobster and egg rolls, slabs of spareribs, fresh whole chicken, and the char siu (boneless barbeque pork). It held everything for all chopping needs—wooden chopping blocks, cleavers of various sizes and weights, and knife sharpeners.

A commercial grill fired up in the morning, in use throughout the day and evening. There were two racks at the top; the upper for grilling steaks, broiling lobsters and shrimp, and the lower to keep platters warm or to save spareribs for the many customers who liked ribs well done and crispy.

Mah Jong diners say that the food was consistently excellent. I attribute this to a family business model steeped with compassion and care. The cooks, all born and raised in China, were sponsored by Dad to come to the United States after the Communist regime took over. The entire kitchen staff, including the dishwashers and the janitors, were loyal to Mom and Dad, who treated them well, gave them respect, and provided them with good salaries so they had extra money to send back home (via

Dad giving a chopstick lesson to a young customer. (Author's collection)

an intermediary) to support their families in China. Dad often asked the entire kitchen staff to come into the dining room after a banquet so the customers could see who made their meals and to offer an appreciative round of applause. Whenever there was a promotional or media opportunity for Mah Jong, Dad invited the kitchen staff to be in some of those photos. Mom laundered and pressed their aprons.

When Dad wasn't roaming around in the dining room, he was in the kitchen checking in and talking to the staff. Dad made sure that all of the waiters allocated a portion of their tips into a communal pot to give to the kitchen staff, establishing equity among those visible to the customers and those who were not. As a result, there was low turnover compounded with high morale in the Mah Jong kitchen. In addition, the issue of shrinkage—through waste or inventory theft—was not as problematic for Mah Jong as it was for other restaurants. Given the sheer volume of liquor and food that flowed in and out of Mah Jong, the temptation for employees to pilfer items was there, but because the front and back of house staff at Mah Jong were treated like our own family members, very few employees felt the need to steal from us.

CANTONESE FOOD: SUBTLETY, BASIC SEASONING , AND A HOT WOK

Dad's hometown of Canton is situated in Southern China along the Pearl River Delta leading to the South China Sea. It is a major port city roughly 100 miles from Hong Kong and is blessed with subtropical weather. Due to its proximity to the sea, Cantonese cuisine is known for its fresh seafood, light mild sauces, and poached/steamed/sautéed methods to not overpower the original flavors. Subtlety and basic seasonings and a hot wok are the keys to good Cantonese cooking. Among the basic staples: ginger, garlic, cilantro, scallions, soy and oyster sauces, sugar and salted black beans.

Unlike Cantonese food, cuisine from Peking, Szechuan, and Hunan, from Northern or inland China where the climate is harsh and cold, are generally hot and spicy. Main staples include chili oil and peppercorns. Wheat flour is a staple in North China where rice is difficult to cultivate, so regions near Peking produce noodles, flour pancakes and buns for their primary starch.

For the Cantonese, meats such as pork, chicken, beef and duck, are main ingredients and often roasted or braised. Every part of an animal is used—from nose to tail—nothing is wasted.

Cantonese cuisine is famous for its Yum Cha, or dim sum, a weekend brunch tradition featuring an array of dumplings and steamed delicacies pushed in carts around the dining tables. The Chinn family strategy is to sit at a table closest to the kitchen since the food coming out is fresh and the carts are full. We became expert lookouts, strategically seated facing all directions and with good reflexes: eating, keeping an eye out to catch the cart pusher's attention and diverting the cart to our table before they got past us.

Today, it is harder to find dim sum service with rolling carts since it takes up space to move the cart through the dining room. It is also cost-saving; there is no need hire extra staff to push the carts. Recently, I've noticed some restaurants offer dim sum on the menu but brought to your table direct from the kitchen. Kathy, Michael, and I—with our keenly-developed restaurant instincts—calculated that while it was economical to dispense with the dim sum carts, there was corresponding lost revenue for the restaurant since it eliminates impulse buying from the cart whizzing by. And it takes longer to order off the menu and wait for it to be delivered to your table, so seating turns over slowly, meaning you can use the table once in 90 minutes as opposed to twice in 90 minutes if using the cart service. Before I consider going to a dim sum restaurant today, I check on their serving method and avoid restaurants without push carts so I don't let my ferocious dim-sum cart-detecting intuition go to waste.

Dad liked to say all Chinese eventually admit that if they want good authentic Chinese food, they'll order a Cantonese meal. Mah Jong's menu was Cantonese, with fresh seafood, meats, and produce ordered on Sundays based on the expected reservations and walk-ins. The food's Cantonese authenticity was proven in every dish, made in-house and by hand. Wonton wrappers were purchased from Chinatown and they were all made fresh by noodle companies. Leftover wonton wrappers were sliced and fried, kept in a warmer, and presented in a bowl with a side of fresh duck sauce and house mustard as soon as the customers had their menus in their hands.

The chefs prepared egg roll fillings each morning and the wrappers were rolled and sealed with an egg wash and kept in the walk-in refrigerator until time to deep fry in peanut oil. One of the secret reasons Mah Jong's egg rolls and lobster rolls were distinctly flavorful was the use of caul fat, or omentum. Omentum is the membrane lining of the animal's abdomen which surrounds the internal organs. Since nothing goes to waste, omentum is used to enhance flavor. Mah Jong chefs put a layer of tissue fat on top of the wonton wrapper and then put in the filling. When it was deep-fried, the caul fat melted into the filling, adding a seductive and irresistible flavor.

The barbequed spareribs were made with fresh pork with all of the fat left on. For special customers' children, Dad offered Mah Jong hamburgers made from chuck steak, freshly ground by the chefs, fried in bacon fat. This was and is the secret to flavorful food: leave the fat on!

When the Chinns went out for Chinese food, it was to Chinatown in the City and on a Monday night (Mom and Dad's day off). We'd never order off the menu. Dad told the waiters to prepare a menu with animal dishes representing something from the sky, land, and sea. Cantonese restaurants have fish tanks stocked with live sea bass, rock cod and, when in season, Maine lobsters and Dungeness crabs. If the fish are moving, they are fresh and you point to the one you want for dinner. The chef scoops the fish out with a net and takes it into the kitchen.

An example of a balanced meal for the Chinns—shared family style—is roast duck or squab with crispy skin served with roasted salt and shrimp chips (akin to puffed potato chips), soy sauce chicken, char siu barbecue pork, sautéed beef with XO sauce, a sweet, smoky, salty condiment originating from Hong Kong said to resemble umami flavors. The XO is a loose reference to XO (extra-old) cognac which signifies prestige and luxury; there is no cognac in XO sauce. Also on the menu might be clams with black bean sauce, fried salt and pepper shrimp (with the skins on), noodle dishes such as beef chow fun or crispy pan fried noodles with an assortment of braised meats and vegetables on top, stir fried green vegetables like gai lan, Chinese broccoli similar in taste to broccoli rabe, bok choy, or snow peas mixed with shitake or wood ear mushrooms, and always plenty of white rice. The centerpiece of a Chinese meal is steamed whole fish, or "yu" which means abundance. We prefer steamed sea bass with soy sauce and sliced fresh ginger. The Chinese believe that the fish is served whole to represent freshness and unity, and to showcase that the fish is fresh. The fish is served with the head facing the guest of honor or the eldest guest. Dad always got the fish cheeks, the sweetest part of the fish. He would eat the eyeballs, too, much to our juicy delight.

We sat at a round table with a lazy Susan so every dish was within easy reach as it spun around. Determined to order plenty of food, our family of five sat at a round table set for 10 and joyfully had leftovers to take home. At the apex of our meals, the lazy Susan wasn't so lazy; it was in constant spinning motion as more dishes were added and we were encouraged to eat and sample while the dishes were fresh.

Even today, with friends at a Chinese restaurant, I ask for a table for double our party size. The Chinese serving platters are large and it is not uncommon to see three of us at a table large enough for six.

We were taught to taste everything on our plate. Mom, knowing what it was like to starve during the war, abhorred wasting food. When we had cracked crab and lobster, she admonished us for leaving any part of the meat in the shells.

FANATICAL HOSPITALITY

My parents instilled important work ethics: show up on time, work hard, be prepared, learn to read body language, address customers by Mr. and Mrs., never by their first names. They emphasized the concept of fanatical and relentless hospitality to make people feel welcomed from the moment they stepped foot in Mah Jong until they got back into their cars to go home. Long before the TV series "Cheers," Mah Jong was the place where everyone knew your name.

Mom often sat on a chair by the gift shop in direct sightline of the front door. She kept an eye on the glass doors and incoming customers. As children, we were taught to stand up, say hello, shake hands, and engage in conversations.

The captains were chosen for their ability to be proactive, easy-going, accommodating, and jovial. As the first staff encountered, the captains' main job was to make each customer feel special, greeting them with a "Hello, sir," "Good evening, ma'am," "Nice to see you Mr. and Mrs. So-and-So," always accompanied by a slight bow of respect. On occasion, the captains, cashiers, and waiters would help certain customers get into or out of their cars. For flourish, Michael and I ran to open the doors for customers as they came in, which put them in a good mood even before their dining experience (they stayed later, ordered more, and tipped well, too). Customers were never greeted informally and no one would even think of a blanket welcome such as the one we use today: "Hey, Guys."

Curious to know why customers kept coming back, other than the consistently excellent food, I spoke with former staff and customers, who unanimously and emphatically revealed that at Mah Jong everyone felt *at home*. Anna Tumpek (cashier and hostess) said, "I remember an older lady, a former high school science teacher with no family, who liked the booth closest to the hostess stand. I asked her if she liked coming to Mah Jong every Sunday and she said she did because this was home to her. She said: 'I've gotten to know some of the waiters, Mr. and Mrs. Chinn, and you come and chat with me all the time. I have a very lonely week and I love coming here.' She was a special lady and I felt there were more people like that who came to Mah Jong because it was their home."

Once you checked your coat, you were welcomed by one of the captains—all in black dinner jackets, white shirts, black pants, and a dress tie. Dick Lang, with his pencil-thin mustache, resembled a short and thin Clark Gable; debonair, gracious, on the serious side, and liked to hang out at the bar with the customers. He loved and specialized in Chinese calligraphy; for Chinese New Year, he created signage and scroll backdrops for the evening's activities.

Watching Mah Jong captain Dick Lang doing calligraphy for Chinese New Year (Author's collection)

Whereas Dick was the dapper captain, Charlie Ma was the inadvertent comedian. Known for his Yogi Berra malapropisms, one never knew what would come out of Charlie's mouth—in fractured English.

Charlie had an easy-going, almost laconic attitude. Nothing fazed him and he was perpetually happy and eager to please. Often difficult to understand, Charlie was known to surprise women coming out of the ladies room with, "Did everything come out alright?" Mom's eye roll was predictable.

When a customer asked where to put his coat, Charlie pointed to the coat room and said, "You go hang yourself over there."

If a customer had dietary restrictions, it might go like this:

Customer: "Can you make this with no MSG, no spice, no cornstarch, and no salt?"

Charlie (proudly): "We can make anything with nothing!"

Some of the more popular waiters were promoted to captain. It was not uncommon for regular customers to ask to be seated at their favorite waiter's station. Harry Chin was a special friend to our family—a calm, gentle, warm man who seemed to possess healing qualities. When one of Mom's pet goldfish took ill and was listless and tilting to one side in the tank, Harry came to our house and with verbal encouragement, special Chinese medicine, and stroking...miraculously cured the goldfish. He made medicine for humans, too. Dubbed "Dr. Chin," he often expressed the desire to run his own restaurant one day. Dad took him under his wing, promoting him from waiter to captain and entrusting him with the management of Mah Jong on Mom and Dad's rare Monday night off.[44]

Most of the waiters and front-line staff used American names, perhaps easier for the customers to remember rather than Chinese names. There were Kim, James, Willie, Henry, and Cowboy. And the cashiers assigned a few nicknames. For example, a 4'10" waiter was dubbed "Tiny," and an elderly waiter, small, wiry, but spry, was simply referred to as "TOG" for "The Old Guy."

THE KOUTENSKYS

Bill and Loretta Koutensky liked to come to Mah Jong after Long Island National Bank closed at 3:00, arriving by 4:00 for an early dinner. Mom watched for the Koutenskys' Cadillac Coupe tail fins driving past the glass entrance and when she saw them pull up, she shouted, "They're here!" in Chinese. Everyone snapped into action.

The Koutenskys had a place of honor at Mah Jong. They sat at the first booth near the hostess stand where they could converse with Mom. My brother and I might hop into the booth to keep them company. Dad, the waiters, the captains, the bartenders all visited the table to say, "Hi."

If Michael and I weren't at the restaurant when Bill and Loretta were there, it meant we were old enough to be home alone after school. Mom would call us just as the Koutenskys were leaving Mah Jong so we could be by the kitchen window to see Bill and Loretta drive past our house, honk their Cadillac horn three times and wave as they drove towards their home in Hicksville.

THE MAH JONG GIFT SHOP

The gift shop was right in the middle of the Mah Jong floor plan. After you checked your coat, you moved to the dining room on the left, straight ahead to the full-service bar, or to the right to Mom's gift shop. You couldn't miss it, which was Mom's intent. She loved her role as curator. The gift shop became a favorite destination for dinner guests and others who knew it was a great place to buy special gifts not found in a department store.

To keep up with the latest trends, Mom went to trade shows in the City. She paid special attention to items of interest to kids. She took me with her to shows and let me pick out toys or games. One of Mom's favorite trade show vendors was Takashimaya for lacquered bowls, tea sets, chopsticks, toys, and games. Other specialty vendors were She Dragon Gate Import & Export (New York), Continental Traders, Inc. (San Francisco), Hong Kong Art Craft Merchants Association, and Orchids of Hawaii.

The gift shop display cases, with adjustable shelves and lighting, featured exquisite hand-made ivory carvings and cloisonné vases on the top shelf. On the middle shelves you might find fine jewelry: jade rings, gold necklaces, and bracelets. The bottom shelves held beaded Chinese slippers (for men, women, and children), Chinese dolls in assorted outfits, and beaded coin purses. Open shelves displayed incense burners, novelty items, and knick-knacks. Glass wind chimes hung on hooks.

There was something for everyone. It was the ideal place to pick up a last-minute gift. After forgetting an anniversary, men might find redemption at the gift shop. Mom often gave long-time customers a 10% discount and, if she learned a customer was celebrating a special occasion, she just gave the items away. Mom often arranged for special last-minute gift wrapping.

Tired of saying, "Be careful!" to kids (and adults), she created signs in bold black letters for each shelf:

Nice to look at
Nice to hold
If you drop it
Then it's sold

The popular fortune cookies were freshly made by a factory in Chinatown. When Dad was picking up the chefs, he also picked up a supply of fresh fortune cookies. One of my jobs was placing six fortune cookies each into parchment bags. The bags were stapled and placed in a bin and sold for 25 cents. After dining, customers could stop by the gift shop and take home a bag of fortune cookies.

Mom thought the popular Mah Jong fortune cookies were perfect for Halloween. On Oct 30, she brought several boxes of fortune cookies home. We sat at the kitchen table with our parchment bags and stapler.

Mom at her Mah Jong gift shop, 1961 (Author's collection)

We put two fortune cookies in each bag, stapled it and lined up the bags to give out the next day. The Chinns' house became the most popular on the Halloween trail, once word got out about the fortune cookies. My mother was lenient to the little kids who came back to the door for more but had little patience for the barely costumed high school kids holding open pillowcases with their gaping maws begging to be refilled with fortune cookies.

"You've had enough. Go home," my mother scolded when she saw these teenage apparitions. Then she'd slam the door. She peered out the window and boasted that she saw kids going through their Halloween bags, tossing out candy and bargaining for our fortune cookies.

"We have the best house!" she said.

Shelves in the Mah Jong gift shop (Author's collection)

CHAPTER 11

DEBBIE'S EARLY YEARS

Long Island is comprised of 291 communities. According to the Long Island Historical Census, the demographic of my hometown of Syosset in 1970 was 99.4% white, 0.3% Asian, 0.1% Black, and 2% Hispanic/Native American/other, [45] mirroring the rest of Long Island's ethnic profile.

A November 17, 2019 article (*"Dividing Lines, Visible and Invisible)"* in *Newsday*, Long Island's major newspaper, reported that Long Island was purposely designed for segregation. Levittown, 8 miles from Syosset, was built by William Levitt after World War II and was America's first suburb. Comprising attractive and affordable housing tracts, it also came with restrictions to prevent sales of homes to blacks.

"The tenant agrees not to permit the premises to be used or occupied by any person other than members of the Caucasian race," one such covenant read. "But the employment and maintenance of other than Caucasian domestic servants shall be permitted."

In a 1954 interview with the *Saturday Evening Post*, Levitt explained his racial exclusion policy this way:

"If we sell one house to a Negro family, then 90 to 95 percent of our white customers will not buy into the community. That is their attitude, not ours. We did not create it and we cannot cure it. As a company, our position is simply this: we can solve a housing problem or we can try to solve a racial problem. But we cannot combine the two."[46]

It was no wonder I rarely saw people of color and the only Chinese people around (other than the Mah Jong staff) owned the laundromats and the other Chinese restaurants.

I wasn't prepared for what school would be like. I recall my kindergarten to third grade experience as extremely lonely. Mom and Dad seldom had time for parent/teacher activities or any of my elementary school activities. Mom got up early to make Cream of Wheat or oatmeal for my breakfast and then went back to bed. I'd walk across the street to catch the school bus. I was the only kid who didn't have a parent waiting with them until the bus arrived.

I was, and still am, a late bloomer: always a shade late to the learning party. I didn't learn how to ride a bicycle until I was about 9. My bike had training wheels while everyone rode bikes with cool banana seats and tall handlebars. I practiced riding with the neighborhood kids and couldn't quite maintain balance until one of the girls stood behind me and wheeled me forward while I wobbled along. Thinking she was running alongside until I got my balance, I looked to my left to find her gone and then I looked straight ahead to see a rose bush. I plowed headfirst into the rose bush and came out gnarled up with greenery. The onlookers laughed, but I was elated! I pedaled about five inelegant spins before my head-on collision. I was proud I could indeed balance myself on a bike, albeit temporarily, which gave me confidence. After several more tries (on the hedge-free side of the block) I graduated from my bike with training wheels by 4th grade.

I was the typical small skinny child who wasn't adept at sports. I rarely got on the A team for relay races. I hated "Duck Duck Goose," the game where you sit in a circle and someone walks around tapping everyone's head, and if they said, "Goose," you had to get up and chase that person around the circle before they took your spot on the floor. I got called "Goose" a lot and I seldom caught up to the bigger kids with longer strides. I was left to tap around the circle. When I tapped a kid to say, "Goose," he or she usually caught up with me before I made it halfway around the circle. I was tense with anxiety, knowing I'd be tapped and, after too many times playing that tortuous game, I didn't bother chasing, I slowed down and just let the kid take my spot back on the floor. I figured if I couldn't be fast, I should at least be polite.

And who the hell invented Dodgeball? Another game where Debbie was an easy target. The object of Dodgeball is for two teams to hit members of the opposite team with an 8" rubber ball. The team that hits and eliminates all members of the opposite team is the winner. The rule was, never hit anyone above the waist. Again, my cursed short height made it hard to find a safe spot to hit and some of the larger girls intentionally aimed at me. They made eye contact and knew I was in trouble. When a large rubber ball hits your face at high speed, it stings and leaves a red welt on your skin. There were times when a ball hit my face and careened off. Pow! My gym teacher pulled me off to the side for a time out, sat me on his knee, and offered words of comfort. I did not want to give anyone the satisfaction of seeing me cry. When I was put back in, I learned to stay behind some of the larger kids as a shield and how to "duck and roll."

I didn't care for kindergarten Show-and-Tell either. What a bore. Someone brought in a rock. Another kid showed off a leaf. No imagination! When it was my turn to bring in an inanimate object, I brought my 3-year-old brother. Mom had slept in that morning and I woke Michael up to say we were going to school. He had no idea what was going on. We went to the bus stop where he was the center of my classmates' and their parents' attention. If anyone questioned why I had a 3-year-old kid with me, I wasn't aware of it.

When we got to my kindergarten classroom, I proudly announced my Show-and-Tell item. Michael just sat there while I described him. Soon after, there was much ado when Principal Hildebrandt came in to the classroom to say that Mrs. Chinn was hysterical. Her son was missing from his bed and she assumed that Debbie been absconded as well. Had I made it to school? Had anyone seen me on the bus? Explanations were made and I was dutifully scolded for creating such a scare. But inside, I felt mighty smug about my creative caper, knowing I had delivered the Best Show-and-Tell item ever.

I loved when Miss Wanda Evans, our school librarian, came into the classroom to read to us. Her voice was low, silky, and comforting. *Curious George*, the *Doctor Seuss* books, *Dick and Jane* stoked my fertile imagination already exercised by my pretend games at Mah Jong. Thanks to Miss Evans, I fell in love with reading. In a 2021 interview, David Ronis, one of my closest classmates from first grade through high school, and now a renowned opera director and singer, recalled, "You and I were in Miss O'Driscoll's first grade class and assigned to seats next to each other for the special reading group which was just the two of us! We were considered the smart kids since our reading aptitude was better than the others. It was Miss Evans who turned us onto books and it was Miss Evans who made reading such an adventure."

My elementary school experiences were accompanied by racial taunts and slurs. A classmate welcomed me into the classroom by pulling her eyes up, clasping her hands, bowing, and saying in an exaggerated fashion, "AHHHH SO!" Others would pull their eyes up, then their eyes down, point to their knees and say, "Chinese, Japanese, American Knees." One bully, who assumed I was Japanese, said his father killed Japanese for sport and I should just "go back home." My desk was across from that bully and during arts and crafts, he ate the white paste out of the jar; after reaching over to try to smear it on my face with a wooden ice cream stick.

My first grade class photo. I am seated in the middle, 3rd from the left. David Ronis is behind me, back row 3rd from left. Also in this photo is the bully who kept trying to smear paste on my face. (Author's collection)

I was a very shy little girl. With each comment or humiliation, I receded into myself and couldn't wait to get to the comfort of Mah Jong where I could hang out at the bar and sell my cigarettes and cigars.

In the middle of a class, a substitute teacher once called on me to ask a question. "Why is it that when I go to a Chinese restaurant and try to drink the tea, that the cup is too hot and you can't hold it? How come teacups don't come with handles as they do in other countries, like England?" The questions weren't posed as malice, just simple curiosity, but I couldn't muster an answer since I hadn't the faintest idea what to tell her. I was also embarrassed to think that Chinese invented teacups this illogical way. Why were my people so backwards?

I told Mom about that exchange when the school bus dropped me off behind Mah Jong. The next morning Mom gave me the answer to relay to the substitute teacher. When the class got settled, I raised my hand to speak and said that I had the answer to the tea-cup-being-too-hot-to-hold question. I said, "My mother said that if the teacup is too hot to hold, the tea is too hot, so don't be stupid enough to drink it."

When I complained to Mom that people made fun of me, she taught me a lesson I've carried with me well into adulthood. "Before they make fun of you, make fun of yourself first. That way, they have nothing to laugh about because you beat them to it." I studied the art of verbal self-judo on late night television by watching comedians like Rodney Dangerfield and Joan Rivers who embellished their foibles and got laughs and applause along the way. Being self-deprecating works best when it is tinged with humor and as I've stumbled through my career and love life, I am lucky to have ample and endless material to work with.

Six-year-old me, however, was just learning to be more emboldened and the timing coincided with Mah Jong becoming famous. Mom and Dad invited some of our elementary school teachers to be special guests during the Chinese New Year Celebration or to come and have a drink after work. This was a way for my teachers to understand how my upbringing, with two working parents—a rarity in those days—focused on getting Mah Jong up and running, fought against my fitting in socially at school.

Some of my teachers became regular customers and were welcomed into our Mah Jong family circle. They looked after me in school. Principal Hildebrandt encouraged me to play with other kids during recess instead of sitting by myself under a tree. He escorted me over to a group of kids playing hopscotch or tetherball and suggested they give me a turn. At last! Two sports activities that didn't include the fear of being chased or hit. I loved tetherball and got so good at it even the big girls wanted to play with me. We smaller kids, for whom the equipment for softball or field hockey was too big, played handball along the side of the school wall. Like tetherball, I enjoyed smacking something hard. The handball was more my size and I learned to keep up with the velocity of the game.

In one version of hopscotch, a teacher placed a penny within the grid, two kids stood at the far ends of the grid, and the object was to take the 8" rubber ball, my Dodgeball enemy, and try to hit the penny. You had one chance to hit the penny. If you missed, you gave up your turn to the next kid in line. If you hit the penny, you could keep it and the teacher pulled out another penny to put onto the grid.

Like a sonar detector, my aim was very sharp and I consistently hit the penny. So sharp, in fact, I kept beating all the kids. Principal Hildebrandt gently suggested I take a rest to let other kids have a chance to play. For once, I was good at a sport, as long as money was a reward. I often left school feeling rich and satisfied with pennies jingling in my pocket. "It was a good day at school!" I would say to Mom before taking out the pennies, stacking them in piles of ten and counting them with her. She said it was good math practice to learn to count in units of ten. We converted the pennies into quarters or dimes and took them home to put in my piggy bank.

Perhaps sensing my worrisome absorption with grabbing pennies during recess, Miss Evans encouraged me to stop by the library. This is where I found the world of *Tom Sawyer, Pippi Longstocking, Harriet the Spy, Charlie and the Chocolate Factory* and *Ramona the Pest*. My favorite was *The Sword and the Stone* by T.H. White, from which I developed a childhood fascination for stories about kings, heroes, fantasy, and magic. I read these books curled up in the back corner of Miss Evans' library so I could pretend to paddle down a river, talk to invisible adventure partners, and wave my invisible sword.

David and I both remember some classmates who casually whispered, "Did you know Miss Evans is black?" It never occurred to either of us that she was black, and actually, as David recalls, "I thought that was cool!" I don't recall knowing as a first-grader what being black meant and I have always wondered what difference this makes to a child. Why are we taught to see people according to the color of their skin? Do children see people in shades or in a different class structure? What was whispered about *me* by my classmates? And where did Miss Evans live, if she was not allowed in Levittown?

Some of my elementary school teachers attending Chinese New Year's dinner at Mah Jong: Principal William Hildebrandt is seated left. Librarian Wanda Evans is seated front right. (Author's collection)

All South Grove Elementary school students were required to take Miss Chieffo's music class; we learned to sing, how to move our arms to conduct in 3/4 and 4/4 time. We gained the early experience of singing in a choir, presented as part of the Christmas program to parents, siblings, and teachers. We learned to memorize the songs since not everyone knew how to read music.

David remembers us marching into the All Purpose Room singing, *We Need A Little Christmas* from the musical "Mame." What fun it was to parade in with such fanfare! After the class play, I discovered I really loved a group creating something with the sum of our various parts. That team environment I envied as a bystander in the sports world was what I gravitated to with music and the arts. The difference was, there was no competition, no score to settle, and everyone was a winner, adding to the mix to blend into a sublime artistic outcome. Best of all, the environment welcomed kids regardless of background, skill level, social status, height or race. And I didn't have to worry about anyone trying to smear paste on my face.

CHAPTER 12

DEBBIE GOES TO CONFESSION

Our local place of worship was St. Edward the Confessor Roman Catholic Church, a mile from our home, reachable by walking along busy South Oyster Bay Road. On Sundays, Mom, Michael and I dressed up in our best attire and walked to church. Dad never attended church; he worked at Mah Jong to prepare for the busy after-church lunch crowd. I wore a white lace dress, a small hat with a chin strap (so it didn't fly off my head when cars whizzed by) and white gloves. I carried a small purse which held a couple of quarters to put into the collection basket when it passed along our pew.

Mass was in Latin and very long. It felt longer in the summer because the church lacked air conditioning. I am sure I looked a mess by the time it came to receiving the Holy Sacrament. When my lace dress was moist with sweat, I started to itch. I ditched the small hat and the white gloves and unzipped a bit of the dress for the cross-breeze at the altar. We were not permitted to speak or whisper which made church very boring. We usually sat in the same area—midway on the left-hand side. I remember kneeling and kicking the shoes of the man in front of me just for fun. He never turned around to snap at me but I thought he might be praying to the saints to make my lace dress more itchy.

Mom bought my first communion dress: white lace, puffy sleeves, a white veil, white purse, and white patent leather shoes with white anklets. She enrolled me in Saturday morning catechism class for my Sacrament of Confirmation when I turned 12. Classes were led by very stern unsmiling nuns in black habits who weren't there to provide comfort and love. It was all business to prepare us for our rite of passage.

We had to stand when a nun walked into the room, we were told to sit up straight, and the learning environment was dour and rigid. Preparing for my Confirmation required learning about the saints and practicing when we were supposed to stand, sit, kneel, and hold up our rosary for the blessing. We were given a book of saints to help determine which saint's name to choose for our Confirmation. This saint would be our spiritual protector and guide. I was transfixed with Saint Sebastian, who was ordered to be killed by arrows for converting his Roman soldiers to Christianity. The picture showed him with arrows piercing his neck and torso. I chose him as my confirmation saint because he was the most dramatic-looking. I was overruled by the nuns, who deemed a female saint the more appropriate choice. So, I went with Saint Anne; Ann is my middle name so it would be easy to remember. Plus, she was Mary's mother and Jesus's maternal grandmother, which I figured is as direct a pipeline to protection as I would need in life.

Going to confession was a prerequisite. What an intimidating experience, going into a dark partition to confess your sins to a disembodied voice. I couldn't think of any sins I had committed in my brief years of existence, and I was already roundly punished for bringing Michael with me to Show-and-Tell. I just said I stole some cookies and the priest said to say some Hail Marys. It seemed efficient enough and that was fine with me. No point staying in that creepy claustrophobic box longer than necessary.

Returning home from first communion (Author's collection)

Returning home from confirmation (Author's collection)

CHAPTER 13

DAD
NEW PROJECTS
NEW ANGLES

Dad opened a second restaurant in Manhattan. Dubbed "Little Mah Jong," it was located in a restaurant district known as "Steak Row" on 45th Avenue near Grand Central Station. Its next-door neighbor was the Pen and Pencil which was adjacent to other restaurants like The Pressbox, The Editorial, and Danny's Hideaway.[47] The prime location offered promise for "Little Mah Jong," but Dad straddled two businesses at least an hour's ride apart. No one knew why he wanted to start another restaurant. It did not last long. Both Mah Jong restaurants suffered from lack of focus and attention.

He also was intrigued by the popularity of baked potatoes and had an inkling to start Greater Tater, featuring baked potatoes with an array of toppings and sides. The concept never went anywhere but it is one example of how Dad's mind was always on the next project or adventure.

Dad, never content with Mah Jong's plateau of achievement, brainstormed myriad new angles to keep the dining and hospitality experience fresh for customers and, as trends changed, he was eager to stay several steps ahead. If not baked potatoes, it would be something else.

THE DAILY RACE FORM

Dad brought home the evening edition of the *Daily News* and *Daily Mirror*. ten-year-old Kathy sat with him to read the paper. Dad read the paper from right to left, not because that is how you read in Chinese, but because the sports section was in the back. Kathy started with the cartoons in the front of the paper. When they met in the middle, Dad taught her about horse racing. Kathy learned about the horses' strengths (strong running in the mud or of a solid breed) as well as how to read *The Daily Racing Form* to determine the winner. Kathy learned math by figuring out the odds.

Living so close to the Belmont Stakes Racetrack[48]—just 20 miles from Syosset in Elmont, NY—was heaven for Dad who loved to play the horses. When off-track betting (OTB) was legalized in New York in 1970, an OTB parlor opened up within walking distance of Mah Jong. When the Mah Jong waiters and cooks got paid, they scurried over to the OTB after the lunch shift to place their bets. They were supposed to come back to Mah Jong by 3:00 to prep for the dinner service but some idled at the OTB a little too long. Mom took note and drove over to the OTB to shoo the lingerers out of the building. Dad, who knew Mom kept watch, had friends place bets for him while he went home to take a nap.

Besides horse racing, Dad loved baseball. Ralph Kiner and Lindsey Nelson were announcers for the New York Mets; Phil Rizzuto and Red Barber for the New York Yankees. Baseball games were often played during the day in the 1960s so Dad set up small black and white TVs at the Mah Jong bar and in his back office.

Communal baseball fever followed the NY Mets' miracle march towards the 1969 World Series. Mom had favorite Mets players: Tommie Agee, Cleon Jones, and Donn Clendenon. She keep them straight by their sequential uniform numbers: Agee, 20; Jones, 21; Clendenon, 22.

I was marginally interested in baseball until Dad took me to Shea Stadium for Game 5 of the World Series on Oct 16, 1969: Mets vs Orioles with the Mets leading the Series three games to one. Shea was packed with over 57,000 (the capacity of Shea was 45,000). In the crowd were Louis Armstrong and Joe DiMaggio. I don't know where our original seats were but I recall Dad smoothly greeting an usher with a handshake in which Dad had a wad of cash. We ended up behind third base roughly twelve rows behind the Orioles' dugout. There were no seats but the usher said we could stand by the corner if we didn't block anyone's view.

We had a perfect spot to watch the dramatics unfold as the Mets, trailing 3–0 at the bottom of the fifth inning, scored 2 runs in the sixth and 1 run in the seventh to tie the game. Ron Swoboda (who made his infamous diving catch the day before in Game 4 at the top of the ninth inning, preventing extra runs which allowed the Mets to advance to Game 5) hit a double in the bottom of the eighth to put the Mets ahead 4–3. One more run was added.

By this time Shea was a wall of yelling and euphoria and when, at the top of the ninth inning, Orioles batter Davey Johnson, with two outs, hit a fly ball to Tommie Agee in left field, the entire stadium reached pandemonium levels. Fans ran out of the bleachers and onto the field to grab dirt, grass, the bases. Some climbed the flag poles, many just whooped and hollered all over the diamond.

It took forever for Dad and me to get out to the car. No one wanted to leave; we had all just witnessed baseball history.[49]

Everyone had Mets fever after that, especially the Chinn family because Ron Swoboda lived in Syosset on Morris Court. Through his and Dad's mutual philanthropic support of Long Island's little league teams, Ron, and his friend, first baseman Ed Kranepool were frequent customers at Mah Jong. In later years, these relationships lead to a new program Dad created utilizing sports personalities to promote Mah Jong.

Pua (Pauline De Silva), one of the Mah Jong dancers, with Ron Swoboda of the New York Mets (Pauline De Silva collection)

CHAPTER 14

LEROY NEIMAN: SIX DEGREES OF SEPARATION

During the mid-1950s, LeRoy Neiman was a fashion illustrator for Carson Pirie Scott, a department store in Chicago for 164 years before closing in 2018. Also at Carson's was an advertising copywriter named Hugh Hefner who had just launched *Playboy* magazine. In 1953, Hefner (known as "Hef," his preferred nickname) commissioned LeRoy to create an illustration for a short story and enlisted him to be *Playboy*'s official artist. It was a relationship that endured for 50 years. I met author Patrick Anderson at a 1993 cast party for *Substance of Fire* by Jon Robin Baitz when I was in my 30s and working at Center Theatre Group in Los Angeles. Pat was a speechwriter for President Jimmy Carter and about to release his political thriller, *Electing Jimmy Carter*. Based in Washington, DC, Pat was living at the Playboy Mansion in Holmby Hills (Los Angeles) while working on Hef's commissioned biography. Pat and I spent most of our evenings at the Mansion since it had everything one could want and more.

My insider's view of life in the Mansion: Wednesday dinners were not to be missed; the chefs made fried chicken from Hef's mother's recipe. Sunday was movie night; we gathered in the screening room after being fed a sumptuous buffet. A couch was prepared in the front for Hef, whose arrival signaled the start of the movie. A full bar was always within reach. Scott Baio and Robert Culp were among the celebrities. After our dinners, Pat and I strolled around the Mansion grounds. We passed flamingos, the aviary and the famous Grotto (the site of wild pool parties, later converted into an arcade for Hef's children).

I joined Pat at one of Hef's holiday parties. It was exactly what you would imagine a Hollywood party to be and, yes, Hef really did wear a silk bathrobe at the Mansion all the time. He and Kimberly had 2 toddlers, Cooper and Marston. I have a lingering image of the boys' toys strewn on the landing on the front stairs directly beneath a seductive nude portrait of their mother.

Over the decades, LeRoy became famous for his paintings depicting celebrities, athletes, sports events, artists, animals, and abstracts. The vibrancy of his brush strokes and use of primary colors was instantly recognizable. He was designated the official artist for the Olympic Games, a role he held from 1972 to 2010.

Dad and Mom collected LeRoy Neiman's work, displayed in our home and at Mah Jong. While sports were the dominant subjects of LeRoy's paintings, Mom's favorite was "Lions Pride;" a lion and lioness with three cubs. Mom said it personified her, Dad, and their three surviving children.

With editor Ginna BB Gordon in front of Leroy Neiman's
Lion's Pride, *2021 (Photo: David Gordon)*

CHAPTER 15

RESTAURANT RESEARCH

Mom and Dad worked every day, all day, except Monday nights, reserved for restaurant research. Sometimes we went to casual places such as Howard Johnsons in Westbury, Cooky's Steakhouse at the Walt Whitman Mall in Huntington, or a local diner (Dad said the best diners were run by Greeks).

I learned to observe restaurant efficiency and developed an intuition for customer service as well as strong aversion to "service with a shrug."

We noticed how long it took to be greeted, how we were spoken to, how long it took for courses to arrive, if the staff were paying more attention to each other or watchful of the customers, when anyone noticed our empty water glasses, and other nuances of customer service. Our family conversations were generally opinions of the meal: "They put too much bread in that little basket; you can't pull the slices out without the other pieces falling on the table," "The ketchup bottle hasn't been wiped down," "The salads are served on warm plates," and Dad's favorite, "They just put the check on the table without asking if we wanted to order anything else—they missed out on getting more money from us." Like Dad, my pet peeve was, and still is, when the fastest thing to arrive at your table is the check.

On special occasions we went upscale to other fine dining restaurants. Mom and Dad became well known as successful restaurateurs, so fellow restaurant owners were delighted to chat and share ideas.

A very special treat was dinner at Trader Vic's in the City, where Arthur Jong's brother, Andy, was the maître d.' We were often privileged to have a prime table and VIP service. We enjoyed a salad made from the new phenomenon, limestone lettuce[50], better known today as butter or Bibb lettuce.

When you entered Trader Vic's at the Savoy-Plaza Hotel on 5th Avenue at 58th, you were welcomed into the land of Polynesia. The décor was Tiki torches, giant clam shells, fishing nets above the ceiling, bamboo partitions, rattan seats, a large outrigger canoe, dark wood interior, and dramatic red and gold lighting.

From 1937–1966, at the nearby Lexington Hotel on Lexington at 48th, the Hawaiian Room featured singers and dancers recruited from Hawaii to perform during their luaus.

Hawaii Kai was perhaps the most famous of Polynesian restaurants in New York and a long-time fixture at Times Square, located above the Winter Garden Theatre at Broadway and 50th. Hawaii Kai was established in 1962 by Joseph Kipness (1911–1982), a Broadway producer whose credits include "High Button Shoes" featuring Phil Silvers and Nanette Fabray (directed by George Abbott), and a string of Broadway productions during the 1970s: "Applause" starring Lauren Bacall, "Seesaw," and "Mack and Mabel" with co-producer David Merrick.

Through Kipness's theatre connections, he engaged the services of Frederick Fox (1910–1991), a set designer for stage, opera, and TV productions. Fox was responsible for set and lighting designs for the Metropolitan Opera and over 200 Broadway productions. An early pioneer of TV set designs, he created the sets for "Your Show of Shows" starring Imogene Coca and Sid Caesar.

Fox created the dramatic interior of Hawaii Kai, including island greenery, waterfalls, capuchin monkeys, and three rooms, including The Lounge of the Seven Pleasures, featuring Polynesian entertainment until 3:00am.

The area that encompassed Hawaii Kai, the Savoy-Plaza, and the Lexington Hotel highlighted a rich Polynesian island experience within the heart of the island of Manhattan.

Part of a nation-wide surge of interest in Hawaii, a U.S. state as of 1959, was the 1963 exhibition at Disneyland called The Enchanted Tiki Room. The Rodgers and Hammerstein musical "South Pacific" opened on Broadway in 1949 and closed five years later in 1954 after an impressive 1,925 performances. The movie adaptation premiered in 1958 and James Michener's "Hawaii" was first published in 1959.

Also in 1958, Rodgers and Hammerstein's "Flower Drum Song," directed by Gene Kelly, opened on Broadway. Some of the dancers at the Hawaiian Room were recruited to be in "Flower Drum Song" including two dancers who were eventually connected to Mah Jong.

The Enchanted Tiki Room at Disneyland featured state-of-the-art technology: animated parrots, singing flowers, Polynesian gods, Hawaiian music. It was mesmerizing and captivating for those just learning about our 50th state.

The Ala Moana Center opened in 1959 on Oahu, a new shopping experience touted as the largest open air shopping center in the world. A Phase 2 opening in 1966 featured live Polynesian entertainment.

Completely swept up in the national fascination with Hawaii and Polynesia, our family went to California and Hawaii for a research vacation in 1966. The trip to Hawaii was transformative, fostering among us an abiding love for and connection to the Polynesian culture.

It was also the catalyst for Mah Jong 2.0. Business had been robust and the small dining room was constantly filled for lunch and dinner. Expansion was necessary. Dad finally ditched the idea of baked potatoes and brought us into the world of poi, pineapples, and the South Seas.

CHAPTER 16

MAH JONG'S FACELIFT 1967-68

Dad engaged architect Michael Spector who, in 1965, established his new design business in his garage in Great Neck, NY.[51] Michael and Dad conceptualized a new dining room at Mah Jong, featuring a Polynesian nightclub inspired by our experiences in Hawaii and Polynesian-themed restaurants. They designed the still-recognizable stone façade facing Jericho Turnpike, with stunning floor-to-ceiling windows and framed by large wooden beams bending into a hint of a pagoda.

Transforming the building from barn to restaurant and nightclub was a remarkable feat. Each stone and rock was inlaid piece by piece by Antovel, a stone and marble company. Photos of the construction show piles of rocks waiting for sorting, measuring, cutting and installation.

Dad's friend, Ralph Papsidero, handled the construction and Bill Koutensky provided the financing. Mah Jong's new dining room was named the "Aloha Room," an homage to the Hawaiian spirit with seating for an additional 150 guests.

A waiting room was created at the front entrance, the coat room enlarged, and Mom's gift shop expanded to carry Polynesian items.

For additional customer overflow, "The Imu Room" was adjacent to the Aloha Room. A 3-foot above-ground imu oven was installed. Taking advantage of the northern exposure, a large skylight provided a constant stream of natural light to the "Imu Room," out of reach of the Aloha Room's floor to ceiling windows. The natural light spilled onto the corner fountain where water sensually dripped down the stones and into a small goldfish pond surrounded by lush plants and foliage. In later years, a large cage was built above the fountain where our blue and gold pet macaw parrot, Pete, presided.

An additional bar and a new cocktail lounge were created in the area where the waiters and I prepped wonton and snow peas. Dubbed the "Bamboo Lounge," it was on an elevated area accommodating 10–12 teak and mahogany tables. They were so beautiful no tablecloths were necessary, plus it was easier and faster to wipe down the sticky and drink-stained tables. The cushioned rattan chairs were accentuated with orange floral decor, the walls festooned with tiki masks, fishing nets and starfish. On each table a red lowboy candle in plastic mesh flickered. The glow of candles and the dim lighting created a romantic seating area.

Dad flanked by the architect team responsible for Mah Jong's south seas renovation. Ralph Papsidero, Arthur Jong, William Koutensky, Michael Spector (Author's collection)

The entrance of the Aloha Room was framed by a bamboo archway with dark redwood and bamboo walls. Two 15-foot tiki statues greeted you at the entryway and more tiki statues were mounted on the walls. The Imu Room was to the right, separated by a sliding glass door, left open for overflow seating or closed for private parties. Some customers asked for the Imu Room during the Polynesian show; they could see part of the show—with a few obstructed sightlines—without the cover charge.

The design project began in 1967 and Mah Jong's grand re-opening introduced the Aloha Room in 1968.

Dad and Michael with the construction workers who are assembling Mah Jong's new facade one stone at a time. (Author's collection)

Above: Artist's rendering of the Mah Jong facelift.

Right: Ad for the Mah Jong Luau (Author's collection)

The interior of the Imu room at Mah Jong (Author's collection)

Aloha Room entrance framed by large tikis

Promo shot for Mah Jong's new South Seas Luau (Author's collection)

CHAPTER 17

AT HOME WITH THE CHINNS

Our family fascination of the Hawaiian culture came home to roost when Dad engaged Ralph to renovate our family home in Syosset. Ralph's friends in the construction business added an extension in the back, replaced the aluminum and wood siding of the house with California redwood and replaced the chain link fence leading to the backyard with a pagoda gate.

CHINN ALOHA ROOM

From Dad's chair by the window in the living room, he could oversee the construction and watch all of the workers. He'd wander outside to check on progress, banter with the carpenters, and revel being amidst the sounds of construction.

When it was finished, our house stood out regally among the uniformity of the ranch and split-level homes in our neighborhood. What once was a set of windows in the rear of the main house became a sliding glass door to the new addition. It led to another sliding glass door and then you stepped into a replica of the bar and cocktail lounge at Mah Jong. Mom and Dad brought home surplus decor items from Mah Jong and the new addition was soon decorated with Polynesian shells, blowfish hanging from the ceiling, decorative leis on the walls, beaded bamboo curtains, tapa cloth wallpaper, tiki masks, teak tables, and rattan furniture. Kathy was away at college before the renovation began; she recalls that when she came home for the summer, she had no idea our entire family was part of a Hawaiian decorative revolution. In her words, "It looked like Hawaii threw up at our house while I was gone."

We simply called it the "Aloha Room" because it resembled Mah Jong's Aloha Room. We set up my upright piano, my electric guitar and amp, Michael's drum set, and our hi-fi stereo system complete with an 8-track player and turntable. With our collection of Hawaiian record albums, I played along to the songs on piano or guitar. There was base heating to warm the Aloha Room in the winter and by turning on the mood lighting, we could transport ourselves to the warmth and balm of Polynesia every day of the year.

Beyond the Aloha Room in our backyard were a koi pond, a redwood deck, and a brick barbeque oven just underneath my favorite tree, which I loved to climb and hide in as a child.

THE MENAGERIE

Pete, our tropical Macaw, slept in the boiler room adjacent to the washer and dryer. When he heard the front door unlock, he squawked, "Hi!" Pete learned to imitate the sound of the doorbell; we'd open the door and no one was there. When we were home, we'd bring Pete out and he'd hang out on the stepladder swaying left and right waiting for us to give him his favorite treat: peanuts in the shell. We eventually moved him to Mah Jong, where he fit nicely into the Hawaiian motif.

Mom collected parakeets and canaries, especially those with vibrant and distinctive colorings. At one time we had over 20 birds in the house. Most of the canaries lived in one large aluminum cage in the living room. Mom's favorite, Manulani, "heavenly bird" in Hawaiian, loved to sing and trill. He had a sweet melodic sound; he loved to show off whenever I practiced piano. Manulani had his own cage, with a 6-inch full-length mirror, hanging in the kitchen on a hook above the 100-gallon fish tank. The parakeets had their own cages in the living room.

Mom collected special breeds of goldfish which originated in China and Japan: the Ranchu, Pearlscale, and Oranda. She visited a tropical fish aquarium in the shopping center near us regularly to see new arrivals and as her fish collection grew, so did all of the accoutrements to keep her fish family happy. In addition to decorative pieces in the tank, Mom added mood lighting for the evenings, purchased special food, medicine, tank filters, cleaning supplies, and every so often, we'd welcome a new member to the fish family. This 100-gallon tank, situated next to the kitchen table by Mom's special seat, was within arm's reach of Manulani so she could feed him his fresh peas snacks and keep an eye on her fish. The TV in the living room reflected in the glass of the fish tank—no need for Mom to get up to watch it. Like her birds, she sat perched at the kitchen table surrounded by her aquarium and her aviary. Her swivel chair allowed her to check on the stove, circle back to look in on her fish, rotate to position herself to watch TV, and reach behind her to grab some fruit off the counter. She was the queen of her fish and bird roost. She was poetry in perpetual circular motion.

Our house was never quiet. Even after Mom covered the bird cages and put Pete back in the storage room at night, the sounds of bubbles in the fish tank emanated from the kitchen. Winky snored. Some of the

Mom and Pete (the parrot, not the husband) (Author's collection)

Mom in front of her 100-gallon goldfish tank at our Syosset home. Note the fish are swimming towards her; they know she is about to feed them. (Author's collection)

canaries could be heard late at night eating their seeds and pooping on the newspaper below. The birds were early risers. We arose to the sound of the birds all chirping and singing. It was impossible to get them to go back to sleep. Once birds are awake, they stay that way all day long. Mom made the rounds to uncover the bird cages and replenish the water and bird seeds. Manulani had a special breakfast of one fresh pea which he pecked at all morning. Mom took Pete out of the boiler room and made him a small bowl of oatmeal.

Growing up around all those animals meant our clothes were constantly covered with dog hair or bird feathers and we did a lot of allergic sneezing. When the Chinns sneezed together at home, it was atonal harmony with accompaniment provided by the chirping birds, the squawking parrot, and the howling dog.

Mom was devoted to our pets and took her pet-care responsibilities seriously. She fretted when Manulani started molting, stopped singing, and went completely bald, possibly from the stress of being around so many other birds or a change in the winter weather in New York. Our vet wasn't specialized in aviary care, so Mom went to her favorite herbalists in Chinatown for medicine. Through trial-and-error and persistence, she found the right elixir and coaxed Manulani back to feathered health.

Mom fed the canaries fresh fruits and vegetables. The birdcage was a sight, resembling a Chinese produce market. Slices of bok choy, snow peas, apples and grapes were typical as well as wads of iceberg lettuce leaves protruding from each side of the cage. In the summer, she treated them to fresh lychees, Bing cherries, and watermelon. Whatever the birds ate, we ate, too.

I had the great misfortune of babysitting the birds when Mom went to visit with one of her sisters for several days. Mom wrote down feeding instructions and I, with teenaged confidence, assured her I had everything down pat. During Mom's absence, my self-absorbed flakiness set in and I neglected to give the birds enough food until I heard a commotion in the large bird cage. The canaries were distressed and flapping their wings and I saw the reason why. A dead canary laid at the bottom of the cage. It was the distinct multi-hued spackled one and I presumed it had died of hunger. Mom knew all the birds well so I couldn't just throw the dead bird out. I came up with the only solution my panicked yet creative mind could muster under pressure.

I found some wire in the supply closet and tied the dead bird's feet to the perch, thinking Mom would assume it was sleeping. I did not realize the other birds smelled death; they all moved over to the other side of the cage. I ran out of time for ideas and when Mom came home, she greeted Pete, Winky, Manulani, and me, then went to her canaries to say hello. She didn't notice anything until a bit later when she looked in the cage closely and saw the stiff unmoving bird. She reached inside to pet it. The bird—with its feet still tethered to the perch—tilted forward and swung like a pendulum until it rested like a bat, upside down.

I tried to convince Mom that the bird would have died anyway due to overcrowded tenement conditions. Still, this ended my short-lived aviary babysitting career.

After I left home and went to college, Mom and Dad purchased a corner lot in Palm Bay, Florida, where they built a home for their eventual retirement. During the summers, they drove to Florida to oversee the construction and, when the house was finished, began to transport items from Syosset to Palm Bay. When I called to see how the move was going, I asked Mom who was taking care of the birds. She said no one; by this time, the other birds had died natural deaths and only Manulani remained. They put Manulani in the back seat of their car and drove him to Florida and back. Most birds fly to Florida; Manulani was chauffeured up and down Interstate 95 in the comforts of the Chinn Chevy Cordoba.

CHAPTER 18

THE NIGHTCLUB TAKES SHAPE

To find the Polynesian entertainment for the new "Aloha Room," Dad was referred to Leia Kirk, a steel guitarist and singer whose recording troupe, Leia Kirk and the Hawaiians, had been prominently mentioned in the Hawaii society columns.

In 1950, the *Honolulu Star-Bulletin* article mentions "in the middle 30s Leia worked with Robert Bell's Hawaiian troupe, which included John Hookano, Dave Kapona, and Bill Lani." Robert Bell's "Hawaiian Follies" was a touring show with a dozen performers that played the major night club and theater circuits in the USA.

The April 11, 1950, *Honolulu Star Bulletin*'s "Reporting From New York" column by Ann Koga reported on an off-the-beaten-track nightclub near the Lexington Hotel in New York where Leia and her husband Bill Kirk held court. The Ringside Cafe, located at 8th Avenue and 49th Street, was within the thriving Polynesian nightclub circuit in Manhattan.

Further, Koga writes, "Leia was born near Hilo, on the Big Island. She is a member of the Hokea family there on her mother's side. She left the Islands when she was a youngster and has played all over the mainland....Last summer Leia and Bill made an album of Hawaiian songs for Signature Records....Leia is one of the first woman guitar players to become a recording star."

Leia frequently mentioned being a regular performer on the TV show, *Arthur Godfrey and His Friends* (1949–1959). Godfrey had popularized the ukulele on radio and TV and often recorded with Hawaiian artist Haleloke, whom he discovered in Hawaii and brought to the mainland to appear on his shows.

Closer to Syosset was the Bali Hai nightclub in nearby Northport, Long Island. Performing at the Bali Hai was slack guitarist Benjamin Poki'i Hele Loa I Ko Aina Kelii Waiwaiole, known as Prince Poki'i. Before statehood, Prince Poki'i was a member of the Hawaiian royalty. He organized and led a group of performers called "Silhouettes of the Tropics" who appeared at the Bali Hai, the Hawaiian Inn in Daytona Beach and

Prince Poki'i on the Mah Jong dance floor with Leia Kirk on steel guitar, 1968 (Author's collection)

Michael and I with Leia Kirk at Mah Jong (before the Aloha Room was built). Leia was one of Mah Jong's regular bar customers before Dad recruited her to lead Mah Jong's polynesian floor show. (Author's collection)

the South Pacific in Hallandale, Florida. Leia recruited Prince Poki'i to join her in the new Mah Jong endeavor.

Leia was an imposing woman, with large bouffant hair, big personality, and a sizable laugh that could be heard over the roar of the bar scene. Her voice was husky, enabled by years of chain smoking; always a cigarette between her fingers and an ashtray never within easy reach. She smoked and puffed, letting the cigarette ashes build to a fiery little tower. When the ashes were on the verge of toppling over, she nonchalantly caught them in one long piece—like a glowing worm—in her other cupped hand.

In my eyes, she was our Hawaiian Ethel Merman.

Recruiting Polynesian dancers was a group effort through word of mouth. The *Hawaiian Room* at the Lexington Hotel in New York City was a main resource. The *Hawaiian Room* dancers Mabel (Mapela) Wong and Betty (Kehau) Kawamura heard of the Mah Jong opportunity and signed up to join the troupe. Mapela and Kehau were in the original 1958 Broadway production of *Flower Drum Song* and remained friends with Gene Kelly, the legendary dancer/director who helmed that production. Kehau often received requests from restaurants, theme parks, malls, and TV shows for Hawaiian dancers. In an email conversation with me in 2019, Kehau recalls, "During the auditions for *Flower Drum Song,* Gene Kelly asked me to help find more Oriental dancers.[52] I knew that all of the best dancers at the Hawaiian Room were directly recruited from the Islands. So I was able to help Mr. Kelly find his dancers."

Kehau and Mapela recruited Olina Brill to join the Mah Jong troupe. Olina's husband, comedian and Hollywood actor/writer Marty Brill, appeared regularly on 60s and 70s TV in both variety ("Ed Sullivan," "Merv Griffin") and sitcoms ("The New Dick Van Dyke Show," "Mary Tyler Moore"). He was a librettist for the Broadway musical "Cafe Crown" (Martin Beck Theater NYC, 1964) starring Alan Alda, Sam Levene, Tommy Rall, and Theodore Bikel. It was a special cachet to be in the orbit of a celebrity and we gathered around the small TV at the Mah Jong bar for a glimpse of his set on Johnny Carson or other TV appearances.

Even though Syosset was a 60-minute ride from Manhattan, the allure of inaugurating a new and exciting nightclub managed by Peter and Nellie Chinn and endorsed by Leia Kirk and Prince Poki'i was quite strong. All three dancers: Olina, Mapela, and Kehau lived in Manhattan and made the round-trip drive to Long Island for the show.

The original dance floor was "in-the-round," with tables in front of and behind the dancers. The band was placed along a portion of the wall. There wasn't enough room for Guitarist Prince Poki'i, well over 300 pounds, to sit next to Leia or the drummer and his drums, so Poki'i stood up and played in front of the small bandstand. A gifted singer and guitar player; a jolly presence on the dance floor for his solo numbers.

OPENING NIGHT ALOHA ROOM 1968

My parents had no qualms about hiring additional staff members and their families. Aunt Daisy spent most weekends working at Mah Jong. She drove in from New Haven and when she lived in NYC, she took the train to the Syosset station where Mom or Dad would pick her up. She was a radiant and charming hostess and pitched in everywhere. As a teacher, she was organized, efficient, and precise. She was always at Mom's side and the Kwoh sisters found great joy working together. Daisy taught customers a few Chinese phrases and when they returned the following week, they asked for Daisy so they could practice and learn more phrases.

Mom and Daisy working together at Mah Jong (Author's collection)

On occasion, Arthur Jong's brother, Andy, came in to help with maitre d' duties. Some of the waiters' children helped out in the kitchen. The parents of the cashiers stopped by regularly, and Mapela's sister, Edna Wong, and Mapela's Aunt Betty were hired as cocktail waitresses for the Aloha Room. If any cashiers had sisters old enough to serve liquor, they were hired as cocktail waitresses. Mah Jong waiters,' captains,' and chefs' sons were put to work clearing tables and bussing dishes. We were known as the "Mah Jong kids"—the children working and playing together in lieu of staying home with babysitters.

Customers took some of the Mah Jong kids on social outings and this was when I learned how to bowl. Several customers were part of a bowling league at the nearby Syosset Bowling Alley, just under a mile away on Jericho Turnpike. They invited us to watch and play a few frames. I loved the lights and the melody of sound. It reminded me of

Above: Original dance troupe in the opening night Aloha Room performance at Mah Jong. L-R, Kehau, Olina, Mapela, 1968 (Author's collection)

*Right:
Leia Kirk with husband Bill Kirk in background, performing at Mah Jong c 1972
(Photo: J.J. Heatley)*

the nightclub environment. When the waiters and chefs brought their teenage kids to hang out at Mah Jong during the summer months, we walked to the bowling alley in the afternoon, played a few games, had a couple of hot dogs, and walked back to Mah Jong in time to get ready to work the dinner service.

During the winter snow storms, the plows created mounds of snow in the parking lot—the time for us to put on our snow suits, grab the large waiters' trays and "tray sled" down the snow banks. The later in the afternoon the better, since the snow turned to ice and we gained speed as we tumbled down the banks towards Jericho Turnpike, never really aware that we might careen into traffic. I don't believe we washed those trays before they next hauled food from the kitchen to the dining tables.

Tropical aromas wafted through Mah Jong on the opening night of the Aloha Room. Leia and the band wore fresh plumeria and pikaki leis. Mom and I, as well as the hostesses and cocktail waitresses, wore Mom's favorite flower, fresh gardenias. A copious amount of rum was poured for the specialty drinks underscored by the scent of fresh pineapples. Many customers wore their best cologne and perfume for opening night. The smell of Sterno was prevalent as the waiters prepared the puu-puu platters (various appetizers in a tiered teak tray kept warm by a flame).

Opening night dinner seating was at 7:00 with the Polynesian floor show scheduled at 9:00pm. Leia and Prince Poki'i arrived around 6:00 for a sound check and warm-ups. They and the drummer were on the bandstand playing at 6:45; the customers heard soft strains of Hawaiian music to put them in the island mood. My job was to say, "Aloha," kiss the customers on the cheek, and hand out plastic leis of various colors. Once guests were settled in for dinner, Leia and Poki'i played a set for dancing to the tunes of *Begin the Beguine, Won't You Come Home, Bill Bailey* and *Hokey Pokey*, among others in Leia's expansive fake book.[53]

The 30-minute set put dining customers in a happy mood. The Polynesian dancers arrived by 7:30, each carrying a canvas bag with their personal show props (feathered gourds, bamboo sticks) and wardrobe bags. When they came in the front door and walked through the phalanx jammed between the hostess counter and the bar, they stood out, exotic and graceful.

While Olina, Mapela, and Kehau were in their dressing rooms, everyone was spiritually transported to the Hawaiian islands. The Aloha Room lights were dimmed, the lowboy red candles glowed, the exotic drinks were served, the dining room—fully decorated with tiki, hukilau nets,

Promo photo of Mah Jong staff and entertainers, 1975 (Author's collection)

Dad taking a curtain call after the opening night performance of Mah Jong's new Polynesian floor show. Greeted with a lei and a kiss from Mapela. (Author's collection)

Shubert Theatre

DIRECTION - MESSRS. LEE and J. J. SHUBERT

RODGERS & HAMMERSTEIN
in association with JOSEPH FIELDS
present
A New Musical

Music by **RICHARD RODGERS**
Lyrics by **OSCAR HAMMERSTEIN 2nd**
Book by **OSCAR HAMMERSTEIN 2nd** and **JOSEPH FIELDS**
Based on the novel by C. Y. LEE

with

MIYOSHI UMEKI

JUANITA HALL ED KENNEY KEYE LUKE
LARRY STORCH ARABELLA HONG

and PAT SUZUKI

Directed by **GENE KELLY**

Choreography by CAROL HANEY
Scenery Designed by OLIVER SMITH
Costumes Designed by IRENE SHARAFF
Lighting by PEGGY CLARK
Orchestrations by ROBERT RUSSELL BENNETT
Musical Director SALVATORE DELL'ISOLA
Dance Arrangements by LUTHER HENDERSON, JR.

THE CAST
(In Order of Their Appearance)

MADAM LIANG .... JUANITA HALL
LIU MA .... ROSE QUONG
WANG SAN .... PAT ADIARTE
WANG TA .... ED KENNEY
WANG CHI YANG .... KEYE LUKE
SAMMY FONG .... LARRY STORCH
DR. LI .... CONRAD YAMA
MEI LI .... MIYOSHI UMEKI
LINDA LOW .... PAT SUZUKI
MR. LUNG (THE TAILOR) .... HARRY SHAW LOWE
MR. HUAN .... JON LEE
HELEN CHAO .... ARABELLA HONG
PROFESSOR CHENG .... PETER CHAN
FRANKIE WING .... JACK SUZUKI
DR. LU FONG .... CHAO LI
MADAM FONG .... EILEEN NAKAMURA

DANCING ENSEMBLE: Fumi Akimoto, Paula Chin, Helen Fumai, Pat Griffith, Mary Huie, Marion Jim, Betty Kawamura, Baayork Lee, Wonci Lui, Jo Anne Miya, Denise Quan, Vicki Racimo, Shawnee Smith, Maureen Tiongco, Mabel Wing, Yuriko.

Above: Dance rehearsal for the 1958 Broadway production of "Flower Drum Song". Betty Kawamura (Kehau) is at the far left

Opposite: Program page for the 1958 Broadway production of "Flower Drum Song". The dance ensemble included Betty Kawamura and Mabel Wing, who became Kehau and Mapela at Mah Jong's Polynesian floor show.

bamboo, tapa cloths on the walls, island fauna by the fountain—resembled Polynesia. As Leia and Poki'i took the stage, the glissando of Leia's steel guitar heralded the intro to *Hawaii Calls*, a song by Harry Owens written for the radio show of the same name.[54]

Hawaii calls, with a melody of love, dear
Across the sea as evening falls
The surf is booming on the sand at Waikīkī tonight

Olina, Mapela, and Kehau danced to popular Hawaiian standards: *Lovely Hula Hands*, *Little Grass Shack*, *Sweet Leilani*, *Pearly Shells*, *Beyond the Reef.*

Prince Poki'i sang *Tiny Bubbles*, a song made popular by Hawaiian entertainer Don Ho in 1966, to which everyone was invited to sing along. This became a standard part of the show and in later years, the waiters, cocktail waitresses, Mom, cashiers, and anyone who could purse their lips and blow were given bottles of soap bubbles and recruited to envelop the audience with "tiny bubbles."

The last number was always a Tahitian dance, a *Ori Tahiti*, characterized by drum beats and fast moving hips. Dancers wore long, heavy straw skirts that waved vigorously with their swiveling hips.

The inaugural show was a resounding success. During the curtain call, Dad was brought on stage where the dancers showered him with leis and kisses. Word of Mah Jong's floor show spread quickly, and reservations became difficult to come by.

Once the Mah Jong floor show got into a groove, customers didn't want to leave. Leia added post-show dance music and the dance floor filled to capacity. Others migrated to Mom's gift shop for souvenirs or to the bars to continue partying. During their set breaks, Leia and Poki'i hung out at the bar and treated to a round or two of drinks. Leia regaled customers with stories of her old days with Arthur Godfrey, her upcoming club dates, tales of Hawaii, and local entertainment gossip.

Olina and Kehau were more circumspect in their interactions with the customers. Olina observed professional boundaries and refrained from joining the bar scene. Kehau, too, abided by the rules: she was there to do a job and when the show was over, it was time to go home. Mapela, on the other hand, was more free-spirited and gregarious. If it weren't for catching a ride back to Manhattan after the show, she would undoubtedly have been quite at home closing down the place with the bar customers.

In an in-person chat with me in 2019, Olina reminisced about the time Dad asked the dancers to chat with a frequent customer who spent good money at the bar. The man wanted to meet the dancers after the show. Olina said it was rare for Dad to ask such a favor and she was willing to consider meeting him in the bar but apprehensive about the "call girl" appearance it might give. Instead, Kehau and Olina sent Mapela, who had no problem chatting up the man and was gone for at least an hour. According to Mapela, when she returned to the dressing room, she proudly beamed, "You gals missed out. He gave me a full dining set and two antique rugs!" [55]

The Aloha Room, and its "can't miss" reputation, was off and running. Its nightclub legend was born. Floor shows were Wednesdays and Fridays at 8:00 pm and Saturdays at 9:00 pm. To accommodate the late owls or those who couldn't get into the 9:00 pm shows, a midnight show was added on Saturdays.

Left: Mapela's relatives were recruited to work: sister Edna Wong and Aunt Betty Wong (Author's collection)

CHAPTER 19

JOINING THE MAH JONG DANCE TROUPE

As a novelty, Michael and I were added to the show. I was 11 years old and my only stage experience—besides being in the school choir—was in kindergarten, playing the planet Venus in Miss Kaplan's musical vignette designed to teach us about the solar system. I loved my Venus costume, basically me stuffed inside a round papier mâché ball. I attempted to wear it home after rehearsal to show my parents but was stopped by the school receptionist who said I couldn't possibly fit up the steps of the school bus without causing a blockade.

I always wanted to be a performer (years of playing make-believe with Mah Jong's furnishings was a warm-up act) and now I was asked to join the Mah Jong dance troupe!

Leia gave Michael the stage name of "Kalani" which means Michael in Hawaiian. I asked her for something not-so-ordinary for me and she came up with "Leimomi" which she said translated into "a wreath of pearls." I thought she said "Aretha Pearls." I was a huge fan of the Queen of Soul, Aretha Franklin, and I felt my Hawaiian name suited me perfectly and even carried a hint of royalty.

Before that, however, as Kehau reminded me in our 2019 interview, "Your father paid the dancers and musicians with checks we signed to get cash instead. You and your mother put wads of bills into envelopes, taped them shut, and gave us our cash at the end of each week. When you saw how much we were paid, you told your parents that if they wanted you and your brother to be in the show, you expected to be paid."

My first venture as my own agent was an easy success. My mother added a wad of cash in envelopes to be given to my brother and me, as well. It was around $50—a sizable sum at that time for two nights' work—and much more than my classmates made babysitting.

After I negotiated with my parents, Michael and I were featured as a duo when Leia broadened the repertoire to take the audience on a "trip to Polynesia." In addition to songs and dances from Hawaii, Samoa, and Tahiti, she added New Zealand to the repertoire. To prepare for battle, the indigenous Maori people of New Zealand used the poi dance to increase their dexterity. The women relied on this ritual to keep their hands flexible for weaving.[56]

And so we began to learn a poi ball routine ("poi" is the Maori word for ball on a cord). Our poi ball was wadded up cloth wrapped in white satin attached to thick braided rope extending approximately three feet. The poi ball dance involves swinging two poi balls—one in each hand—in geometric patterns without tangling up the rope. Olina, Mapela, and Kehau taught us the basic moves of simple twirling and "double-dutch." Much space is needed for poi ball twirling, so I took the balls with me to school to practice during recess, and I practiced in Mah Jong's parking lot. Eventually I learned how to hold both ropes in one hand while keeping the poi balls in fluid motion. I wasn't nearly as proficient as the dancers who used four poi balls—two in each hand—which always received an appreciative round of applause. Midway through the number the stage lights were switched to ultraviolet so the satin poi balls glowed in the dark.

My costume was a simple red satin one-piece shift that barely stayed on since it was meant to be anchored by a bust line; I was still wearing t-shirts, and a training bra was two years away. A red floral headdress was placed over my butch-cut short hair, and I had no grace whatsoever. I was a gawky, plain, prepubescent girl in the midst of beautiful and exotic Polynesian dancers. Mapela taught me about stage makeup and tested different shades of eye shadow and rouge on me. Leia found a shoulder-length wig. I eventually learned to put on my own false eyelashes. (Every several months I walked to the local drug store to buy a fresh set of false eyelashes; I wore them out fast. I wonder what the cashier thought since, at the same time, I paid for my Bazooka gum and *Archie* and *Superman* comic books.)

After we learned the poi ball routine, Leia suggested a new number for Michael and me: *Happy Talk*, from the musical *South Pacific*, sung by the character Bloody Mary. Juanita Hall was the first African American to win a Tony Award for Best Supporting Actress for her role as Bloody Mary in *South Pacific* on Broadway which ran for 1,945 performances from 1949–1954. In a small twist of Mah Jong fate, Juanita Hall played Madame Liang in the 1958 original Broadway production of *Flower Drum Song* directed by Gene Kelly. In that production were Betty Kawamura and Mabel Wing who became Kehau and Mapela at Mah Jong.

South Pacific was the featured production at the Jones Beach Theater, an outdoor amphitheater in Wantagh, NY, during the 1968 and 1969 seasons, thus familiar to Long Islanders and a nice tie-in to Mah Jong's Polynesian floor show.

Jones Beach Theater, with a capacity of 8,000+ seats, was a favorite summertime destination for Long Islanders and tourists. Shows were outdoors in the evenings, providing a relief from the summer heat and humidity. The stage was situated on the bay with a moat separating the audience from the actual stage. The Guy Lombardo Orchestra led the show when a spotlight shined on an area far to the right, like a bright moon on the Bay's surface. The light picked up some motion on the water: Guy Lombardo himself, dressed in a captain's hat, being sped across the bay towards the stage. He got out of the boat, turned to the audience to take a bow, and proceeded to lead the orchestra and audience in *The Star Spangled Banner,* signaling the start of the show.

Although Jones Beach is just 14 miles south of Syosset, my parents went only a handful of times. When *South Pacific* was announced as the main stage production, my parents were eager to see it. The Aloha Room had just opened in 1968 and we were collectively enthralled by all things Polynesian. Through one of Dad's connections, we secured seats in the center section, one of the rare occasions our family went out to see a show together.

A Jones Beach production was on a magnificent scale and brand new to me. I had not been introduced to this kind of artistic experience. I was in awe of the size of the amphitheater and the backdrop to the production, the vast view of the Bay. The staging elements often included movable set pieces floating in and out on a barge. The lush sounds of the orchestra, the gorgeous voices, the dancing, the open air, the collective experience of being together to watch a story unfold, the excitement after intermission as we waited for the house lights to dim to half and then settle in for the second act—the entire majesty of that live theatre experience was ingrained in my psyche. I wanted to be in show business! These early seeds were planted for my eventual career as an arts executive. Throughout my career, I have led initiatives to introduce arts and culture to youth starting at a very young age, because I know first-hand how impactful these experiences can be.

Right: Promo shot as Leimomi (my stage name) for my first dance number: the poi ball routine. (Author's collection)

Below: Mah Jong's dance troupe: l-r: Pua, Kehau, Leia, guitarist Sam, Olina. Kneeling: Drummer Tama, me, Chief Taofi, Michael ca.1970 (Author's collection)

Above Left: Performing my fire torch number (Author's collection)
Above Right: Dancer Donna Brent (Author's collection)
Below: Some of the Mah Jong dancers reunited at the home of Olina and Marty Brill. With Olina, Michael, and NaPua, Las Vegas, 2019 (Author's collection)

Dancing the Tinikling number. Donna Brent is holding one end of the pole, Mom (unseen) is holding the other end. (Author's collection)

Above: With Pua, Donna and Michael in our Easter parade outfits (Author's collection)

Opposite, clockwise from upper left:

Dancing to "Silver Bells" during the Christmas show (Author's collection)

Dancing with the uli'uli gourds (Author's collection)

L to R: Dancers Pua, Donna, Cathy and I flank Mah Jong's chef in a promo shot for Mah Jong's Imu Room and luau.

CHAPTER 20

FAMILY MATTERS

Mom and Dad embraced the Mah Jong troupe and workers as part of the Chinn family. Leia, who preferred not to eat before singing, and the musicians, continued to play sets for post-show dancing. The waiters set a special table for the troupe, who were encouraged by Mom and Dad to order anything off the menu after the show. Mom and Dad's generosity to the troupe extended beyond paying well and providing a warm and nurturing work environment. When I visited with Olina and Marty at their home in Las Vegas in 2019, a stunning vase in their foyer looked vaguely familiar. Mom and Dad gave it to Olina over 50 years ago simply because she often admired it in the Mah Jong gift shop. Olina said she couldn't possibly accept it but Mom and Dad insisted. Olina and Marty made many household moves during their lifetime, but they could not part with the vase; a beautiful reminder of a special era with the Chinns and Mah Jong.

CHINESE AND THE JEWS

Mom said the Jews and the Chinese have been close throughout civilization. She and Dad felt a special kinship with our Jewish customers and Kathy is somehow naturally facile at speaking Yiddish. Mom and Dad extended special courtesies to kosher Jews who requested food be placed on paper plates or Pork Fried Rice be made without pork. Yom Kippur was usually a slow day but Kathy recalls, "Dad would see our Jewish customers driving into the parking lot to wait for the sun to set. Then a mad rush of Mah Jong customers raced in to order spareribs, shrimp, pork fried rice…the works!" Christmas Day was notoriously busy so we enjoyed a brief family Christmas morning at home before Dad headed in to ready Mah Jong for the Christmas brunch and dinner rush. Mom, Michael and I followed and spent Christmas in the company of our Jewish friends.

Mom posited that both cultures were rooted in strong family traditions, that matzo balls and wontons were really the same when you put them in a bowl of broth, and that "Chinn" was Chinese for "Cohen." I recited this to friends, joking that perhaps Mom nipped too much Rock & Rye Whiskey, which she prescribed for a sore throat.

There is, however, truth in Mom's insistence that the Jews and Chinese are actually one civilization. The Kaifeng Jews, in China's central Henan Province, are believed to have settled there before 1127, arriving from either Persia (Iran) or India.[57]

"The Kaifeng Jews are the descendants of Sephardic Jews, who immigrated to China millenniums ago, and the Han Chinese, indigenous to the Middle Kingdom. The Jews of Kaifeng, according to stone inscriptions, were composed of 70 clans (or families) when they first set foot in China; after nearly a hundred generations, and numerous instances of social, political, and natural upheaval, their population has declined significantly, leaving a headcount of barely 1,000."[58]

My DNA test results from Ancestry.com indicate that 3% of my ethnicity originates from Korea, 85% from Southern China, and 12% from Eastern China, where the Kaifeng Jews are based in Henan Province. It is just under 700 miles from Shantung Province, the roots of my ancestors, who possibly lived as Kaifeng Jews and perhaps account for that 12% of my DNA.

The story of the Kaifeng Jews found its way to the United States when a 1966 musical called, "Chu Chem" (composed by Mitch Leigh who, the year before, had enjoyed box office success with "The Man of La Mancha"), opened and closed in Philadelphia, PA. The book was by Ted Allen, based on his travels to Kaifeng. "Chu Chem," a play-within-a-play spoof, was roundly panned. Ernest Scheir of the *Philadelphia Evening Bulletin* wrote, "...confused and tasteless. . .thoroughly unpalatable...bizarre and unedifying...like blintzes and soy sauce...a better title might be 'The King and Oy.'" [59]

"Chu Chem" was resurrected in 1988 at the Jewish Repertory Theatre in New York, then moved uptown to the Ritz Theatre where it previewed on March 17, 1989, opened on April 7 and closed five weeks later on May 14, 1989.

CHAPTER 21

THE NIGHTCLUB

DANCE TROUPE CHANGES

By 1969, the dance troupe was changing. Mapela was the first to leave. She and her husband Richard lived in Chinatown and were ready to raise a family. The long and late-night commute from Manhattan to Syosset was becoming difficult. Before leaving, she mentioned one of her Hawaiian dance students, 19-year-old Donna Brent, who would be an excellent replacement. During their modeling days for corporate promotions, Mapela was Miss Chung King, and Donna, Miss Hawaiian Punch.

When Mapela announced her departure, it left a big hole in the troupe's personality. She was so flamboyant on stage and off and she loved to talk, nearly nonstop, to anyone. All the dancers were gorgeous; Mapela, chosen 4th Princess in the 1958 Miss Chinatown USA pageant, was stunning. Kehau and Olina would saunter in from their cars with their costumes and canvas bags filled with dance props. Mapela, however, bounced in swinging her bags, purse, and arms while greeting everyone all the way from the front door, past the hostess stand, continuing on to the bar, and finally into the dressing room. I looked forward to her entrance. Some of the waiters deliberately parked themselves at the bar to gawk and be among the first to welcome Mapela with a few words of admiration. During the winter months, Mapela came in with big coats with lots of fur, which took up much of the small dressing room. She was hard to miss.

Mapela was replaced by Puanani De Silva (Pua) who lived in nearby Huntington, a much closer commute. Pua was of Portugese, Hawaiian and Chinese lineage. She caught the eye of *Look* magazine at the age of 21 and was featured in a 1959 edition of Hawaiian models in Hawaiian bathing suits at scenic locations on Oahu, Kauai, and Hawaii. Prior to that, she was an airline stewardess. When she joined Mah Jong she was married to Bob Horowitz and had two young children, Kat and Jimmy, close in age to Michael and me. Bob spent his weekends on hunting trips, so Pua brought Kat and Jimmy with her to Mah Jong and they became part of the Mah Jong kids. During our 2021 Zoom chat, Kat recalls, "I sat at the bar and hung out by the waterfall or the gift shop. Your mom let Jimmy and me pick out dolls and toys we wanted!"

In a 2021 interview with Pua, I asked her how she started at Mah Jong. Pua said, "Mapela and Olina wanted me to work with them at Mah Jong. Your father asked me to work there but I couldn't work within 7 miles of Bali Hai since I was on contract with them. I couldn't work for a competitor within 7 miles even after I left. Then one night in 1970 Bali Hai burned down. Your father immediately called me and said, 'OK you can come and work here since there's no Bali Hai! I started right away."

Pauline De Silva (Puanani)
(Pauline De Silva collection)

Olina was the next to leave. Marty's popularity as a stand-up comedian led to additional bookings at clubs and cruise ships and they wanted to be together more often than apart.

Kehau went back to school and became a lab technician for Lenox Hill Hospital. Pua was the new leader of the troupe and Donna became a regular. Replacement dancers for Kehau followed, but Pua and Donna remained the constant talent. Pua choreographed, curated with Leia, sewed costumes and procured props.

Donna's gregarious personality—exotic, playful, silly, and quirky—filled the void of Mapela's departure. Post-show, she and Pua liked to hang out at the crowded, lively, smoked-filled bar, where they were the center of attention. Loud conversation and laughter were joined by the constant sound of blenders, martini shakers, clinking glasses, cash register bells, shouted drink orders, and buckets of fresh ice cubes poured into the bar sinks. When all remnants of restraint evaporated and all libations were consumed, customers often broke out into song.

I was envious of the bar scene. It looked and sounded like so much fun, but I was too young to participate. After getting out of costume, I helped in the coat room and gift shop, sold cigarettes and cigars, took over cashiering duties, and worked with Mom counting cash. We batched up the money to put in Dad's office safe.

Every now and then I sidled over to the bartender and asked for a Coke from the soda gun. While I waited, I watched the action. I marveled at people who didn't know each other earlier in the evening, now unified in happiness. The banter was melodic and transfixing. Breaking the spell, Mom put me back to work counting money and cleaning up.

POLYNESIAN NIGHT CLUB IN FULL BLOOM

By 1970, the nightclub was in full bloom. Leia kept things fresh for return customers by constantly changing the line-up of the show. Holiday themes were opportunities to go wild. The Christmas show included *Mele Kalikimaka (Merry Christmas).* The dancers wore red satin sarongs with matching bras accented by white boa feathers and a white lei. Fire dancer Chief Taofi was Santa Claus, and Michael dressed as Rudolph, prancing to *Santa Claus is Coming to Town. (I'm Dreaming of a) White Christmas* and *Silver Bells* were mixed in with the standard show repertoire.

The Easter show preparations was a team effort. Pua made large Easter bonnets. Mom bought a supply of PAAS egg dye tablets and Dad brought home cartons of eggs. What a fun job—spreading all the cooked eggs onto the kitchen table and to mix and match with colored dyes! I secretly dyed messages onto the eggs: "Let me out!" and "I'm cracked, get the yolk?" and "Egg Foo Old" were some of my witticisms.

For the *In Your Easter Bonnet* dance, we wore long satin gowns with large hand-made Easter bonnets made of crepe paper flowers and silk bows. Midway through the number, we handed out Easter eggs from our baskets, including the eggs with my jokes. My whimsical egg messages became a popular tradition. I added, "Mom, is that you?" and "I'm egg-cellent!" and "A practical yolker!" to my collection.

The Aloha Room and the floor show gained popularity. The stage was moved to provide space for more tables and to expand the dance floor.

TRIP AROUND THE WORLD

Leia's "trip around the world" included a stop in the Philippines, introducing Michael and me in a traditional Philippines Tinikling dance, featuring two long bamboo poles laid horizontally on the floor. At Mah Jong, the poles were placed atop a piece of wood to provide elevation. Two people held the poles at each end, beating in rhythm and sliding the poles back and forth. Michael and I jumped in and out of the poles before they closed in on us. The slow music made the dance look easy but as the pace picked up, the poles slid in and out faster and faster, then higher and higher. It took a lot of coordination to not get our ankles caught in the poles. We held hands and then separated while twirling outside of the poles before jumping into the poles safely. Pua and Donna worked the poles and sometime Mom pitched in. She often lifted her side of the poles higher than necessary, trying to catch our ankles. Sometimes she succeeded.

I learned dances involving feathered gourds called uli'uli, brightly colored rattles resembling sunflowers with bright yellow feathers in the center surrounded by red feathers. Underneath is a small gourd filled with seeds or small pebbles, with a handle wrapped in rattan. The percussion and a flurry of color is produced by holding the handle and rapidly rotating the wrists between the 12:00 to 3:00 position while dancing. *The Hawaiian War* Chant[60] is perhaps the most recognizable number using the uli'uli.

We danced with paired pu'ili, splintered bamboo sticks roughly 2 feet long. We beat the pu'ili together, tapping them on our shoulders, on the floor, or reaching to tap each other's pu'ili, while tapping out the beat to the song *Nani Wale Na Hala*. All this required good peripheral vision.

Many routines required quick costume changes. To stall for time, Leia announced special celebrations and bantered with the audience. The cocktail waitresses casually asked about anniversaries, reunion, birthdays, or engagements. After Leia announced the special occasions, she led everyone into a rousing rendition of *Happy Birthday/Anniversary.*

A favorite segment of the show was the audience participation. Leia asked for free hula lesson volunteers. The ladies came up onstage first, with coaxing from the dancers, Mom, and the waiters. Then the gentlemen, who didn't need much nudging; the dancers approached them and many couldn't resist. Men were asked to take off their jackets and Leia led the band in a striptease intro. The dancers knelt down and rolled up the men's pant cuffs. They placed shell crowns on their heads and gave them straw hand tassels. Once they were fully draped in Hawaiian props, the men were asked to limber up by kneeling down and rising up several times. In most cases, they were lubed up with Mai-Tais and Daiquiris and a few toppled over, helped up by one of the dancers. They were led in a gentle Hawaiian hula lesson before the band picked up the pace with ferocious drumming. Each man soloed with a dancer; the fastest hip shaker received a special mention by Leia. This was a crowd pleaser; regular customers might ask Mom or the waiters to send word to the band—someone from their table should be approached for that piece!

CHIEF TAOFI: SCREAMS FROM THE WOMEN AND SQUEALS FROM THE SQUEAMISH

A Polynesian show is incomplete without a sword and fire dancer. Chief Taofi, a true Samoan chief, thrilled and terrified the audiences with his knife routine and flame throwing. A gregarious man at heart, Chief was usually mobbed with fans after the show and loved to wind down at the bar and hold court. He often stayed until closing time, somehow managing to safely make that long drive home to Queens.

The small dressing room was not good for unisex purposes, so a nook was created for Chief Taofi just outside the dressing room wall in front of the emergency exit. By today's rigid accessibility standards, this was certainly not legal. The nook was an adjunct restaurant storage space for tablecloths, candles, and cleaning supplies. Taofi, who stripped his street clothes and put on a small loincloth, used the back of the nook behind a folding screen. On warm summer nights, Taofi liked to step outside the emergency exit to warm up and used the outside steps as his smoking lounge.

The dancers' dressing room was perhaps 4 feet deep and 15 feet wide. A set of mirrors ran the length of the wall and the dancers used a long built-in shelf as their make-up/vanity stations. Their personal belongings and all of their costumes hung on a modest number of racks. Quick-change costumes dangled on several hooks on the back wall. Polynesian costumes and props can be bulky: large and heavy grass skirts for the Tahitian numbers; feathered gourds, head-dresses, bamboo torches, 12-foot-long bamboo poles for the Tinikling dance;[61] bonnets for the Easter-themed show—all of these and more were stuffed into that small dressing room.

Between the dancers and the stage were waiters hustling to deliver food, a waiters' and busboys' service station, bar customers ogling the dancers, the lookie-loos who snuck around the back to watch the show, and a beaded curtain offering no privacy whatsoever. Sometimes, while we were getting changed, customers ambled into the nook thinking it was the bathroom.

Regardless of the season, each show ended with the fire dance and the Tahitian 'ōte'a. Chief Taofi came out of the dressing room with two swords, the tops and bottoms wrapped with cloth pre-soaked in benzene. He'd drop one sword at the back of the stage and move around the audience asking for a light. If no one came forth with a match or lighter, Taofi dipped his benzene-soaked sword into a table candle, igniting the top of the sword like a torch. His accompaniment was simply the pounding rhythm of the drums in 4/4 time. After Taofi twirled the sword, he held it vertically and

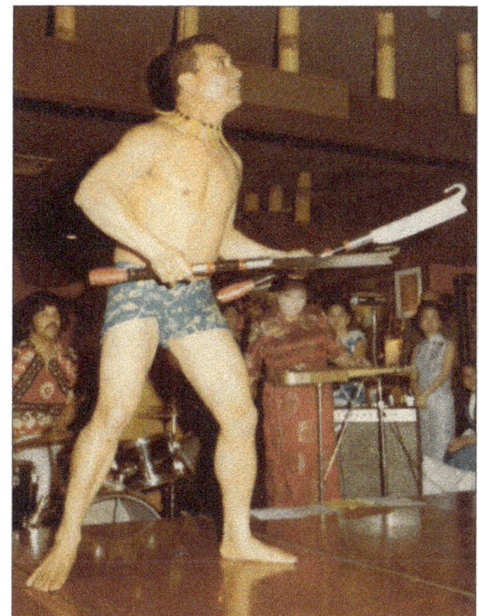

Chief Taofi's fire and knife dances (Author's collection)

let it drop, catching the sword by the flame. He'd squeeze the flaming rag and his hand, slightly on fire, lit the bottom of the sword. Audible gasps were heard as he continued to twirl the sword—now lit on both ends. The drum beats quickened as Taofi treated the sword like a baton: throwing it in the air, flipping around to catch it behind his back, making one-handed circular patterns before rolling on the floor and finally landing on his back with his bare feet raised. Slowly, he put the lighted sword on the soles of his feet. There were screams from the women and squeals from the squeamish.

He'd kick the sword off his feet, roll around on top of it a few times and, just when you thought it was over, he'd grab the second sword (unlit) and hold both swords horizontally, moving them under his armpits as the second sword caught on fire. He twirled the swords in patterns before reaching up to hook the swords together while swirling them over his head. At this, those in the front row, within inches of flying fiery swords, collectively recoiled. After unlatching the swords, Taofi twirled a few more times before going into a backward flip—just the top of his head and the soles of his feet on the floor while he did figure eights with both swords. He moved the swords slowly under the arch of his back, jumped up, did a few more twirls and ended the number with both swords raised high above his head. The performance took at least 10 minutes and was *the* crowd-pleaser.

Once he finished and put out the flames, Leia announced, "Ladies and Gentlemen! Chief Taofi!" Taofi took a breath and a bow to rousing applause before preparing for the final number: the Tahitian 'ōte'a, an exhilarating, rapid, hip-shaking dance accompanied by drums and the beating of a hollow Samoan log drum called a Pātē.

The Pātē was set on a folding waiter's stand. Taofi used two short, thick sticks to pound out the rhythm. Beating the sticks at the outer edge of the log drum yielded a higher intonation; the middle of the log drum produced a deeper pitch. When Taofi beat the rhythm he used every inch of the drum, including the ends. After a full fire dance, his drumming stamina was remarkable. Sweat poured off his body as the dancers ran through the Tahitian routine. I came on midway through the dancers solos, moving in a circle and towards center stage where I dipped low—my knees nearly touching the floor—while constantly shaking my hips to the beat of the drums. After my brief solo, the drumming tempo accelerated, the pounding of the drums got louder (the drum cymbals now in use), and we ended with a flourish.

By this time, the audience had enjoyed over an hour's worth of non-stop entertainment.

Above: On the right, I am doing a Ori Tahti (Tahitian dance) solo while Taofi beats the Pātē (Samoan drum log) and Donna awaits her turn.

Leia Kirk (Author's collection)

These two pages: Performing at Mah Jong during the ages of 13–17. (Author's collection)

Performing at Mah Jong, age 16

CHAPTER 22

I BECOME A REGULAR
OR
THE FIRE WASN'T THAT HIGH... JUST UP TO MY CALVES

Michael didn't want to stay in the show. He was at the gawky stage with orthodontic braces, and he never did like to call attention to himself. When he dropped out in 1970, I became one of the regulars, joining Pua and Donna. Chief Taofi and Leia thought that Debbie performing the sword dance would add a unique element to the show.

One of Chief Taofi's featured routines involved a Samoan twirling knife, which resembles an elongated cleaver with a hook at the end. Taofi made his entrance by racing on stage with a full blood-curdling warrior cry, the knife held high in one hand, a pineapple in the other. After he strutted around the stage bantering with the audience, he lopped off the top of the pineapple with his knife in one fluid motion. He offered the open pineapple to a guest in the front row and proceeded with his knife dance. He twirled the blade close to his body as he flipped it in the air, catching it behind his back while avoiding the blade. He twirled the knife between his legs, making sure the hook didn't catch on his calves. He added a second knife and tossed them both in the air, hooking the knives together, creating a frightening scene—the stage was so small he often came close to hitting the singers' microphones. This, and his fire dance, were the only segments of the show where photography was not allowed; the flashes from the cameras might distract Taofi.

Considering this peril, I was stunned when Leia and Taofi asked me to learn this number. My parents didn't think it was a big deal; they thought it added value to the line-up. Perhaps this was a not-so-subtle punishment for sneaking off to watch the bar scene or not up-selling cigarettes.

Taofi provided a smaller knife, three feet in total length with a polished wooden handle and a dulled blade but sharp hook. It weighed over five pounds. I learned the routine during the summer. Taofi drove from

Queens to Syosset on weekdays to teach me and, since Mah Jong was always busy, we rehearsed on the redwood deck of our house.

He taught me a special routine using only one knife (thank goodness) and I learned how to best balance the knife to build up maximum twirling speed. My routine began with figure eight movements, spinning the knife in one hand and then behind my back, switching the knife to my other hand and twirling the knife between my calves a couple of times. Then, I carefully tossed the knife up under my leg, catching it with the same hand before giving it a quick backward flip and then tossing it in the air and catching it behind my back.

We rehearsed until my arm muscles were well past sore and I was strong enough to do the number with relative ease. By the time Taofi thought I was ready, our redwood deck was nicked and dented from all the times I dropped the knife.

Performing the sword dance was a different story. I wore my glasses during rehearsals so I could see the knife easily. We never wore glasses during a performance and I didn't have contact lenses, so I did this routine with my raw 20/200 eyesight. Sometimes the hook caught my thigh or I dropped the knife after trying to catch it behind my back. Taofi told me to just keep going and have fun.

Above: My nephew Chris holding my knife - notice the hook at the end (Author's collection)

Left: My knife dance routine at Mah Jong (Author's collection)

Fun?

I was a nervous wreck and went on stage knowing that at some point I would drop the knife, but it was well-received by the audience because it was rare to see a teenaged girl knife-dancing. The Debbie Sword Dance stayed in. My routine led into Taofi's routine. When he came on stage he asked the audience to give me a round of applause. A very kind gesture for this clumsy teenager.

Leia liked to mix it up, so next she and Taofi thought I should learn a fire dance. Now I was certain they were out to get me. There was no way I could do a routine like Taofi. Not with my eyesight. Hadn't I been through enough with the knife dance?

Taofi envisioned a fire pit prelude to his sword fire number. This involved me, dancing around the stage to the sound of the drums before slowly stepping onto a pit of fire. To prepare, I built calluses on my feet by walking barefoot outside as much as possible, especially on pebbles or any hard uneven surface. I practiced on the hot asphalt of our driveway, on the sidewalk and, after a while, Taofi said I was ready.

Back to the redwood deck we went.

He placed a large industrial wok on a two-foot-tall metal stand. I practiced by stepping up into the wok, getting my balance, doing some hand motions, and then stepping down slowly, one foot at a time. After I got used to that, it was time for the fire. He soaked rags with benzene in the wok and lit them. The fire wasn't that high, just up to my calves. The same calves that got caught on the hook of my knife.

Taofi said to step up into the fire on one foot, step on with the other, stay two seconds, then step off with one foot and then the other. He demonstrated with feet thickened by years of fire dancing.

Do you know how hot fire is on the soles of your feet? It is painfully hot no matter how thick your calluses. I managed to step up but leapt off before even getting the other foot onto the benzene-soaked rag. Taofi used the garden hose to spray cool water on the soles of my feet. Then we'd try again. I got a little better at it and could stand in the fire for two seconds, then three more seconds, without yelling in pain.

After much rehearsal and now a nicked, dented, and *charred* redwood deck, I told Taofi I just couldn't do this number. I didn't want deformed feet. I told Taofi that no one would take me to the prom if I was disfigured. My dramatic pleading convinced Taofi and Leia and I never performed the fire pit dance at Mah Jong.

CHAPTER 23

BAND EVOLUTION

By 1971, Bill Kirk's poor health meant he couldn't continue. He was obese and his beer drinking between sets didn't help. He would pop a Peppermint Lifesaver before going back to perform. He'd blow in my face and ask if I could smell beer. I could, but I always said, "No," so he'd get out of my face and up on stage faster.

Bill was replaced by an assortment of guitarists until 17-year-old musician Billy Pratnicki joined Leia and Willie, the drummer. In 1974, a 16-year-old keyboardist, Johnny Rubino, was added. Each band member earned $125 per week for three nights' work), a hefty sum in those days, plus free food.

DINNER AFTER THE SHOW

Our family dined after the shows and the dinner rush. We sat in a booth closest to the hostess stand so we could answer the phone, tend to cashier duties, help someone at the gift shop, or welcome a take-out customer. Every customer or staff member was attended to, even if it meant we bobbed up and down. We kept a watchful eye on the dining room, bar, gift shop, and lobby.

We ordered whatever we wanted from the chefs. Our favorites were "Mah Jong Steak," a top sirloin cooked medium rare and served on a hot silver platter. When the waiter dropped vegetables on the platter, it sizzled, and the smell of steak wafted around the dining room. We also liked Lobster Cantonese (Maine lobster stir fried in black bean sauce). When Chico was in the kitchen, we ordered Clams Casino. On Saturday nights, we ate after the midnight show, often at 1:30am after I got out of costume. The dancers were treated to dinner at the bar but many of them ordered take-out for their commute back to NYC.

On our way home we headed over to Town and Country Diner, just around the block from our house. We ordered coffee and cheesecake, biding our time until the Sunday morning papers were delivered by courier to the diner—our cue to finish our dessert and head home, often well past 3:00am.

Sundays were hard. I slept in until noon and tried to concentrate on schoolwork before going to Mah Jong by 5:00. Sundays were just as busy as any weekend night. It was also the busiest take-out night. Often the take-out wait was over an hour, but most customers knew to call ahead. Many bided their time by shopping at Mom's gift shop.

By Monday, I was barely functional. I had to operate on a different sleep pattern from the weekend and concentration was extremely challenging. I was a miserable student. Math and science classes were scheduled in the morning. Choir and drama rehearsals were mercifully in the late afternoons and evenings, and I thrived in those courses partly because my internal circadian restaurant rhythm had adjusted by late afternoon.

Dad & Mom, Chinese New Year celebration, 1972

MOM LEARNS TO CUSS

In 1970, Mah Jong was ten years old. By day, it was a favorite lunch destination for local politicians and business executives. By cocktail hour, the bars teemed with workers on their way home. Evenings were busy with take-out. Wednesdays were Luau Nights. Weekends were maddeningly busy. Even if you made a reservation for dinner on weekends, you still waited an hour for slow customers to finish their meals.

Mom worked at the hostess stand on an elevated platform with a microphone and a big red hard-bound calendar. The microphone allowed us to call the names of diners waiting by the front entrance or in the gift shop or bar. The book held the reservations and, in theory, there was a limit to how many tables we could handle per hour. But mostly, reserved customers didn't mind biding their time at the bar or the gift shop. At the height of dinner service on Fridays and Saturdays, the front entrance was packed. Mom shooed away customers who tried to peek at the waiting list on the red calendar. Some tried to bribe her or the captains but Mom could not be bought.

The cashiers and I helped work the crowd. It was so loud no one could hear Mom when she announced a table. We made our way through the crowd to the front entrance, the gift shop and the bar, constantly shouting out names, such as "MR. SCHWARTZ, PARTY OF 4, YOUR TABLE'S

READY!" because people couldn't hear or see us among the crowd. Mom sent out Stacey Krinsky, the tallest cashier with a booming voice. Like a periscopic prison searchlight, Stacey scanned the dining room from her position at the hostess desk to report on diners finishing up or paying their check. This gave Mom a head start to alert the waiting customer.

Anna Tumpek vividly recalls working at the hostess stand on Saturday nights. "The sheer size of Mah Jong was astounding. It was incredible how many people we served on weekends. People waited two hours for a seat on a Saturday night!

"I hostessed with your mom. It was hilarious. She would say 'Suega!' (I later learned this was Chinese for *idiot*). I asked what that meant and she said, 'I can't tell you. Good Catholic girls shouldn't know that.' Working the hostess desk was insane. Your mother said, 'Just smile, they won't get mad at you, they'll get mad at me.' This was very true. On a Saturday night, parties of six or ten without a reservation came in off the street; there was already an hour wait *with* reservations. They were desperate to get in. They asked about the Aloha Room cover charge and many paid to sit down for dinner even at a premium."

Most customers were gracious, some were not. On occasion, irate customers hurled racial slurs, demanded special attention, or issued threats: "I know people who can shut this place down." We were told to "Go back to where you came from" or "We don't want your type here." This inspired Mom to ask me to teach her some curse words. She didn't get the origin of "Sh>t" or "Fu%k" and why they were considered bad words. She heard some customers utter this at the bar which piqued her curiosity. I taught her some phrases, "Fu%k You" or "You're a piece of Sh#t" and said these were most effective when spoken forcefully. "Asshole" didn't mean much to her.

When tables weren't turning over fast enough and customers complained about the wait, Mom replied, "What do you want me to do, kick people out of their tables?" To help speed table turnover, whoever was available cleared the tables, bussed the dishes, set up the fresh tablecloths and place settings. Mom would tell the customer, "She's cleaning your table now." The customers followed us and hovered while we madly cleaned up and reset the tables.

One very stressful Saturday night as I was clearing a table with one of the Mah Jong kids, I overheard commotion over the loudspeaker. Muffled sounds, then background voices engaged in an argument, then Mom's voice at top volume: "SHIT YOU!"

I was so proud.

CHAPTER 24

OTHER FAMOUS PEOPLE 1960-67

Mah Jong was a celebrity magnet, starting with Congressman Steve Derounian (R-NY2), who gained national attention serving on the House Congressional Subcommittee quiz show scandal investigation during the 1950s. Congressman Derounian was part of Mah Jong's opening day ribbon-cutting ceremony on August 4, 1960.

In 1963, Thomas Tien Ken-sin, with his entourage, paid a visit to Mah Jong. Thomas Tien had been a priest at Tsingtao's St. Joseph's Church, Mom's school and where she, Daisy and Edie and their mother Kate took refuge during the Japanese occupation of 1937. Father Tien was later ordained Bishop of Tsingtao in 1939 by Pope Pius XII and eventually elevated to Cardinal in 1946, becoming the first Cardinal from China and the Far East.

Just as the Communists were gaining political control over the Republic of China in 1948, Cardinal Tien left Peking and traveled to Shanghai to seek medical treatment. This went against the approval of Pope Paul XII, who believed a pastor should remain with his congregation. He was ordered by the Vatican to return to Peking, but was advised by the National Government of the Republic of China that it was too risky since Peking was falling under Communist control. If Cardinal Tien returned to Peking, he could be tortured, killed, imprisoned, or held for ransom, given his direct relationships with the Vatican. By 1949, conditions worsened in Shanghai and Cardinal Tien flew to Hong Kong. Caught between the dangers of returning to Peking, his frail health, and escaping to Taiwan, Cardinal Tien was a man without a country.

Cardinal Tien spent the rest of his life in exile in the United States, Hong Kong, and Taiwan.[62] In addition to sharing Tsingtao roots with Mom, Cardinal Tien became the Board Chairman of Fu Jen Catholic University (Mom's alma mater) from 1960–67, after it had been relocated from Peking to Taiwan following the Communist takeover of China.

Mom, a devout Catholic, was overjoyed to learn that Cardinal Tien would be in the New York area and that he specifically wanted to stop by Syosset to reunite with her, an old hometown parishioner from Tsingtao.

He and his priests contacted a few local friends to have dinner at Mah Jong. The back room was reserved for a private gathering with over 30 guests. Mom wore a fine cheongsam (Chinese dress) to mark the auspicious occasion. Mah Jong was just three years old and Cardinal Tien's visit accentuated its blossoming social prominence on Long Island.

At the time of his visit to Mah Jong, Cardinal Tien was in swift-failing health. Traveling was arduous and his taking the time to come to Mah Jong was a wonderful honor. He died four years later at the age of 76, in exile in Taiwan.

Cardinal Tien's colleague was Paul Yu-Pin. In 1936, at the age of 35, Yu-Pin became the Bishop of Nanjing (Nanking) , at that time the capital of China. When the Imperial Japanese Army gained control of Nanjing in 1937, a $100,000 bounty was placed on Bishop Yu-Pin, already in the United States setting up employment agencies to match American teachers and doctors to jobs in China.

He left China in 1949 as the Communists were taking over. Yu-Pin spent time in the United States raising funds for refugees who escaped Mainland China and settled in Taiwan. Between 1950-1960, the Catholic population of Taiwan expanded from 5,000 to 200,000.[63] In 1960, at the request of Pope John XXIII, Bishop Yu-Pin was asked to re-open Fu Jen Catholic University in Taiwan after it had been shuttered during the Communist takeover.[64] He was appointed the University's first President to serve with Cardinal Tien, the University's first Chairman.

Yu-Pin was elevated to Cardinal by Pope Paul VI in 1969.

Thus, in a period of 10 years, Mah Jong was visited by China's only two cardinals.

Dad's Kiwanis Club and King Wah connections aligned him with the powerful heads of the local unions: Jack Kiernan from the Nassau Electrical Contractors Association (NECA), Joe Kramer from the Electrical Workers Union Local 25, and Joseph P. Tonelli from the International Paperworkers Union. Monsignor Richard Hanley, the founding editor of *The Long Island Catholic* was also aligned with Joe Kiernan and Jack Kramer as arbitrator and as Chairman of the Industrial Relations Board of the Electrical Construction Industry.

Reservations were made weeks and often months in advance, especially during the holiday seasons, so getting a table at Mah Jong on the weekends was difficult. People tried to slip large amounts of cash into the captains' hands hoping to get preferential treatment. Many customers came in claiming to know Dad or a member of his inner circle.

Above: Mom, Dad, Michael and I with Cardinal Yu-Pin at Mah Jong (Author's collection)

Above: Mom and Dad with Cardinal Tien at Mah Jong, 1963 (Author's collection)

Right: Dad and Mom with Cardinal Yu-Pin and Joseph Tonelli at Fu-Jen University fundraiser at Mah Jong (Author's collection)

Nino Loiacono brought an entourage to dinner and Dad arranged to have his party seated towards the back dining area. Nino was Vice President of Local 318 and a close associate of Paul Castellano, a leader of the Carlo Gambino crime mob. Castellano was known as the "Howard Hughes of the Mob."

We were accustomed to minding what we said and did in front of Uncle Nino and Aunt Rose. One evening they invited Mom, Dad, Michael and me to dinner at their house in nearby Plainview. Uncle Nino and Aunt Rose picked us up and drove us there in their large car. Before we got into the car, Mom warned me, "Don't say anything when you are in the car." Mom revealed years later that she thought the car was bugged.

On another occasion, two imposing-looking men came in to Mah Jong claiming they were part of Nino's dinner party. Their names weren't in the reservation book. Dad asked them to prove they were legitimate guests. After some verification and validation by Nino, Dad said they needed stop off at the coat room to check their coats. They went to Mom at the coat check room, gave her their hats and coats. Before they took off their gloves, Mom said sternly, "Hand over your guns." Dutifully, the two big burly men did what they were told and gave my 4'10" mother their weapons before she allowed them into the dining room.

One night Dad announced that Nino would be bringing over a group of people for dinner. Special arrangements were made for their private table in the back, guest names recorded in the reservation book, and a special guest would be in attendance. Mom told me, "Whatever you do, don't look at his face."

It is hard for a naturally curious teenager to follow those instructions. I was working in the coat room and awaiting Nino's entourage. Nino came in first, checked his coat and hat, did his customary handshake with me (after he released his grip, there was usually a crisp $50 bill in my hand), and went to greet Dad. The rest of the party came to the coat check area to divest themselves of their outer garb. Try as I might, I could not maintain discipline. I looked up to catch a glimpse of the next person checking his coat and found myself staring at a shiny grayish-brown wad of skin where the face was supposed to be. There were slits instead of eyes and I didn't see much of a nose. The mouth was taut and twisted. This man could not have been more than 30 years old. I froze in horror and kept staring at him until Mom came over and jabbed me with the coat hanger to tell me to take his coat. I learned later that he had crossed someone in the mob and was pulverized as a warning.

AARON FROSCH

Dad engaged with several lawyers at Mah Jong. One of them was Aaron Frosch, a prominent entertainment lawyer who handled Marilyn Monroe's business affairs, her divorce from Joe DiMaggio, and served as the executor of her estate after her death in 1962. Aaron's other clients were veteran stage and screen actors Rex Harrison, Elizabeth Taylor and Richard Burton, among others. He was on the board of directors of the Rebekah Harkness Foundation (now known as the Harkness Foundation for Dance). In 1967 he served as Co-Chairman of Mayor John Lindsay's Committee for the New York Shakespeare Festival.

Aaron was friends with our friend, Ralph Papsidero and our family became close friends with Aaron. In a letter dated April 22, 1974, Aaron was concerned about our family affairs and wrote to Dad:

> *Dear Peter,*
>
> *"As you know, I frequently see Ralph. Each time I meet with him, we speak of you. As a result of our personal relationship and on the basis of our mutual relationship with Ralph, I feel a close friendship with you.*
>
> *Therefore, you must excuse my concern over certain of your affairs and I trust you will not think I am prying.*
>
> *From time to time, we have discussed a Last Will and Testament for you. My offer of this as a gift to you and your family for Christmas 1972 still exists...*
>
> *"...I bring this to your attention, not only from the viewpoint of your own protection but from the viewpoint also of the security of your wife, your children, your family...I understand from Ralph that you are the owner of a Condominium in the State of Florida.....Consideration also should be given to the establishment of Trusts for the benefit of your children...."*

Aaron's estate was in Quogue, Long Island, slightly midway between Syosset and Montauk Point (the most eastern tip of Long Island). He hosted Liz Taylor and Richard Burton at Quogue on several occasions[65] and during an attempt to help facilitate the reconciliation of their turbulent marriage in 1973. Pua shared a memory: "Ralph used to drive for Aaron and he was asked to pick up Liz and Dick from the airport, per

Aaron's request. Ralph said he was driving them out to Quogue and Liz asked Ralph, 'Love, do you know where we can get a bit of refreshment?' so Ralph drove them to Mah Jong so they could have a drink. We had just finished a show when Ralph walked in with them. Your father arranged a private table in the main dining room and we were all told to just act cool. Ralph, however, wasn't impressed with them."

Comparing dance notes with choreographer Donald Saddler at Mah Jong's Chinese New Year celebration, 1975 (Author's collection)

When Ralph was not available to pick up Liz and Dick from Kennedy Airport, Dad asked my Uncle Teddy to go instead. According to Kathy, Teddy was not impressed with the celebrity couple, either. He used a Chinese phrase to convey his experiences with them in the car: "Yo lao, yo cho" loosely translated, "Not only are they old, they smell bad."

In 1975, Syosset High School's senior class musical was *No, No, Nanette*. I was cast as Betty, one of the floozies. I was in the number *Telephone Girlie* but I memorized the entire score by listening relentlessly to the 1971 Broadway cast album. I had *No, No, Nanette* fever. I listened to the album, played the score on my piano, watched my classmates rehearse their numbers, and dropped in on the dance rehearsals in the high school cafeteria even though I wasn't in any of those scenes. I loved performing at Mah Jong, but in my view, this was legitimate theatre and I was one of the principal characters. This could be the start of a fabulous song and dance career. How I'd matured since my stage premiere as the planet Venus in kindergarten!

Dad told Aaron about my falling deeply in love with the arts in high school. I was part of the high school choir and was discovering new friendships through both choir and theatre. Mom added that I was a big fan of the Broadway cast recording of *No, No, Nanette* (featuring Patsy Kelly, Bobby Van, Jack Gilford, Susan Watson, and the indomitable Ruby Keeler) and that I knew all the songs. Aaron said that his friend, Donald

Saddler, did the choreography for the Broadway production and had won a Tony Award for his work. If he could work things out, he would bring Donald to Mah Jong for dinner so I might meet him.

Mom and Dad didn't mention this possibility, likely because they thought I would bounce off the walls in anticipation of meeting a Broadway luminary. Donald Saddler was one of the original members of the American Ballet Theatre and a chorus dancer in some of MGM's great musicals of the 1930s (*The Great Ziegfeld, Babes in Arms*, and *The Wizard of Oz*). Jerome Robbins became his mentor. Donald choreographed Jerry Herman's *Milk and Honey and* became Robbins' assistant for the 1950 Ethel Merman vehicle *Call Me Madam*. And now, *No, No, Nanette!*

On Chinese New Year, Feb 11, 1975, Aaron and his family were our guests at Mah Jong's annual extravaganza. He brought Donald Saddler. After I finished performing and got into my evening dress, I sat down for dinner with the cashiers. Aaron came over and introduced me to Donald. I thought it was going to be a quick handshake before Donald went back to his table. Plates of food were brought over to me since I hadn't eaten yet and Donald asked for an extra plate so he could join me. Incredibly, we compared dance notes. He was interested in the Polynesian dance steps. I chatted animatedly about *No, No, Nanette* and how I yearned to be a tap dancer. I wanted to be like Ruby Keeler: an understudy one night, a star the next! He so kindly indulged a hyper-excited teenager; I was just 18, but I felt grown up beyond my years.

Later, after graduating from college and starting a career in the arts, I corresponded with Aaron. When I began to produce Equity-waiver productions in Los Angeles, I sent Aaron press clippings and show programs. Ever the gentleman, he always wrote back.

In 1980, I was a producer with Theatre 40, an Equity-waiver theatre in Beverly Hills. (As a producer for this theatre company, there was no monetary compensation; the title was it, for doing most of the administrative organizing and grunt work. Since I was just getting started in my career, I gladly accepted the impressive sounding title to beef up my resume).

One of the shows I produced was the West Coast premiere of *Philemon*, written by Tom Jones and Harvey Schmidt, the team who created *The Fantasticks*. I figured Aaron knew them and I sent him a courtesy note.

His note to me, dated November 25, 1980 and printed on his letterhead, was sent just before he was diagnosed with the onset of cerebellum degeneration, a form of multiple sclerosis.

Aaron R. Frosch
445 Park Avenue
New York, N.Y. 10022
to me at Theatre 40, PO Box 5401, Beverly Hills, CA 90210)

Dear Debbie,
I am impressed with your production of PHILEMON.
I trust you will inform me when you participate on other projects.
With every good wish,
Sincerely yours,
(his signature)

He had the letter dictated and personally took the pains to sign his name, nearly illegible but written with determination.

A subsequent letter to me, dated March 18, 1981, just as he was retiring due to failing health:

Dear Debbie:
I received your warm letter recently. I have sent a copy of your letter and this to your mother.
I am glad you value my advice. I will seek to make it good advice.
I am impressed with your artistic accomplishments. Your experience as a Producer and Stage Manager should bring you, before long, to New York.
Your parents are very proud of you, which they are hesitant to show. They speak of you often.
I look forward to seeing you in New York before not too long.
Naturally, if we ever come to California we will visit you there.
With every good wish.
Sincerely,
Aaron

Aaron's condition deteriorated. We kept in touch until 1988, when I wrote to let him know I finally got my first professional job in the arts as the Special Events Manager for San Francisco's American Conservatory Theater, producing and directing major galas and community events. I sent Aaron copies of invitations, newspaper articles, and photos of my work. I did not hear from him. Mom and Dad later said he was slowly slipping and fighting at the same time.

He passed away on April 29, 1989 of cerebellum atrophy. He was 64 years old.

TONELLI

Joseph P. Tonelli was a Mah Jong VIP. He was a close acquaintance with Uncle Nino and served as President of the United Paperworkers International Union, and Vice President of the Executive Council of the AFL-CIO. President Lyndon Johnson appointed him to the Social Security Advisory Board in 1964 and President Nixon appointed Tonelli to the Air Quality Advisory Board of the Environmental Protection Agency.

He was involved with a number of humanitarian causes, catching the attention of Cardinal Yu-Pin, who made arrangements with Cardinal Terence Cook (Archbishop of New York) to designate Tonelli a Knight of Malta. A formal black-tie gala was held in the ballroom of a New York City hotel; the occasion was to raise funds for Fu Jen University in Taiwan. American comedian, radio host, and nightclub performer Joey Adams was master of ceremonies and Dad, representing Mah Jong, was asked to sit on the dais with Tonelli and other renowned guests.

Cardinal Yu-Pin later arranged for Tonelli and his grandchildren to have a private audience with Pope Paul VI. Shortly after returning to the States, a dinner auction party was held at Mah Jong to auction off the Cardinal's personal collection of art objects and paintings. The proceeds of the evening were donated to Fu Jen Catholic University.

In recognition of Tonelli's efforts as a fundraiser for Fu Jen University, the Tonelli Science Building was established on the Fu Jen University's new campus in Taiwan in 1972. Upon its dedication, Fu Jen University described it as "named after Dr. J.P. Tonelli, a faithful Catholic and passionate admirer of Chinese culture. He generously funded the establishment of this three-story building."

CHAPTER 25

CHINESE NEW YEAR

Mah Jong opened to the general public every day and evening of the year except for one annual occasion: Chinese New Year, a holiday revered by the Chinese people honoring our ancestors, families and the start of a new lunar year. Depending on the lunar calendar, Chinese New Year typically falls during January or February.

Preparations began in the summer. Traditionally, Mom and Dad took us to the Chinatown tailors to order Chinese clothes for the new year. Mom and Dad went their separate ways in Chinatown; Dad loved to roam around the food markets and tea shops; Mom was at the fabric shops choosing material for our cheongsams and Michael's changshan.[66] We had our measurements taken and chose the color of our Chinese New Year outfits.

By fall, our custom-made attire was ready and the feeling of anticipation was like Christmas just before opening presents. I couldn't wait to see and try on the finished product. Adjustments were usually necessary since I grew a little taller after the original fitting, but everything was ready by Chinese New Year day.

From the age of 6 through 10, I preferred the more comfortable silk pantsuit but as I got older (and developed a figure), I wore cheongsams with a preference for pink. Mom, on the other hand, loved darker colors since the embroidery stood out dramatically. Dad wore his standard black suit, white shirt, and a tie.

Mah Jong's preparations also began early, in association with the Chinese Center of Long Island (CCLI), a cultural organization established in 1960 to preserve and study Chinese heritage, language, art, and traditions. Dad's business partner, Arthur Jong, was the Board President from 1964-67 and introduced Mom and Dad to the Center's important work during this era, when China was under Mao Tse-Tung's Communist rule on the advent of its Cultural Revolution. The students answering Chairman Mao's call for this revolution were known as Red Guards. They operated a campaign to eradicate the "Four Olds" (ideas, cultures, customs, and habits), beginning the widespread destruction of cultural heritage sites and the persecution of artists, scholars, and those with ties to the West.

The mission of the Chinese Center of Long Island resonated deeply with Mom and Dad. They began the longstanding tradition of making Mah Jong's Chinese New Year celebration a fundraising event, the proceeds benefiting the Center's efforts to foster Chinese cultural awareness and appreciation on Long Island. The Center arranged for raffle prizes, handled the publicity, and provided traditional Chinese entertainment—fireworks and lion dance ceremonies.

Mah Jong was responsible for everything else: building the altar, taking reservations, handling dinner seating logistics, hiring extra chefs, waiters, and hostesses, setting up the dining room decor, and preparing the menu for a 12-course banquet, including a whole roasted suckling pig, to serve over 150 guests.

The altar, an important component of the dining area, was created by placing two dining tables together, set on a riser, and draped in red tablecloths. It was the first thing customers saw when checking in at the hostess stand. You couldn't miss it. Everything burst with red, the color associated with good luck for Chinese New Year. Behind the altar, embroidered cloth banners with Chinese characters extended good wishes and prosperity. Dick Lang created Chinese calligraphy artwork for welcome signs at the front door. The altar centerpiece was the whole pig, surrounded by incense, fruit, candles, chopsticks, rice wine cups, and paper money—offerings to our ancestors.

Dad considered the altar a sacred area and reverenced the lighting of candles and burning of paper money to send up to our ancestors. Mom added a porcelain statue of Kwan Yin, Goddess of Mercy, to offer thoughts of compassion. I realized how seriously Dad took the altar symbolism when a customer did something egregious (I'm not sure what) and Dad burst into anger. He lunged at the man, yelling, "If anyone wants to f*ck with that altar, they need to f*ck with me first." Dad had to be held back. The customer quickly apologized, not knowing what he had done wrong. That was the first and only time in my life I ever heard Dad use an expletive.

During the weeks leading up to Chinese New Year, the entire Mah Jong staff focused on its preparation after the restaurant closed for dinner. The energy was distracting, making it hard for me to concentrate on school. All I could think about was the excitement waiting for me after I got off the bus behind the Mah Jong parking lot. I would switch gears and join my parents and the Mah Jong staff in producing this extravaganza. Michael and I were excused from school for three consecutive days: one to prepare for Chinese New Year's Eve, one day to work the entire Chinese New Year's Day and Evening Gala, the other to recover, since the celebrations continued well into the early morning of the next day. As I succinctly summarized in my 7th grade essay regarding "Our New Year's Celebration" for Mrs. Winter's English class, "At the end of all of this, you must go home and rest for a few days."

Mom tracked the reservations and took care of guest seating according to their requested tablemates and VIPs. Long Island National Bank supplied new crisp $1 dollar bills. She studied the reservation list for customers with young children or grandchildren and prepared Hong Baos—lucky red envelopes—by placing one or two dollar bills inside. She handed these out to the adults to give to their children and grandkids when they got home.

The captains studied the table configurations, assigning the more experienced waiters to the VIP tables. The lobby was converted into a second coat check area, and extra wooden coat hangers brought up from storage. I organized the coat check tags in numerical order and put them on hangers accordingly.

Chinese New Year banquet dishes were presented on platters, served family style or passed from guest to guest. For tables of 8–12, several communal platters were set for groups of 4–5. The gift shop became the Chinn family and special guest dining area; the cabinets were replaced by a large rectangular dining table to accommodate 12–15 people. This was where Mom's cashiers, hostesses, and our family sat for dinner, except Dad, who never sat down to eat. Instead he chatted with guests at each table. Special guests at the gift shop dining room table included my aunts, uncles, and cousins. It was a wonderful bonding experience.

CHINESE NEW YEAR FESTIVITIES

Happy New Year! Gung Hay Fat Choy! (my father's Cantonese dialect) and Gung Xi Fai Cai (my mother's Mandarin dialect).

Invitations to Mah Jong's Chinese New Year celebration were coveted. The guest list was our key clientele, although the list grew as Mah Jong became famous. A waiting list formed as early as the previous Thanksgiving. At first just the main dining room, accommodating 140 guests, was used for Chinese New Year. Later, due to popular demand, we opened up the Aloha Room.

The evening started at 7:30pm. Everyone was more than prompt; some allowed extra time for winter weather driving and a good parking spot. Others knew if they got there early, they could enjoy a drink at the bar.

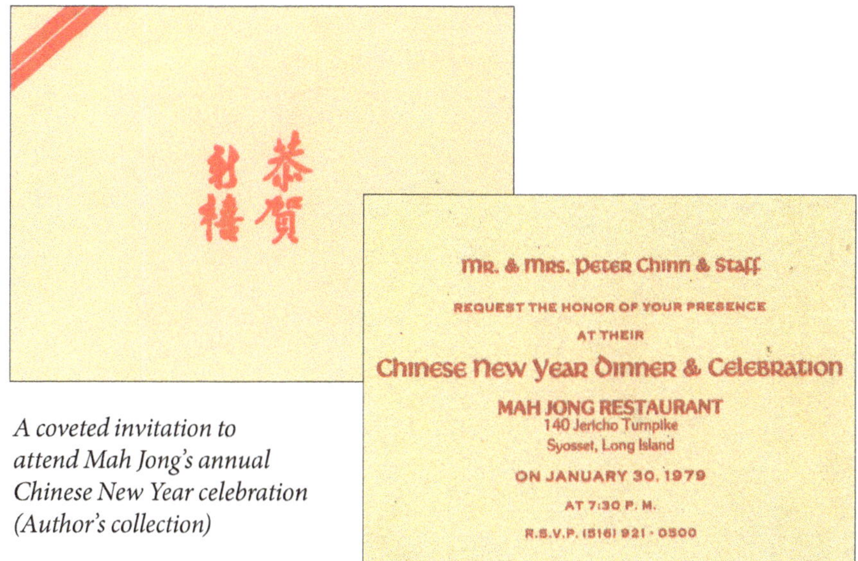

A coveted invitation to attend Mah Jong's annual Chinese New Year celebration (Author's collection)

This meant a general rush of customers arriving at the same time. Mom, the cashiers and I spent our time from 7:00–7:30 in the coat room taking in heavy coats, furs, hats, and gloves.

Once guests got table assignments and were escorted to their tables, the dining room was a sea of noise; voices, laughter, glasses clinking, blenders blending and the martini shakers shaking.

While guests settled in, members of the lion dance group prepared for their entrance in the Mah Jong parking lot. The dance troupe huddled outside in the blustery January or February winter air, dressed in thin sweatshirts, black pants, and soft cloth shoes. They would work up a sweat once they slipped inside the lion costume.

The lion represents power, wisdom, and wealth—fortuitous symbols to welcome a new year. In the lion dance, the lead dancer holds the heavy head of the lion; 30–40 pounds depending on the head's size and decorative items. It requires strong upper body strength and sturdy legs since the lion bobs and weaves its way along the route, crouching and rising up while shaking its head. It is so physically difficult that often two or three dancers take over mid-way through the dancing ceremony.

The lion body was 30 feet long and made of silk. The longer the body, the more luck it symbolizes. Dancers crouched underneath the fabric at 5–6 foot intervals positioned at different angles so the lion can "slither" its way along.

Dad and Mom posing with the lion's head, Chinese New Year celebration at Mah Jong (Author's collection)

Once the lion dancers warmed up, fireworks started in the parking lot. At first just a couple of 'pop' sounds, and then nonstop crackling. More fireworks were added to the mix and then the ceremonial drums, gongs, and cymbals. Once we heard the drums, Mom and the captains cleared the path for the lion to enter the Mah Jong dining room.

The first to arrive were the drums on wheels. Keeping time to the steady beat, the gong and cymbal players were right behind. More fireworks in the parking lot sent the lion in.

The ferocious lion head was most prominent. Its bulging eyes (manipulated by the dancer inside the head) moved from side to side as if taking stock of the room. The lion made its way to the altar where Dad waited with a long pole with a string entwined with numerous $20, $10, $5, and $1 bills at the top and a head of fresh cabbage at the end—the "offering" to appease the lion. The lion rose up on its legs (the dancers inside the body stood on top of each other to give the lion more height to signify its power) and the dancer in the lion head maneuvered the mouth so the lion would eat the cabbage, spit it out, and go after the money.

It was mesmerizing to see Dad tease the lion by lifting the pole out of reach. The lion retreated and tried again. Dad lifted the pole even higher and the lion pawed at the ground and tried again. The drums, cymbals, and gongs beat faster, as if to replicate the lion's heartbeat. And it was LOUD! When the lion finally got ahold of the money, it was "satisfied," and the drums muffled a bit while the lion moved into the dining room, thrilling those close enough to pet it.

Then, as if to say, "I've had enough," the lion moved out of the dining room. The drums, cymbals and gongs followed. Later, the head of the lion was brought into Mah Jong to stand watch over the festivities, a logical place for photo opportunities.

That got the festivities going. Next, a ritual blessing of the Eight Immortals performed by representatives from the CCLI and Dad. In Chinese mythology, the Eight Immortals transcend the human state and are endowed with powers to guard against evil. They are known as He Xiangu (the only female of the Immortals), Cao Guojiu (believed to have lived during the Song Dynasty), Li Tieguai (an apprentice of Lao Tzu, the founder of Taoism), Lan Caihe (patron of beggars), Lü Dongbin (clever scholar), Han Xiangzi (patron saint of musicians), Zhang Guolao (believed to be a real historical figure) and Zhongli Quan (alchemist).[67]

After the altar blessing, welcoming remarks were made by the CCLI representatives, then Dad was introduced and warmly acknowledged as the host. Mom didn't like to speak in public; she was self-conscious about her English and preferred to stay in the background. However, everyone knew it was Peter and Nellie Chinn who produced the event and Mom held court where she felt most comfortable: behind the scenes, making sure everyone did what they were supposed to so things ran smoothly.

The banquet service began by 8:30. Each banquet dish was brought out one at a time so the guests could slowly savor their way through the menu. In a traditional Chinese banquet, noodles and fried rice are served towards the end so you don't fill up too fast during the meal.

TYPICAL CHINESE NEW YEAR BANQUET AT MAH JONG

Minced Chicken in Bird's Nest Soup or Winter Melon Soup
Treasured Pork Rolls
Jaded Capon or Squab
Beef Medallions
Sweet and Pungent Baby Ribs
Five Flavor Filet of Bass or Brocade of Titi Shrimp
Braised Duckling
Longevity Noodles
Barbequed Roast Pig
Yang Chow Fried Rice
Almond de Creme

CHINESE NEW YEAR ENTERTAINMENT

The entertainment by the Chinese Center featured traditional Chinese songs and dances, lost on me since I don't speak Chinese, but I was enthralled with the costumes and make-up of the dancers. The ribbon dancing was my favorite; the dance my cousin, Wa-Wa, performed as a young girl. Many of our family gatherings featured Wa-Wa performing the ribbon dance and it was fascinating to see fabric swirling in stunning geometric shapes.[68] The Center's dancers moved with grace throughout the Mah Jong dining room. I wondered if the ribbon would get caught on a customer or a passing waiter.

In 1969, Mah Jong added a special Polynesian floor show to the Chinese New Year's entertainment. It was a tighter set-up: smaller bandstand and smaller performance area adjacent to the altar. We managed to do all of the numbers, including Chief Taofi and his sword/fire dance, ending with the Tahitian number.

After the show, around 10:00, the CCLI held a raffle and door prizes. Meanwhile, we dancers got out of our costumes and put on long gowns,

typical Chinese New Year banquet at Mah Jong, 1979 (Author's collection)

CELEBRATING THE

MONDAY & TUESDAY

January 29th & 30th, 1979

PROGRAM

7:30 p.m.	FIREWORKS
	DANCE OF THE LION
	RITUAL CEREMONY
8:15 p.m.	WELCOME ADDRESS
8:30 p.m.	DINNER
	ENTERTAINMENT
	DANCE MUSIC
10:00 p.m.	RAFFLE

YEAR OF THE RAM 4677

CHINESE NEW YEAR BANQUET MENU

八仙賀年 BLESSINGS OF THE EIGHT IMMORTALS
綠珠冬蓉 WINTER MELON SOUP
大讌三元 MAH JONG GRAND TRIUMVIRATE
錦繡蝦仁 BROCADE OF TITI SHRIMPS
鴛鴦碧樹 YING YANG CAPON
羅漢集會 LO LAN FESTIVAL
楊州燴飯 RICE OF YANG CHOW
穿標金牛 BEEF MEDALLIONS
八珍扒鴨 BRAISED DUCKLING
五掷大魚 FIVE FLAVOR FILLET OF BASS
金猪擡盆 GOLDEN BARBECUED PIG
杏仁香露 ROCK SUGAR ALMOND DEWS

WE WISH EVERYONE
A HAPPY AND PROSPEROUS NEW YEAR
MAY ALL YOUR WISHES BE FULFILLED

Peter Chinn

not formal ball gowns but a step above a casual muu-muu. Some dancers joined the family table for dinner or ate with friends by the bar. The energy never really reached a final climax—every hour was as exciting as the one before. All five senses were stimulated in one way or the other and when the evening was officially over at 10:30, hardly anyone left. There were long goodbyes, people lingered at tables to finish conversations or ambled over to the bar for more drinks. There was impulse buying at Mom's gift shop and lots of well-wishing to the Mah Jong staff. Mom and the cashiers took their positions at the coat check room. Generous tips went into a basket, and there were more extended good-nights as guests made their way out the door.

By midnight, the Mah Jong staff could finally relax and celebrate. Dad locked the front door and turned off the lights on the outdoor sign, Mom took her post at the cash register where she counted the coat check tips, the cigarette and gift shop sales.

Most of the guests were gone . The few still at the bar watched the waiters quickly clear dishes and glassware off the tables. With great speed, the tables were set up for all-night gambling. Out came the dominoes, dice, poker chips, and decks of cards. Out came wads of cash from the waiters' pockets and the communal tip jar. The waiters and captains took off their jackets and ties, the chefs came out in their aprons, packs of cigarettes and ashtrays were set up, unfinished bottles of scotch and bourbon from the banquet were brought over, and everyone took up a place to play and bet at a table of their choice. There were 4–6 people at each table and usually 6–8 tables.

What had been an upscale dining room barely an hour before was transformed into a gambling den.

Clack, clack, clack! was the constant sounds of the domino tiles on the tablecloths. At another table the decks of cards were shuffled for poker. Everyone spoke Cantonese, yelling and shouting at each other as the bidding became more manic, winnings were claimed, and losers burst out in frustration.

I was allowed to watch up close but told not to speak; it might bring bad luck. I stood next to a player and whenever he was on a winning streak, he would turn and give me a dollar or two since my presence was regarded as good luck. When I first started hanging out with the gamblers, I was about 7 years old and considered cute and hard to resist. The dollar bills came in easy; all I had to was stand, watch, smile, and wait for pay dirt. Then I would go to the other side of the table and do the same thing.

By the age of ten, I had gained a particular interest in the poker games. I learned to watch the action of the cards, the body language and the facial expressions of the gamblers. Not everyone was good at keeping their hand a secret. I noticed that the ones dealt poor cards usually puffed their cigarettes extra hard or fiddled with their poker chips. I would size up a player and keep tabs on how he was doing and when I sensed the cards were moving in his favor, I casually ambled over to stand next to him, trying to be cute, sweet, and innocent. Before long, dollar bills flew into my hands!

Dad joined the gamblers once he finished reconciling paperwork in his office and by that time it was 3:00 or 4:00am. I wasn't tired at all—I was juiced up, having received many Hong Baos along with my haul at the gambling tables.

While Dad stayed into the morning to gamble, Mom took Michael and me home. After we got undressed and before going to bed, Mom took out all of the Hong Baos and my gambling money from her purse and we counted how much I took in that night. One year, I counted at least $200 which, in 1968, was a hefty amount to earn for just standing around and smiling, even for call girls. I figured that worked out to be $75/hour (the minimum wage in New York that year was $1.60/hour).

At this very early age I developed an enduring preoccupation with gambling. Dad loved to play the horses and cards. I gravitated to blackjack as did Michael, who also became proficient at pai gow and poker. Many of my vacations as an adult have been spent at blackjack tables at Tahoe and Las Vegas. The constant din of gambling sounds and the camaraderie at a blackjack table remind me of the nightclub and gambling noises of my youth, and comfort me.

Mom liked to watch the Mah Jong staff gamble, too. She cheered them on and silently admonished them if they played a bad hand. She took a liking to gin rummy and we played many rounds after work and on weekends. She was so fast and she always won. When my younger cousins came to visit, Mom taught them how to play gin rummy and she showed no mercy. Those poor kids lost all the time, but Mom figured it was a good way to teach them how to count and to be gracious losers.

The Chinn family celebrating the Year of the Snake at Mah Jong, 1965
(Author's collection)

Left: My solo dance number: Narcissus Queen (Author's collection)

Below: Dad, Michael and I with Bill and Loretta Koutensky at Mah Jong's Chinese New Year celebration, 1967 (Author's collection)

Bottom: Special guest Robert Oxnam at Mah Jong's Chinese New Year celebration. With Daisy (center) and Mom

福

Opposite page top: Lion dancers warming up in the Mah Jong parking lot (Author's collection)

Opposite page bottom: Posing with the lion dancing troupe. I danced with the little lion head to my right. (Author's collection)

Above: Dad teasing lion with money

Below: Lion dancers entering the Mah Jong dining room.

CHAPTER 26

DID NOT COME HOME LAST NIGHT

Dad's gambling habits extended beyond Chinese New Year. Sometimes he stayed past closing time to play a few rounds with the waiters. Unfortunately, he seldom alerted Mom to this fact. I was about 8 years old when I awoke on a Sunday morning and went into the kitchen for breakfast. Mom sat at the table casually doing her crossword puzzle. Before I sat down, something on the kitchen wall caught my eye. Scrawled across the entire wall in thick black magic marker were words documenting Dad's egregious act:

DID NOT COME HOME LAST NIGHT

Mom acted as if nothing was amiss and I asked her what was going on. She looked up from her crossword puzzle and just pointed her pen at the wall, as if to state the obvious. Dad eventually came home. He looked at the wall and went right to bed, thus agitating Mom even more. She left the writing up for several days, refusing to wash it off so Dad could be reminded of his sins. Eventually and begrudgingly, Mom scrubbed the wall.

Another night Dad stayed out gambling with the Mah Jong staff, I thought, "Uh-oh, Mom's getting the magic markers out." To my surprise, she spent most of the time in their bedroom and I heard lots of rustling in the closet. The next morning, I went out the front door to catch the school bus and saw piles of clothing on the curb. Upon closer inspection, they were all Dad's trousers, some with the crotch cut out.

Dad came home on time after that episode. He usually left for Mah Jong at 11:00am, came home around 3:00 for a nap, and went back to work from 5:00pm to midnight.

The gambling bug never left Dad. He still played the horses at the local Off Track Betting shop, but he was more discreet when gambling at the restaurant. Financial pressures of Mah Jong were constant and would further escalate during the next big event in the life of Mah Jong.

FINANCIAL PRESSURE COOKERS

Since Mah Jong opened in 1960, Dad financially flew by the seat of his pants. Cash flow was a perpetual worry. Kathy helped Dad by handling accounts payable. He was impressed with her neat handwriting and thought she would be good at writing out the checks to vendors.

Dad attempted to pay bills on time. He'd mail a check but would "forget" to sign it. When the vendor returned it, Dad signed the check, put it in the envelope, popped it in the mail but would "forget" to affix a stamp, giving him enough float time to get cash flow regulated.

Mah Jong's financial pressures created marital pressures. Mom and Dad frequently fought at home. Mom complained that Dad seldom spent time with the family, we had few family vacations, and we were always working.

One summer when Michael and I were in grade school, we idled at home while Mom and Dad were at Mah Jong. We watched TV and ate junk food. Mom came home on her 3:00 break and when she saw that we never got out of bed the entire day, she didn't get mad at us. She got mad at Dad. She told us to get dressed because we were leaving the house. She drove around, we went to a movie and stayed away from Mah Jong until it closed. Using her key, she opened the door and told us we were going to sleep that night in the restaurant. She never told Dad where she was. He tried to reach us and thought we had been abducted. I recall sleeping on the banquette using a tablecloth as a blanket. The next morning, Mom drove us home. We were met by a furious Dad. Mom scolded him by pointing out that the children have no social life and do nothing but watch TV. After that, we took a few more family trips but we were basically latchkey kids if we weren't at Mah Jong.

Another fight involved a kitchen knife. Kathy was preparing to go to Smith College and we had planned to take her shopping. Mom, Kathy, Michael and I started out for the car but Dad stayed petulantly at the kitchen table. We came back in and Mom asked Dad what was going on. He waved his hand to say, 'You go on without me, you don't need me." We sat down at the table; Dad at one end, Mom at the other, the three of us in the middle. We watched while Mom and Dad had a verbal tennis spat culminating in Mom insulting Dad's mother. At that, Dad took his coffee cup and threw the contents at Mom. Mom turned to the three of us to say, "You see what a violent man he is?" She grabbed the butter knife from the table and lunged at Dad. Fortunately, the blade was dull. We jumped in to separate them and I took the knife away. Dad left the house and Mom called Teddy to ask him to come over right away. Teddy left his work in the City and drove to Syosset to reconcile Mom and Dad. We three sat on the front lawn wondering what would become of us.

Dad was not a demonstrative man. Mom complained that he never bought her any flowers or expressed affection for her. Upon the occasion of their 25th anniversary, Leia and the band wanted to dedicate a song to Mom and Dad. She asked Mom which song to play to which Mom replied, "My Way" where the lyrics mention: *let the record show, I took the blows and did it my way.*

That summed up Mom's idea of her marriage.

Dad planned a surprise for Mom: he'd take her to Vancouver for their 25th anniversary. Mom was miffed to not be consulted or even asked where she would like to go for the occasion. Dad purchased the airline tickets and secured the hotel, but Mom refused to go. Dad asked Daisy to encourage Mom to change her mind. Mom, however, was determined to stick to her principles. Not wanting to waste the money invested in this trip, Dad invited Teddy to join him. Teddy checked in with Mom to see if she minded. By now she was smoldering and snapped, "I don't care." Peter and Nellie's 25th anniversary was commemorated by Peter and Teddy's stag adventure to Vancouver.

Mom was restless as she neared the end of her 40s. She felt inferior to her sisters, who she thought married men of more distinction. She thought she was the ugliest of the Kwoh sisters. Although she and Dad owned Mah Jong together, Mom was seldom consulted on Mah Jong business matters, compounding her feelings of neglect and isolation. It was therefore no surprise when she announced she had signed up for self-assertiveness classes in an adult education program at Syosset High School.

She was a changed woman after that. She had long been careful with her money, but she now expedited plans to ensure her own financial independence. Mamie introduced her to a stockbroker named Nancy who provided advice and tips on what to buy and what to sell. I doubt Mom had a strategy for buying stock but she did quite well for herself. In 1998 she asked me, "Have you ever heard of the company A-O-L?" I said I had; they had just bought a company called Netscape. Mom said she recently bought a bunch of AOL stock and I asked her why she bought it if she didn't know what the company was. She replied, "I needed a stock that starts with the letter A. I have all the other letters in the alphabet."

CHAPTER 27

THE GIFT SHOP GOES POLYNESIAN

Mom ordered pre-cut synthetic paper in an assortment of colors. When the boxes of paper arrived at Mah Jong, she took them home and, while relaxing at the kitchen table, created multi-hued leis to sell in the gift shop. The whole family got into the act for this wonderful ritual to sit with Mom creating colorful leis, which were displayed on hangers above the main counter in the gift shop, just steps from the Aloha Room entrance.

On her beloved Singer sewing machine in her bedroom in Syosset, Mom hand-made the waiters' new Polynesian Aloha Room uniforms, a thrill for her. The local Syosset fabric shop didn't carry Polynesian designs, so she drove to the garment district in the City. Through persistent research she found bolts of fabrics suggesting Polynesian themes: mostly bright florals and tapa designs from Hawaii.

Mom measured each Mah Jong waiter from wingspan to height and custom-designed jackets with ample room for stretching and moving. She provided double pockets for pens, writing tablets, and reading glasses and made them deep enough to hold cash tips. She left room around the neck. Her goal was jackets resembling the "aloha shirts" she admired in Hawaii, providing a visual counterpoint to the traditional Mah Jong dining room where the waiters wore formal buttoned up jackets, waistcoats and clip-on bow ties. When you walked into Mah Jong, to your left would be the fine dining ambiance and to your right, you were thrust into Polynesia. Not only did Mom make the Aloha Room waiters' uniforms, she laundered and ironed them for the next shift.

Mom holding one of her hand-made leis for sale at the gift shop

Mom also made Aloha shirts for the musicians and hostess dresses for herself, the cocktail waitresses, and me; we chose the patterns and off she went to her Singer sewing machine to make the long gowns we wore on Saturday nights.

She made Mao-style jackets, in bright colors and designs as opposed to drab gray, for the cashiers to wear over their street clothes.

In honor of Mah Jong's 10th anniversary in 1970, Dad created commemorative paper currency to be redeemed for a discount at the gift shop. In lieu of a national leader, Mah Jong's currency featured a photo of me framed in an oval and a serial number. Another paper currency had Michael's photo in the oval. There was also an image of the Haizhu Bridge which spans the Pearl River in Canton, a nod to Dad's birthplace, now known as Guangzhou. Haizhu Bridge was built in 1933 and was the source of immense pride, ending the practice of sampans of crossing the sea, which put many lives at peril in frequent regional winds and storms. The bridge had a new mechanical device which allowed the middle section to rise, making way for the passage of tall ships. Haizhu Bridge was famous and became a target for the Japanese who bombed and damaged it in 1938 and again in 1949 during the Communist takeover. Haizhu Bridge is still standing today and represents one of the few historical structures connecting modern Guangzhou to its historical roots in Canton.

Debbie Bucks: The front and back of commemorative currency honoring Mah Jong's 10th anniversary (Author collection)

The back of the Mah Jong currency was printed with a sketch of the Mah Jong building and the notation that it was redeemable for "10." Left to interpretation was whether it was 10% off or worth 10 cents.

Dad harbored tender memories of his brief time growing up in Canton. It is no wonder he featured the Haizhu Bridge on this Mah Jong currency as a sweet tribute to his hometown.

FROM CUSTOMERS TO CASHIERS

Mom mentored young girls, hiring high school students as hostesses and cashiers. She felt it was a good for them to learn how to work in a customer relations industry. Her main resource for finding workers was from Mah Jong's customers.

As Stacey Krinsky tells it, "How I got hired was funny—from the time I was a little girl, my parents and two sisters and I went to Mah Jong every other Saturday night for dinner. One night, there was a call at home asking if we were the Krinskys with three girls (there were five Krinskys in the phone book and we were the last). My Mom knew it had to be Mrs. Chinn who asked if the older girls needed a job. We were close in age, but my two older sisters had part-time jobs and so my Mom volunteered me. Mrs. Chinn was slightly apprehensive since I was barely 15 and would have to serve drinks, which was illegal. However, I was tall for my age, had already worked in my dad's stores, and my sister worked at the local cinema near the police precinct and was friendly with all the cops. That was enough for Mrs. Chinn. I started that Friday."

Mom asked nearby Mercy Catholic Academy to announce that she was looking for another cashier. Anna Tumpek was a high school junior and had just turned 16, the legal age to be hired in 1969. Anna heard the guidance counselor mention that Mah Jong was hiring high school girls. In a 2021 interview with me, Anna recalled, "I thought, *That's just down the street from me. I think I'll check this out.* The guidance counselor asked where I lived since I wasn't yet able to drive and I told her I lived right down the block from Mah Jong. She said, 'Great, you got the job, be there at 5:00 on Saturday and ask for Mrs. Chinn.'

"I had no idea what job I got and what I was supposed to do. I got there and was scared out of my mind. Your mother said I would be a cashier and that some of the older cashiers would train me...and that I would get dinner. That was the best! I had never eaten Chinese food in my life. They brought out Chicken Chow Mein and I thought, 'What *is* this?' I had never seen a dish like this but I tried it and liked it. When I got to know your mom better and they brought in a new cashier, I would ask her, 'What are you going to bring out for dinner?' Your mother said, 'Chicken Chow Mein," and I said, 'NO! If they haven't had Chinese food before, give them Pepper Steak or something more recognizable.' Your mother started introducing new dishes to us which is how we learned to appreciate authentic Cantonese food."

Hiring the high school girls attracted their parents and siblings who became regulars at Mah Jong. They, like all customers, became an extension of the Chinn family.

One of Anna's classmates, Joanne Giannoni was a cashier for a short period of time. Unfortunately, Joanne and her friend were in a horrific car accident. The friend was killed and Joanne suffered brain damage. As Anna recounts, "Your parents always sent food over to her house and called her parents to ask about her. I remember how thoughtful your parents were to take care of Joanne's parents."

Mom's method of training was basically throwing you into a situation and letting you use your head to figure things out. All of the former cashiers I interviewed used the same two words to describe Mom: "tough" and "fair."

She made every cashier tally up take-out orders and calculate the tax manually. No one was allowed to use an adding machine; Mom felt it was an excellent way to learn to use your head to do calculation. Cashiers learned to properly hand back the change to the customer. These days, if you pay by cash, cashiers put the loose change on top of the bills and—as if it were a dessert topping—plop the thermal paper receipt on last. It takes time to undo the pile and it is cumbersome especially for those with limited hand mobility, such as arthritis. At Mah Jong, cashiers were taught to show the change, count it out, give it to the customer and then count the bills.

I lament the loss of cashier etiquette and training. With the use of ATM cards and digital payments, we've lost the ability to mentally calculate change. As noted by Anna, "Nowadays, when you pay for something that is $5.05 and you give the cashier a $10 bill and a nickel, they can't comprehend what to do."

Mom's strictness was accompanied by a devilish grin. Anna said, "She wanted us to learn how to use chopsticks and we had to practice. During Chinese New Year when we all sat down for dinner, for the love of Pete, she wouldn't let me have a fork. She made me use chopsticks! She wouldn't even let me keep the soup spoon. All that food in front of me and the only way to eat it was with my clumsy chopsticks!"

Above: Mom's cashiers and hostesses at Mah Jong's Chinese New Year. Deb Colton, Lynn Kologi-Youngs, Carol Tumpek are at far left

Left: Anna Tumpek, Mah Jong hostess and cashier (Author collection)

Below: Mom and hostess/cashier Stacey Krinsky (Stacey Krinsky collection)

Many of my high school teachers were regular customers. Among them Jane Schmitt, my science teacher. She and her husband, Wil, came nearly every week for luau night. Having no children of their own, they gave a select number of young girls cultural and travel opportunities—with parental permission, of course.

One of those girls was my classmate, Lynn Kologi, a frequent guest of Jane and Wil's at Mah Jong for dinner and the floor show. I interviewed Lynn in 2021 and she revealed the true breadth of the Schmitt's generosity for nurturing the lives of young girls. "I met Jane in 8th grade; she was my science teacher. I was the only person who said good morning to her and I offered to help her clean up. That started our friendship. Since she and Wil never had children, they thought it would be a nice idea to take young women on educational trips across the country. Jane offered to give my parents solid references. I went on cross country camping trips, to the ballet, opera, ski trips. We went to California and England, they taught us about geography and history. They basically adopted me. When I got married, my husband joined us on our trips."

Jane and Wil extended that generosity to me and while I was never able to spend much time away from Mah Jong, they treated Michael and me to dinners at their home and grown-up cultural experiences in New York City. My first experience of the opera world was at the Metropolitan Opera with the Schmitt's.

I was transfixed by the majestic opera house, surrounded by so much gilded decor, glass, and pomp and circumstance. Jane and Wil peppered us with questions about how we felt about the production and the plot line. This was before the now-standard supertitles to help follow along with the text (in English). I was in way over my head but these cultural experiences stretched my avid curiosity about music, singing, and theatrical productions.

Mom was impressed with Lynn's maturity and good manners and made a beeline to recruit her to be a cashier. As Lynn recalls, "Your parents did things the right way. They hired the right people and treated them with respect. They were strong and hardworking people. They had good business sense. Your mother was on top of things. She was always watching that cash register and making sure things were done correctly! She was excellent at training people. Your mother always told us to greet people with a smile and say, 'Welcome to Mah Jong' and when you seated them say, 'I hope you have a pleasant evening.' If they weren't happy, try to accommodate them."

Anna's parents, Anton and Anna Tumpek, instilled a deep love of music in their girls, all of whom played an instrument and took private lessons at the Burt F. Arden School of Music in Hicksville. The Tumpek girls were such inspirations to me that I begged my mother to enroll me at the Arden School of Music to take piano lessons after school.

I assumed it was going to be easy to learn piano but I was assigned to a no-nonsense teacher. Mrs. Udeyni had a full day of teaching; by the time she got to my lesson, she was ready to enjoy her snack: a banana that had ripened considerably over the course of the day. She'd use the banana to smack my wrists if they were not in the proper playing position. My next instructors were more mellow but even today, the scent of bananas incites a pavlovian instinct to check my posture and sit up straight.

Deb Colton recalls, "I worked at Mah Jong during my freshman year at Post College, 1975–76. I remember how hard your parents worked. They were working machines. Your father was like an Energizer bunny. He never stopped moving. Your mother was very strict, very kind, very fair. I couldn't stay for dinner with the other cashiers since I had (theatre) rehearsals but your mother sent me off with lots of egg rolls which I shared with the tech crew at Post. It was so kind of your parents to feed us and we could eat all we wanted!"

Every cashier had to keep busy even when there was a lull in activities:

Deb Colton, "I remember dusting a lot. I dusted the gift shop. Your mother always gave me Windex and paper towels, and off I went to dust the glass shelves and counters."

Anna Tumpek: "When it was slow, I would walk all along the gift shop. I loved the gift shop. I loved the carved ivory; I would stop and study the intricacies. I loved when we got stuff in and I had to dust those shelves constantly!"

- PART FOUR -

Growing Up

Mah Jong dining room renovation and new entrance, 1976

CHAPTER 28

THE MAH JONG EXPANSION CONTINUES

The nightclub expansion greatly boosted business and all dining rooms, the Bamboo Lounge, the Imu Room, and bar seating were completely filled on Friday and Saturday nights. The volume of take-out orders also grew, plus requests to cater business lunches, school graduations, weddings, summertime backyard parties, and reunions. On the nights with no floorshow, the Aloha Room, with its romantic tropical decor, was often booked for private events and was a popular venue for wedding receptions. Local society pages mentioned Mah Jong in wedding announcements and this, too, increased bookings. Mah Jong was popular for brunch after Sunday church services. It was common to see priests come in, have a drink at the bar, loosen their collars, and settle in for lunch. Nuns ordered take-out and usually asked for Mom 's menu recommendations. As a sign of pious solidarity, she threw in some free wonton soup, egg rolls, and fortune cookies.

In 1974, Dad introduced another new concept at Mah Jong, incorporating his love of sports. At the suggestion of Jim Heatley, one of Mah Jong's photographers, Dad started a live afternoon radio show broadcast from Mah Jong. According to Pua, "Jim hung out at Mah Jong, probably because your dad fed him. Your dad loved sports and hosted all the sports guys who came in to Mah Jong in the late afternoon."

Along with free food, Dad enticed the sports players to be part of the radio interviews by creating awards for them. Ray Wilson, publisher and owner of *New York Today* and *Long Island Today* magazines, broadcast his Ray Wilson Radio Show with celebrity interviews from Mah Jong's Aloha Room.

Ray Heatherton (who starred in the TV variety series as "The Merry Mailman" from 1950–1956) was the emcee of the Long Island Breakfast Club which broadcast from nearby Adelphi University during the late 1970s. He was also invited to be part of the Mah Jong radio broadcast. Jim Heatley's press connections at *Newsday* attracted more publicity, especially among the sports fans.

Ray Heatherton and Pua during Mah Jong's live radio show (Pauline De Silva collection)

Reflecting on the business ingenuity of Dad's generosity, Pua recalls, "All the celebrities came because your dad gave them food and booze. Politicians came with celebrities like Dustin Hoffman because Mah Jong was the place to be seen. There was not enough help during the late afternoons during the radio show and your father paid me $20 to come in and help. He never asked me to do anything for free. I appreciated your dad asking me to run a few errands to get $20 here, $20 there. That extra money helped a lot. Your father invited me to join him to attend events since your mother was taking care of you and your brother. So when we went out to present or accept a Restaurant of the Year award or represent Mah Jong to honor a local celebrity, your dad paid me just as if I was going on a club date. He raised the cash to $45!"

Dad had the constitution of a philanthropist. He supported and was fond of several non-profit organizations: Easter Seals, Muscular Dystrophy Association, Little Sisters of the Poor, and the Little League. He helped raise money by hosting their fundraising parties at Mah Jong, donating dinners for their auctions, and sponsoring the North Shore and Syosset Little League leagues. After the games, the teams would come to Mah Jong and Dad treated the boys to free appetizers. Mom and Dad sent food over to the doctors and nurses working the emergency shifts at Syosset Hospital, just across the street from Mah Jong. The Nassau County police and firefighters were given special discounts on take-out orders. Whenever local businesses and non-profit organizations approached Mom and Dad for support, they always said yes. Their spirit of philanthropy was deeply ingrained in my siblings and me and we grew up learning how to be generous and supportive members of our communities.

Mom and Dad balanced their generosity with equal doses of modesty and humility. They knew that if you made a child happy, you kept the parent happy. Quietly giving a child a free toy from the gift shop made them feel important and many of those children, now grandparents, have told me that they still have that yo-yo, coin purse, doll, or other gift shop item. If anyone was short on cash, Mom and Dad let them make it up next time. When we learned that someone's child was at Syosset Hospital, Mom dropped off toys or fortune cookies at the nurse's station as get-well gestures. The seeds of my career path as an arts activist/CEO, in which I build coalitions of support, were certainly planted by these examples of empathy set by my parents.

By the early 1970s, Mah Jong's in-dining, nightclub, bar scene, take-out, and catering business was firing on all cylinders. More delivery trucks came through, cars were double-parked to pick up orders or for last minute gift shopping. While Mah Jong doubled the number of dining rooms, bars, and cocktail lounges, it had outgrown the number of available parking spaces.

The next big Mah Jong event was buying the commercial property next door. The Paddock Inn, owned and operated by Gus Pierson, was a favorite spot for local politicians. Mr. and Mrs. Pierson were getting on in age and wanted to retire. Gus came to Mah Jong and asked Dad if he had any interest in buying the property.

According to Dad, "When I heard the price, I thought he was out of his mind. But soon some Greeks bought it and turned it into "Fisherman's Luck." They didn't last long and sold it to a steak house in nearby Mineola. Months passed and I noticed he wasn't doing so good either. I saw the restaurant owner one day and told him that if he ever decided to sell, to let me know. I had made up my mind to buy it. It seemed that if I didn't, someone else would. Sure enough, he made an offer to sell and I took it. I had no business buying. I had no money. I put a little down and took over his debts, notes from Pierson, notes from Fisherman's Luck, and more notes from the steak house."

Aaron Frosch and Ralph Papsidero proposed that a motel on the site of the old Paddock Inn/Fisherman's Luck building would complement Mah Jong. It might encourage diners from the eastern and western tips of Long Island to stay longer for dinner and a nightcap without the worry of the 1–2 hour drive home, especially during the winter months. Knowing Mom's favorite flower was gardenia, Dad wanted to register the new company as the "Gardenia Corporation." It was taken, so Dad opted for "Gardina Corporation, Incorporated."

Dad began to secure a zoning permit for the motel. As when Dad built a dormitory for restaurant employees at King Wah and Mah Jong, he worked hard to placate neighbors who expressed concerns about too many Chinese people coming into the area. Mah Jong's success was not welcomed by some of the residential neighbors. During the late 1960s and early 1970s, the U.S. was at war with Vietnam and the Viet Cong's brutality in the killing of the American soldiers was televised into U.S. homes. The "Yellow Peril" stereotype had long preceded the Vietnam War, but its racist roots took hold in parts of white suburban America, where anyone who looked Asian was often considered the enemy. Also, white people generally could not tell Japanese, Chinese, Koreans, Vietnamese, and other Asian ethnicities apart.

When the public hearing was held for Dad's presentation of the zoning plan and application to Nassau County, some of Dad's supporters went to offer endorsements of the motel project. Peter Chinn was booed by the project's opponents. The complaints against our family reached a point of concern. In my 2021 interview with former cashier Stacey Krinsky, she recalls, "There was strong opposition against your dad building a motel. People were angry and upset. Also, a lot of people knew that you and Michael were sometimes left home alone. One night after we finished up at Mah Jong, I drove you and Michael home and a car slowly followed us out of the parking lot and through the back streets towards your house. I was scared for your safety and I went into your house to call your mother who was still at Mah Jong. Your mother said it was OK. She said we were followed by Nino's guys who were there to protect us and we were being followed for a good reason."

The booing at the public hearing was a rare rebuke of Dad. He and Mom were beloved longstanding members of the community.

One of the worst things for the Chinese is embarrassment or humiliation. It's referred to as "losing face," or dignity. The public embarrassment of proudly offering a bold vision for Mah Jong to bring economic vitality to Long Island only to be vilified was a profound blow. When Dad lost face, our family lost face. Dad was dejected but his sense of determination prevailed.

He and Ralph modified the scope of the motel project, including the removal of the two planned tiki torches at the motel entrance. The opposition was worried about smoke, expressing concern that the torches might ignite wildfires.

The second application was approved but only for one year. Dad had to secure financial footing for the project, otherwise the permit would be voided.

At this time, Bill Koutensky caught a cold that turned into pneumonia which lingered. He did not feel the need to see a doctor until it was much too late. He died of lung cancer on August 25, 1971. Ironically, he never smoked and he couldn't stand smoking. "No smoking" sections in restaurants or offices did not exist. Everyone smoked, all the time. Flashback to that first meeting at Linck's Cabin, when my godfather, Rocco Setaro, set up that first lunch for Dad and Bill Koutensky to meet to secure a loan to start Mah Jong; Rocco's warning to Dad, "Don't smoke," was prophetic.

We were on a family vacation in Florida to research Disney World's new Polynesian Resort exhibition when the phone in the hotel room rang. Dad answered and listened, put his hand to his head, turned to Mom and said, "Mr. Koutensky just passed away." We returned to New York that night. Loretta arranged for Bill's wake to be at their home in Hicksville. We paid our respects but not before arranging to send over a buffet of food for family and guests for the vigil. Mom was bereft at the loss of Bill, whom she credited as the man who gave the Chinns the opportunity of a lifetime. After Bill's death, without fail, the Mah Jong chefs made Loretta a bone-in whole ham, roast beef, slabs of spareribs, and dozens of egg rolls. Mom or some of Bill's favorite waiters delivered it to Loretta's house and spent time with her before her family gathered for the holidays. Mom faithfully brought flowers to Loretta on her birthday. This tradition continued until Christmas 1998. Loretta Koutensky passed away in February 1999.

After Bill's death, the new President of Long Island National Bank was overheard to say that when Bill Koutensky died, Peter Chinn died with him as far as the bank was concerned. Upon hearing that, Dad's first thought was that the mortgage for the motel just went out the window.

He did not bother to apply for a mortgage loan with Long Island National Bank. Instead, he turned to a union pension fund. Joe Tonelli had mortgage surplus funds set aside. Dad applied through Tonelli's lawyer, Charlie Mintz, and was endorsed by Uncle Nino. Lo and behold, Dad was approved for far more than he had asked for. Construction got underway to raze the Fisherman's Luck building.

Unbeknownst to us, this coincided with an FBI investigation into Joe Tonelli for allegedly embezzling $300,000 in his union pension funds. He had been named in two other federal indictments. Also named was Anthony Loiacono, our Uncle Nino.

Tonelli was also accused of spending $50,000 of union funds to pay lawyers to intercede with the Department of Justice to have the case sidetracked. A third charge against Tonelli was conspiring with Nino and others to get kickbacks from union pension funds. Additional charges included falsifying expense reports to the Union. This was major news by the NY press and television stations.

Charlie Mintz called Dad to say he had quickly pulled his mortgage application out from the file of Tonelli's office so the FBI investigation wouldn't lead to Mah Jong. Still, there was a trace of Mah Jong associated with Tonelli and Dad was interrogated by the FBI. He was instructed not to leave the country and was put on notice that he might be asked to testify at Tonelli's trial. Dad never had to testify; there was plenty of other incriminating evidence.

Tonelli was formally indicted in July 1978 and in November 1978 sentenced to three years in prison. According to the *New York Times* article, "A Weeping Tonelli Given Three Years for Embezzling his Union's Funds," Tonelli's lawyer is quoted, "The President of the United States (Richard Nixon) got an absolute pardon. To put this man in jail makes a mockery of justice," to which the presiding judge replied, "But Mr. Nixon was not before me." [69]

According to Dad, Tonelli was back in the union movement after he got out of jail.

The years between buying the property and the construction, which left a hole in the ground, were a constant drain on Mah Jong's finances. The town's tax lien on the property had been bought by a Mr. Katz who served notice that he intended to exercise his rights.

Dad quickly approached Loretta Koutensky through her attorney Ben Shepps. Ben hand-delivered the check to Dad to pay off Mr. Katz in full.

Mah Jong had a balloon payment due on a mortgage with Suburban Federal. Dad and his lawyer, John Tessier, looked for a bank willing to give Mah Jong a new mortgage. The prevailing rate at that time was about 19%. No bank was willing to give Mah Jong a mortgage; as noted on the rejection letter, "his [Peter's] earnings already committed to debts and carried a piece of land with no income."

Determined to find a solution, John Tessier and another one of Dad's lawyers, Bill Merritt, met a broker representing an East Coast family restaurant chain called Friendly. They were willing to lease the Gardina property for one of their franchises. Dad and his lawyers drove to the Friendly corporate office in Wilbraham, MA, signed the paperwork and returned to Mah Jong that day. For the first time, Mah Jong was getting rent for the Friendly property to help pay off notes, and to reimburse Mrs. Koutensky, Nino, and others.

Dad secured a mortgage from Sunrise Federal Savings at a reasonable rate. However: he had to put our house on the line. Even with the rent from Friendly, we were not out of the financial woods.

CHAPTER 29

THE UNEXPECTED END OF MY CHILDHOOD

In 1970, I was thirteen and experiencing the Dance of the Hormones. My breasts were developing. I wasn't sure what was happening. Mom just said, "Time to move to a training bra." That was easy to understand.

But my first period terrified me. I woke up and saw red on my underwear and the bed sheets. Why am I bleeding? I thought I was dying. I wouldn't need a coffin; I imagined myself buried in a jar of my fluids instead. No one told me to expect this. No one assured me this was a natural female transition.

I wore a Kotex pad clipped to a sanitary belt. Shaking my hips in the Polynesian floor show with this underneath my grass skirt was like sitting on a damp sponge perched on a blender. In the Tahitian number, dipping my knees while shaking my hips, I tightened my thighs. I was petrified of the unthinkable in front of an audience. Kathy, home for a holiday visit, asked me why I wore such old-fashioned pads from the 1950s. Belatedly, she taught me all about Tampons.

My childhood innocence came to an abrupt and traumatic halt that summer.

I write about this not as an exposé, but because what happened to me continues to be a too-frequent occurrence among young girls and women. I hope that by sharing my experiences, I might serve as an inspiration to other girls who—like me—teeter precariously between despair and hope while scrambling to find the right footing for the necessary steps towards survival.

For privacy and because the perpetrator of this event is a member of my family, I refer to him as "Brian."

It started innocently. 17-year-old Brian visited us for the summer months and was put to work at Mah Jong. I hadn't seen him since we were kids when I was upset that he wouldn't share his toy submarines with me. I thought he was arrogant, but we were teenagers now and would have the chance to start anew. As an extra special treat, Dad planned a family road trip to Montreal in June so Brian could join us.

He fit right in at the Mah Jong exotic nightclub environment. He was gregarious, boyishly charming, so much fun, and easy to talk to; he knew so much about a variety of subjects. I thought he was a perfect older brother, even just for a few summer months, and I loved listening to him talk. I trusted him.

While he was visiting with us, Brian broke that trust and crossed the boundaries of decency to become the unwanted first sexual experience of my life. He forced his tongue into my mouth and went on to coerce my naïve self into his arms. Even though I balked and tightened myself up to keep him away, he soothed me to relax and whispered that I would eventually like it.

I had no training for this. I was thirteen, on that brink of girl-to-woman, and no one had given me any tools to deal with, or even any conversation about, the first encounter and this rite of passage.

BAM. In an instant, my childhood was over.

He came into my bedroom. The act was sudden and painful. When he returned to his guest bedroom, I was no longer a virgin. I buried my face into my pillow and quietly sobbed so as not to awake the household. I comforted myself by practicing how to tell Mom in a way that wouldn't bring wrath unto me or Brian.

The next morning, I told Mom what I could muster with my limited vocabulary: that Brian came into my room, into my bed, and did bad things. I didn't go into details, figuring she would understand. I couldn't describe statutory rape. I did not yet know those words.

Mom told Daisy that "something happened" and they separated us for the rest of his stay. They didn't tell Dad. They planned for Daisy to sit between Brian and me in the car on the rides to and from Montreal. Dad arranged three hotel rooms: one for him and Mom, one for Daisy, and one for the kids—Brian, Michael, and me. Mom said "No." She wanted Daisy and me to share a room and the boys would share a room.

No major confrontation happened. We continued with our work routines. No one asked if I was OK. Nobody asked if I needed help. No one held me in their arms to soothe the fright away. In fact, nobody talked to me at all. I kept on dancing—putting on my happy stage face during the shows, wondering if I should ask one of the dancers for help. But the dressing room was chaotic. There wasn't the chance for personal conversations—we had a show to do and it was all business.

Even though I was visible to the public, as a victim of sexual assault I was invisible. Why was everyone silent? Won't anyone sit and talk to me? Was this incident not as awful as I experienced? Why was Brian protected and given preferential treatment? I questioned my self-worth. Why am I even here? Who even cares? And I realized that maybe, just maybe, I was a disposable human being.

I considered going to confession, but I didn't want to be in a small enclosed booth. With a man. That I couldn't see. My sexual rite of passage should have been glorious and memorable. So many questions raced in my mind. I was afraid of questions that might be asked—"How did it happen?" "When?" and "Why?" Or worse, "Why did you let this happen?"

I had no answers. I was in emotional solitary confinement.

The summer and the Montreal trip came and went, and still, no one checked in. The incident had been brushed aside. Brian returned home none the worse for wear.

That Christmas, Kathy came home from college. She recalls Mom and Daisy at the kitchen table goading each other to "tell Kathy what had transpired during the summer."

When she was finally told, she asked, 'Did you take Debbie to a doctor?" Then Kathy learned that no one told Dad because he would have sent Brian home. Kathy's response to Mom and Daisy was an incredulous, "So what?"

Kathy remembers, "I came into your bedroom and said to you, "Mom and Auntie Daisy just told me. Have you been to a doctor?" And you said, 'No…..'"

The next year, my cousin Wa-Wa died. Deeper into the morass I went. I slogged through school and work. The reality hit me: I was damaged goods.

After I learned the truth about Wa-Wa's death, specifically that she had committed suicide (more on that later), I began to think that killing myself was the only way out of my dishonor. I had lost face, I placed shame on my family, I was 13 years old, and then I began to wonder if perhaps suicide ran in our family.

Some of the Kwoh siblings wondered if Wa-Wa had been sexually abused. While no one proved it, this remained a family speculation. In my mind, being abused equaled a road to suicide, but I wasn't sure where to start. I'm truly a late learner. I didn't know how to buy a gun or how to match up the bullet. There were no pills at home for an overdose. On the contrary, all we had at home were Dad's Chinese herbs designed to keep you alive and healthy.

The holidays came. The merriment of the season was hollow. I was now 14 and so morose that Leia took me out of the show. She just had me introduce a number or two. A devastating blow to my ego.

With no identity and nothing to lose, I decided to go for it.

It was a school night. Michael and I were home; he was in the back room getting ready for bed. Mom and Dad were at work. I took a knife from our kitchen drawer and tentatively held it against my stomach, thinking Hari Kari would be a dramatic way to go. I stood over our kitchen sink and pushed against the knife. I couldn't get enough thrust and got out the stepladder to give me more height. The knife was old, rusty and dull, with a flimsy handle. The blade snapped off when I slipped and lost my footing on the stepladder. Mom used a knife from the same set to lunge at Dad when they had their terrible fight at the kitchen table. Obviously, we didn't bother to sharpen our kitchen knives.

I heard Mom's car pull up and I figured I'd try again later. Later came in the form of another method: I tried staying outside in our backyard with no clothes on in the dead of winter, thinking I could develop pneumonia and slowly die. That attempt barely lasted a couple of minutes. Winky kept barking at me through the living room window. She whined, pawing at the back door in distress. I came in to calm her down before Michael could hear the commotion. I wasn't old enough to drive a car or I could have driven myself into a tree. I dialed the operator but ended up comforting *her*; she was so concerned about me ("You are one of the youngest callers I've helped") that I apologized for taking up her time before hanging up.

My subsequent suicide attempts during that year were quiet, persistent, futile, and clumsy. I truly was inept. How did Wa-Wa get her gun? Saint Anne was giving me a sign: I was doomed to be reminded of my carnal sin for the rest of my life. I picked the wrong Saint for my confirmation; I should have ignored the nuns and gone with Saint Sebastian and his arrows.

Tired of failing, I realized I had to go in another direction. If I could not succeed in snuffing out my life, I'd try to excel at living. I wasn't ready for therapy; I couldn't bear to relive the memories of feeling suffocated and helpless in my bedroom with Brian pinned on top of me. Instead of receding into irrelevance and pity, I focused on my guitar and piano lessons with the goal of accomplishing something no one in my immediate family could boast. I would not go in the direction of math and science—the anchor points of achievements among my aunts and uncles and cousins. I didn't have an aptitude for math or science anyway. I was marginally good at singing, dancing, and performing but I was determined to go all-in.

I entered high school. Music and the arts were central components to our educational experience and Syosset High School churned out many alumni artists of note. I began to take advantage of my high school's arts programs.

I joined the choir, took private singing lessons and learned about expansive breathing and positive visualization. This helped counteract the claustrophobia I developed as a result of being silently raped; a condition I have lived with ever since. I continued with private guitar and piano lessons and gained confidence to enter music competitions. I won trophy after trophy, and I felt I just might be good enough to become a professional classical musician.

I took my usual refuge in the school library, this time immersed in the history section on Polynesia, Hawaii, Samoa, New Zealand. I listened to Dad's collection of Hawaiian songs and played along on my guitar. I borrowed Leia's fake book of Hawaiian songs, copying the chords and lyrics into my own notebook, an expansive three-ring binder filled with detailed choreography notes down to precise hand and feet movements.

I also tracked all of Mah Jong's monthly show repertoire, lyrics from my favorite Polynesian songs and details on climate conditions in Polynesia at various times of the year. When I read through this binder in 2021, I realized that this was not only a therapeutic outlet to channel my creativity, but one of the ways to escape my rugged hell. I used this binder to transport me away from Long Island and towards a nirvana of paradise in song, mind, motion, and calm.

Sitting at the piano bench and playing music was therapeutic. I practiced piano and guitar hours upon hours every day. It softened my anxiety and fears. I've often said that music is one of humanity's most powerful tools. The softest of notes can stir the soul of a nation towards action and can equally dismantle the veneer of the toughest of humans and reduce them to tears. For me, it did both as I began to crawl through the grieving process of losing my childhood.

Mah Jong customers had inquired about my absence from the floor show and eventually, I was put back in as a regular. Leia even compassionately featured me for a brief guitar solo for a Christmas number. My confidence increased. People were paying attention to me. I was being acknowledged, and it felt cathartic.

Being immersed in the arts in school and performing weekly at Mah Jong pulled me up and gave me a renewed purpose to reinvent myself as a functional human being.

It is no hyperbole to say that the arts saved my life.

CHAPTER 30

INDEPENDENCE

My last year dancing with the Mah Jong troupe was summer 1975 after I graduated from high school. It was a bittersweet double graduation. High school is where I began to emerge from my shell and listen more acutely to my heart's clarion call to find peace and salvation in the arts.

At Mah Jong I learned about the hard and soft skills needed to develop exceptional customer relationships, strong work ethics, the building and sustaining of broader networks, an intuition for creating better business efficiencies, how to work with an ensemble of artists, and the personal thrill of performing.

It was time to move on, to find a new environment in which to grow. I had advanced with my piano classes and competitions and felt qualified to apply to the State University of New York at Purchase as a music major. During the weeks leading up to my piano audition, karma appeared during gym class field hockey. The hockey stick was far too big for me to grab and I tripped over the end of the stick and jammed my finger. It wasn't broken, just injured enough so I couldn't audition.

I had to pick another major quickly and chose theatre. I again applied to SUNY Purchase but was turned down.

There was a map of the United States on my guidance counselor, Mrs. Allen's office wall. I looked at New York to the right and glanced all the way to the left and asked, "What's that state over there?" She said, "California," but, she cautioned that it was still recovering from a 1969 major oil spill off Santa Barbara, at the time the worst oil spill in U.S. history (later surpassed by the Exxon-Valdez disaster in 1989). The environmental impact was not yet determined and she thought it would not be safe.

The more I looked at the map the more I wanted to move far away from home. California was about as far across the United States as I could go. No oil spill was going to deter me. I applied to the University of Southern California with a declared major in theatre. Accompanied by a healthy dose of hubris, I was certain that, with all my performing credentials as the planet Venus in elementary school, an alto in the school choirs, a floozie in the high school musical, and the years spent as a hula dancer, I was now qualified to be an actress. In reality, I was accepted only because Dad agreed to pay the full tuition. He was proud that I was accepted to USC not for my pursuit of acting; he, the rabid sports fan, was impressed with USC's excellent football team.

I set out to drive cross-country to California by myself, determined to move far away so I wouldn't be tempted to come home, and to become, at Mom's urging, independent. In doing so, I missed out on long weekends at home and high school reunions since I could not afford the airfare.

I did come home for Christmas in 1975 and was put into the show for a couple of numbers for a reunion, but it wasn't the same. I felt like the new girl coming to school when everyone was already in their social groups. That was fine. It meant I was emotionally able to say goodbye to that part of my youth. I left Mah Jong at its pinnacle and I did not want to be around to watch it move towards its close.

After I left, Cathy Casserly replaced me as a regular. Chief Taofi pulled back and was replaced by Joe Salito. Donna left and was replaced by Cathy's sister. Pua remained the constant thread.

TRAUMA DOES NOT TAKE A HOLIDAY

During my freshman year at college, I had the opportunity to talk about what had happened in my bedroom when I was 13. I was visiting Brian's mother, who asked me, "Is it true what happened with you and Brian?" She said, "Your mother told me about 'the incident.'"

I calmly and clinically told her that her son came into my room and raped me. She gasped and put her hand over her mouth. She had only been given softly veiled references; this was the first time she was hearing the clear truth. And it was from me—the victim. I said, "But I didn't get pregnant and I'm fine." She called Brian and angrily berated him.

Brian came to his mother's home and apologized. "I'm so sorry, he said to me. "I did a stupid thing, I didn't mean to hurt you." I reassured him that it was fine. I cannot believe the words that next came out of my mouth: "I'm glad my first experience was with you."

I was more concerned with how *he* felt than with acknowledging my own admission. I had been spiritually weakened and the only way to recover was to deny the severity of the incident.

He apologized, I forgave him, and we moved on. We actually became friends and I socialized with his girlfriend and friends on long weekends

The Chinn Family

and holidays while I was in college. He eventually married and we all enjoyed a very warm friendship.

In 1995, Brian and his wife visited with me in San Francisco. Kathy, Michael, and my nephew Chris were in town. While we gathered in my flat, Brian and I found each other alone in my living room. He said, "I am again so very sorry for what I did to you and I hope it has not affected how you've grown up. I would feel awful knowing that it did." Then he said to 10-year-old Chris, who had just entered the room, "You're not going to understand this now but don't make the same mistake I did."

Kathy and I talked about this episode in more depth in 2021. "They tried to make fun of the trip to Montreal in a light-hearted way. They said they would put a bucket of water over your hotel room door just in case he tried to walk in. Dad had no idea what was going on. I was into women's lib[eration] at the time and I could not believe they favored him over you. He was 17 years old! They should have stopped it right there and sent him home. They protected him over you. They should have told Dad. The main issue was: Did they take you to a doctor? The issue was not putting a bucket of water on top of a hotel room door. This is not how you give a girl confidence and security."

As Kathy continued to recount the details: "To this day, I don't get it and you can tell, I'm *still* worked up about it."

Brian harbored guilt and remorse over the years and I once again assured him that all was fine and that what was in the past would remain there. Everything had come to a gentle resolution.

Or so I thought.

To use a restaurant metaphor, memories of trauma arrive like demanding customers who show up after the restaurant is closed insisting to be fed and refusing to leave. Such was the case when talking to Mom in 1995, twenty-five years after Brian stole my virginity. The conversation was not focused on Brian at all but when discussing our family at large, the doors of the memory vault flew open and I angrily spewed explicit details of my rape to Mom. She, too, was caught unaware. There was an awkward silence, followed by my realization that Mom had no idea what actually happened when Brian was in my bed. Years of innuendos, euphemisms, dysfunctional communication, and a fortress of silence minimized all that transpired during the summer of 1970. Now, a tsunami of belated emotions, angry accusations, denials, confusion, and hurt feelings created an irreparable chasm between Mom and Brian's mother. The rift was so deep that, in spite of a 70+ year relationship, for the rest of Mom's life they never spoke again.

For years, I harbored guilt for being the catalyst for this family divide, especially for the pain it caused Mom to lose one of her closest friends. But, as part of my own personal growth, I accept now that being a rape survivor means the road to recovery is littered with collateral damage; my mother was caught up in that residue. My determined evolution towards survival includes finding ways to co-exist with sensory memories which continue to induce my sense of claustrophobia, panic attacks, fright, extreme self-deprecation, and frustrated outbursts.

I am fortunate to have finally reached a new plateau of peace and grace thanks to those who served as my guardrails. Some of those reliable anchors have been my sister and the man she married.

Christmas at Motel 14 (Kathy's home in Maplewood, NJ) with family members representing Big Center, Paul Ernest, and Frank Kwoh's families. Dora is seated in the middle, wearing purple.

CHAPTER 31

THE GENTLE INFLUENCE OF MY SISTER

KATHY AND MARIO

Kathy and her future husband, Mario, met in 1979 when she was applying to medical school. Mario was married at the time and Kathy recalls, "Mario said he wanted to go to medical school but he didn't have family to encourage him. He found out I was an older student (30 years old). Every time I got a rejection, he took me to lunch. I realized we had an attraction. I started New York Medical School in July but I was waitlisted at University of California at Irvine. I made the decision to stay at NY Med School and the next thing I knew, Mario showed up saying he left his wife and 'I want to be with you.'" Mario's ex-wife, Julie said, "You seduced him with medical school."

Kathy and Mario lived in Valhalla, a hamlet in Westchester County near Bertha and Paul's White Plains home, and near Bell Laboratory where Mario worked. "I spent a lot of time with Auntie Bertha and Uncle Paul. I introduced Mario to them and Auntie Bertha pulled me aside and said, 'Don't let this one go!'

"Mario adored Uncle Paul and never tired of hearing stories of his youth and adulthood. Uncle Paul knew every famous person in the 20th century, and they knew him: President Eisenhower, Winston Churchill, President Truman, Pearl S. Buck, Herbert Hoover, Marian Anderson, to name just a few. In a conversation with Uncle Paul, Mario asked, 'Of all the people you've known, who is the most impressive?' Uncle Paul said, 'Eleanor Roosevelt,' Uncle Paul asked Mario, 'Who is the most impressive person you've met in your lifetime?' Mario said, 'You!'"

In Mario Slazak, Kathy found a winner of a man, gem of a husband, and the most popular member of our family. He knew about my episode and i found solace in our private talks as he gave me the encouragement to keep moving forward. All of the aunts, uncles, and cousins adored his quick wit, and it was hard to top him when it came to telling a joke. He had an endless stash of stories and jokes he'd rattle off, leaving everyone in stitches. Mario was of Polish and German descent and Mom affectionately

Mario and Kathy in front of one of Mom's bird cages at our home in Syosset.
Mario holding his newborn son, Christopher, November 1985.
Mario with Dad, Mom, Kathy (not pictured, Michael) in front of more of Mom's bird cages.

called him "Meathead" after the character played by Rob Reiner in the hit TV series, *All in the Family.*

Mario and Kathy were married in 1984 in a simple ceremony attended by Daisy and Michael, and set up home in Maplewood, NJ, which proved to be centrally located for family reunions. Michael moved in, as well. When looking for homes, Kathy said she found one that was stone-colored but Mom didn't like it. She said it was the color of Lowell's face when he was sick.

At Kwoh family gatherings, proactiveness was a cardinal rule. Woe be to anyone who didn't jump up to help. In fact, Mom and Daisy kept tabs on who sat around like a sloth. It was unseemly and disrespectful. Mario fit right into the Kwoh expectations and practically sprinted to help anyone in need.

Kathy, Mario and Michael's Maplewood, NJ home at 14 Highland Avenue had a deep backyard and was set in a leafy suburb along the train line to/from New York City. Mom dubbed the home "Motel 14;" that's how many people could sleep across all 4 levels, inclusive of attic and basement.

On November 8, 1985, an excited Mario called me at work saying, "He's here! He's here!" Kathy had delivered a baby boy, Christopher Lowell, and Mario added, "He looks just like your mother. He has big balls and big feet."

The house was filled with aunts, uncles, cousins, friends as well as copious amounts of food, music, games, and warm company. I wish I had been able to spend more time on the East Coast, but my career in California was just starting to take shape and I couldn't afford the time or expense to make frequent trips home.

I saved up for Christmas to be spiritually refueled even if just for a couple of weeks. Mom and I had a chance to get to know each other again—this time as adults. I was in my late 20s, the age when the Kwoh siblings had begun to assimilate in the U.S. Their stories were coming into sharper focus in my mind while at the dining table listening to my aunts and uncles build on each other's memories, often segueing into a childhood song or getting up to dance. I loved to pan around the table, to take note of their personalities and to hear their blended voices which sounded divinely symphonic, and I thought, "someday I should write a book about all of this."

THE PREMONITION: GINA THE GYPSY

Kathy recounted an eerie story about an impromptu visit to a fortune teller who foretold what was on the horizon for our family. "Mario and his friends from Bell Labs often had lunch on Restaurant Row in Manhattan. One day, on the way back to the car, they happened to see a Fortune Teller sign. On a whim, Mario went in where he was greeted by Gina the Gypsy. Mario said there were odd sensations as she read his palm. She told him, 'You are worried about your children,' which was true; he was just divorced with two young girls."

Mario returned home and told Kathy that she had to go see Gina the next time they were in the City. "So," Kathy continued, "we had dinner at the same restaurant as his Bell Lab workers and walked by the storefront to find the "Fortune Teller" sign. However, the sign was gone. Gina's husband was the superintendent of the building and when we rang the buzzer, we were let in.

"We knocked on Gina's door and her husband answered. Mario asked for Gina but was told that she was not home. But Mario saw her hiding in the back. Gina finally came out and was reluctant to do a reading. After Mario persuaded her, Gina finally did a reading in the lobby. She read my palm and gave a cursory standard reading. Mario said, 'NO! Read her other hand!'

'It was obvious that Gina didn't want to read because she sensed that something was not right, but Mario kept insisting she read my palm. 'The man you love' said Gina, 'he is not yours. *Even if he is yours, he won't be yours for long.*'

"Everything she read in my hand was bad. You have a cousin who's sick. I see a cousin of yours will die soon..."

– PART FIVE –

Seismic Shift

Early gathering of Kwoh elders and my cousins, 1964. Front row: Di-Di, Michael, me, Wa-Wa. Seated: Paul Chih-Meng, Mom, Edie, Grandmother Kate, Mamie, Bertha, S.C. Back: Dora, Daisy, Kathy, Nancy, Mei-Mei, Bonny, Teddy, Ni-Ni. Rear: Emily, Jesse . Not in photo: May, Vivian, Roy (Author's collection)

Daisy with the Meng family at Mah Jong. L-R: Di-Di, Ni-Ni, Mei-Mei, Daisy, Paul, Wa-Wa, Bertha, 1970

CHAPTER 32

MY COUSINS

Of the 14 Kwoh cousins, I am the second youngest. All I knew about my cousins were how accomplished they were even when as teenagers and young adults. My cousins were the children of parents moving into careers in the fields of nursing, engineering, cultural heritage, diplomacy, arts, education, and restaurant hospitality. The Kwoh siblings never intended to move to the United States when they were teenagers and in their early 20s. By all accounts, they had happy and simple childhoods along the coast of Tsingtao and were content to stay there or in Peking/Beijing. The threat of war and persecution, however, forced them to leave China without much advance planning. They struggled to finish their education regardless of the hardships. Therefore, a non-negotiable expectation among my cousins and me was the importance of a good college education.

My generation honored that. The Kwoh siblings would be immensely proud. My cousins established prominent careers as researchers, scientists, teachers, lawyers, doctors, in technology, business/accounting, and the outlier—me—who went into the field of nonprofit arts leadership.

Sadly, there are no photos of my cousins all together in one place at the same time. Geographical distance precluded a full generational reunion in our lifetime. The closest thing to a group photo was in 1963 when 12 (out of the 14 surviving members) gathered at Bertha and Paul's home for a family reunion.

Several of my cousins died before they reached their prime years. The Kwoh siblings, who survived the gruesome atrocities of the Japanese occupation of China, could not have imagined that some of them would outlive their children. As I experienced the losses of my cousins, I bore witness to my aunts and uncles as they demonstrated nearly superhuman durability, stoicism, acceptance of fate, and in some cases, denial. Tragedy coalesced the Kwoh siblings and showcased the indomitable power of sibling unity.

Two of my cousins committed suicide. They were brother and sister. The violence of their deaths is inexplicable as it is haunting.

VIRGINIA (WA-WA)

I was closest in age to Bertha and Paul Chih-Meng's daughter Wa-Wa and her brother Di-Di, which gave Mom and Bertha the opportunity to visit each other in White Plains and Syosset. Through us, Mom and Bertha grew particularly close and bonded by their children.

Wa-Wa was a close playmate and my pen pal. She gave me horseback rides as she crawled across our living room. We practiced handstands and cartwheels in the backyard. Many bruises were soothed when Wa-Wa, Michael, and I piled into our bathtub. We created tsunamis and tidal waves while Winky, our dog, tried to get in on the action. On rare summer weekends at Bertha's home in White Plains, Wa-Wa, Di-Di, Michael, and I did typical kid stuff: rode bikes, counted ladybugs, made a fortress in the basement organized by Wa-Wa, the Inventor of Fun.

Wa-Wa was a favorite of Mom's. She felt that Wa-Wa, as the second daughter, had been bypassed by Bertha and Paul for attention and affection. Elder daughter Mei-Mei received the lion's share. Mei-Mei was an accomplished classical pianist, which aligned with Bertha's musical passion.

As Wa-Wa moved into adolescence, her *joie de vivre* was replaced by troubled rebellion. The horseback rides and bathtub tidal wave rituals ended. One summer, she transitioned from a fun-loving goofy kid into a deeply sullen teenager. The ease of our banter as young kids had disappeared, replaced by stiltedness. I was 9 years old and far removed from her current reality. She was around 14 and had taken up smoking. We sat in the backyard of our Syosset home one hot humid summer afternoon and I found it strange that she wore a long sleeved t-shirt and a denim jacket. She finally took off her denim jacket and pushed up her t-shirt sleeves. To my horror, I saw big welt marks on her wrist and naively asked her what happened. She showed me other parts of her forearm and said it was where she snuffed out her cigarettes and cut herself with razor blades. I asked her why her wrists were so swollen and she casually said, "I tried to kill myself."

I don't know how my 9-year-old self processed that news. I only remember my first impulse was wanting to care for her. She didn't say much and shrugged it off. That was the end of our backyard banter.

I later told Mom and asked if we could adopt her. I pressed Mom for details about what would cause someone to want to harm themselves. In typical euphemistic fashion, which was how our family communicated, I was told that Wa-Wa was very sick. "Sick?" That propelled me to deeper worry and anxiety.

Family gatherings were held, but Wa-Wa was always "busy," or "tired," or "going through typical adolescence." What was not said was that Wa-Wa had been institutionalized. She underwent electric shock therapy, a form of psychiatric treatment where electrodes are attached to the scalp to deliver an electric current to the brain.

The next time I saw her was the summer she was 17. She was given a day pass to reunite with Mom, Michael, and me at Bertha's home. By this time, I was an adolescent age 12 and I wasn't sure what to say for fear of setting off emotions. We conversation-surfed, talking about anything except what was profoundly evident: a teenager increasingly disenfranchised from her family and no one with the skills or courage to connect with her.

Mah Jong's popularity limited Mom's availability to visit White Plains, so the gatherings with Bertha became less frequent. In 1970, soon after Mah Jong opened the Aloha Room and for Mah Jong's 10th anniversary, Mom and Dad invited the entire Meng family to attend the floor show. Photos show the Mengs wearing leis and enjoying tropical drinks. Paul and Bertha beamed, and there were joyful smiles on the faces of Ni-Ni, Mei-Mei, and Di-Di, but only a vapid hollow stare from Wa-Wa.

One day in 1971, a package arrived at our home from Bertha, who had sent it several months earlier when she was overseas with Paul. Confused, Mom called Bertha to ask why the package was sent. I came home from school to find a note from Mom on the kitchen table. She said she was going to White Plains to visit with Bertha who wasn't feeling well; she'd be back in a couple of days. Michael and I couldn't figure out why she'd be gone so long. I assumed that Bertha or Paul was on the verge of dying. Days went by and Mom didn't come home, didn't call, and my imagination manufactured all sorts of dramatic scenarios.

Early Saturday morning I woke up to find Mom had returned home. She was sitting in the kitchen and said she had something to tell us. "Wa-Wa passed away." I couldn't believe it. "What happened?" I insisted. Mom only said she died in her sleep and that she went peacefully. The bone-crushing sorrow, fueled by my 14-year-old hormonal surges and compounded by confusion made me inconsolable and yet, Mom's demeanor was absolutely marble-esque. She didn't cry, she didn't say much of anything except to reassure me that Wa-Wa had gone to a better place.

I didn't know what to make of that. I wondered why she had to leave in the first placc. Mom, Daisy, Mamie, and Teddy led the efforts to support Bertha and to get ready for the memorial and funeral service. Walking into the funeral parlor amid hushed and muffled voices, I saw the open casket. In the casket Wa-Wa was holding a bouquet of flowers from Michael and me. I kept looking at her wrists but they were covered by her long-sleeved dress, and her neck was covered with high-collar lace. I saw Ni-Ni approach the casket and I was transfixed by his soft caressing of the top of Wa-Wa's head. *Such tender brotherly love*, I thought. The entire Meng family were understandably grief-stricken. I still could not understand how Wa-Wa died peacefully from whatever sickness she had.

After some time passed, Mom invited Bertha to Syosset to get her out of the sad confines of her White Plains home. Bertha took great interest in my piano and guitar practice; she drove me to my lessons and sat in on my classes. Mom asked me to play the piano for Bertha at home. I wasn't very proficient at classical music so I played "The Long and Winding Road" by the Beatles, "Bridge Over Troubled Water" by Simon and Garfunkel, and other soft tunes I played to help me cope with the aftermath of Brian. Bertha, sitting next to me on the piano bench, bent over and wept and I wasn't sure what to do. Mom said, "Keep playing," which was hard since I felt I was torturing Bertha with these tunes. But music was cathartic to her and she asked me to play some more. Knowing she was a teacher, I asked how I should play a certain chord, did I get the right phrasing during a certain measure, or if I was following the right tempo. My questions were a brief distraction from her misery, but I ran out of questions and just continued playing while Bertha cried.

About a year later at Mah Jong, I rummaged through Mom's purse for reasons I can't recall and found a small folded up article. I opened it and was stunned to read a newspaper clipping reporting that the autopsy reports verified that Wa-Wa, daughter of Chih-Meng and Bertha Meng, had committed suicide by a self-inflicted gunshot wound to the head.

I immediately confronted Mom to ask, 'WHY?" Not, why did it happen? But, why wasn't I told? I demanded details. What I finally pieced together was a tragic family story.

At their White Plains home, time with my cousins was great fun, but when Paul was in the room, there was expected obedience and reverence to which he was due. A sense of formality prevailed. The children spoke Chinese and Dad remembers that when we had a family gathering at Mah Jong, Ni-Ni guzzled Coca-Cola because the children were not allowed to have soda at home. I also remember their house was cold and Bertha particularly parsimonious with meals. We assumed it was because she was on a teacher's salary and Paul worked for a non-profit organization.

When we went to their home for Thanksgiving, Mom brought extra food because, she said, Bertha never made enough.

This is not to suggest untoward actions occurred within the Meng household, but there was speculation that something was just not right. The age difference between Bertha and Paul? Cultural pressures among children raised in white Westchester County and yet living within a strict Chinese culture at home? Bertha's seeming subservience to Paul? Did the China Institute's demands upon Paul compete for time with his children? Genetic imbalances? To this day, everything is inconclusive and conjectural.

Wa-Wa's psychiatrist had contacted Bertha and Paul the night before she died to alert them to watch her closely. He was worried about their recent session. We learned later that 19-year-old Wa-Wa was somehow able to buy a shotgun and smuggle it into the house.

The next day while Bertha was teaching her third grade class in the nearby town of Armonk and Paul was in another part of the house, Wa-Wa went into Bertha's bedroom (Paul and Bertha had long maintained separate bedrooms), took out the shotgun, inserted the barrel into her mouth, and pulled the trigger.

Paul heard the blast, discovered Wa-Wa's body and called the police. The police were dispatched to Bertha's school where she was told the news. As Bertha walked into the house, the phone was ringing. It was Mom calling to ask about the mystery package.

Mom didn't know why the package arrived when it did or what prompted her to call Bertha at that exact moment. She called Teddy to notify the other siblings to meet at Bertha's house, left a note for Michael and me on the kitchen table, and raced to White Plains. Mom, the first of her siblings to lose a child when Lowell died as a toddler, gravitated intuitively to Bertha to provide the solace and understanding that only the two of them could understand as mothers united in grief; part of a club they never wished to join.

I remembered how peaceful Wa-Wa looked in the casket and realized, with more clarity, that the embalmers had done a remarkable job of putting her head back together. And the sight of Ni-Ni softly caressing his sister's head, where the bullet exited, became all the more poignant.

PAUL (NI-NI)

I remember Bertha and Paul Chih-Meng's eldest son Ni-Ni as shy, softspoken, gentle, and tender-hearted. With an 11-year age gap between the two of us, I was not as fortunate as my older cousins to get to know him. One of the rare times I spent private time with him was in 1974 when I was a high school student doing summer stock at Northwestern University. Ni-Ni was attending Ohio State pursuing a master of science in chemistry and physical education.

He learned I would be in Chicago for the summer and called to suggest that he come to Northwestern to have lunch with me. That was a big surprise and, of course, I accepted. I wasn't sure if he reached out because he knew I had been close to Wa-Wa, or if he was in need of a connection to her. He met me in my dorm room with his instantly recognizable smile which resembled Bertha's. We made some small talk before going to a nearby coffee shop. He kindly expressed interest in what I was studying, but we never discussed Wa-Wa's passing or how he was adapting to her loss. Instead, we enjoyed each other's company, and I was smitten by the attention of someone far more intellectual than I would ever hope to be. I wistfully imagined him as an older brother, wondering what my life would have been like had Lowell lived.

We wrote postcards to each other for the duration of the summer and alas, life, school, distance, and other interests intervened, and we went our separate ways.

He found a passion for scuba diving and became a certified diving instructor at the physical education department of the University of Florida (Gainesville). He taught canoeing, sailing, scuba diving, and lifesaving. By all accounts, he was thriving, happy and had a girlfriend. He was highly regarded by his students and was an active member of the Cave Diving Section of the National Speleology Society.

I was working in an office in Los Angeles when the receptionist came to my desk to say there I had an urgent call. It was Mario relaying the news: "Your cousin just died." We had so many, my first question was, "Which one?" "It's Ni-Ni. He was electrocuted in the shower."

Jesus.

What a tragic accident. As more details emerged, the news got worse. We learned that Ni-Ni had died in an apparent suicide. As Mom and Daisy put it simplistically, he bought some wire, fastened it to a live electrical outlet, tied the wire around his head, and went into the shower. Mom vaguely said it was because of money pressures and extortion from a competing scuba diving company. Their blurry explanations suggested that no one really knew what caused Ni-Ni to kill himself, that it was too painful to discuss, and/or there were deeper circumstances to be revealed.

It was all of the above, with particular emphasis on the latter.

The newspapers were sensationalistic. *The Independent Alligator*, an independent school newspaper reporting for the University of Florida (UF), opened with a lead article on its front-page May 27, 1982 issue: "Paul Meng was found dead, face down in a pool of water, in a Florida Gym shower stall on March 22. He had electrodes taped to his forehead and an electric switch in his hand. The UF Police Department was called and declared the death suicide by electrocution."

It was speculated that the class fees went towards a project of Ni-Ni's: the construction of a small concrete structure, 20 x 12 feet, near Florida Pool/Gym to house an industrial air compressor, to offer full scuba repair services, and to provide scuba/diving equipment to other UF departments.

The auditor demanded that Ni-Ni and his fellow instructors produce receipts and proof of how they used the money they collected for their courses.

Ni-Ni tried to resign twice: once on February 22 when he wrote to his department chairman, Clarence Moore, who refused to accept Ni-Ni's resignation. Ni-Ni tried again to resign on March 22, the day he died, and less than a month before the final audit results were to be released.

A MOTHER'S ANGUISH

Eleven years earlier, Bertha was interrupted while teaching her third grade class by the White Plains police to inform her of Wa-Wa's suicide. Bertha was again teaching in her classroom when the White Plains police came to tell her that now her eldest son had also likely committed suicide.

Since the University of Florida audit was a public document, the University was required to release it to the press. The mysterious circumstances surrounding Ni-Ni's death gave rise to lurid gossip, defamation, rumors, and innuendos at the University of Florida and in the local media.

With relentless determination, Bertha—at the age of 66—channeled her energies into a fervent campaign to clear Ni-Ni's name. The speed and intensity by which she pursued her quest was nothing short of remarkable.

On May 30, two months after Ni-Ni's death, Bertha wrote a letter to UF President Robert Marston requesting another probe into the investigation. "I beseech you to initiate an investigation so my son's good name will be restored." Bertha enlisted the help of close family friend, Elizabeth Luce Moore (Beth), whose brother Henry R. Luce was the founder of *Time* magazine.

Beth Moore, in her letter to Marston, asked him to "make a simple dignified statement to the family that will also be issued to the public at large. That such a person (as Paul Meng) should have been vilified by the local press, with innuendos of scandal, has of course added intense distress to the trauma the parents were suffering over Paul's death," wrote Moore, "Any family would be mortified by such innuendos, but the Chinese are particularly sensitive to an attack on the good name of the family. To clear the name of their son is therefore of utmost importance to them—as it is to all of us who have been his friends and admirers."

With surgical precision, Bertha took apart the audit and listed its fallacies point-by-point while reprimanding the local news media: "Based on this (audit) report, the news media have been reporting sensational scandals inside your university and have smeared your dedicated staff, particularly my son, who had done so much to elevate the standard of his department and his students," she wrote.

By July 8, 1982, four months after Ni-Ni's death and as a result of Bertha's efforts, University of Florida officials came around to question the accuracy of the audit, admitting it was "incorrect" and "full of innuendo."

The audit, which caused such angst to Ni-Ni, was magnified because he couldn't produce the requested receipts totaling $509.14.

Five hundred nine dollars and fourteen cents drove Ni-Ni to claustrophobic despair and into the Florida Gym shower stall.

Bertha and Paul, and some members of our family, have never been fully convinced that Ni-Ni committed suicide. Nothing to the contrary has been proven and there have been no arrests or evidence to suggest this was a staged suicide, as his former girlfriend posited. I believe he—a most gentle man—was overtly bullied, which drove him to that god-forsaken place of profound emotional hell. President Marston's indictment of the gossip-infused stories that *The Independent Alligator* fomented was too little and too late.

Against the abject sadness of the death of two of Bertha's four children—only elder daughter Mei-Mei and youngest son Di-Di remained—and more untimely family tragedies on the horizon, the Kwoh siblings tightened their web of support for each other. All the hardships they endured during childhood just made them stronger.

AND THEN, MARIO

It was unfathomable to think that the laughter, love and support Mario brought to the family would begin to ebb when we received news in 1987 that he was diagnosed with leukemia. He was 37 years old. Chris was a toddler. Kathy had just started her career as a doctor and obviously had her hands more than full. Mom and Dad spent more time in Maplewood to help out while Mario underwent chemo. Michael, who had evolved into a sturdy family anchor, grew particularly close with Kathy, and I felt helpless being so far away.

I got the call from Mom that Mario had passed away at home at the age of 39 on April 29, 1989. Motel 14 filled up with family to begin the unspeakably sad task of supporting Kathy and 3-year-old Chris. Once again the aunts and uncles convened and rallied, but a rare supernova was prematurely extinguished from our lives.

The words of Gina the Gypsy who foretold Ni-Ni's death and who was reluctant to read Kathy's palm were prescient: "The man you love...he is not yours. Even if he is yours, he won't be yours for long."

My cousin, Jesse Kwoh, with my sister Kathy, San Diego, 2010

With my cousin, May. (Author's collection)

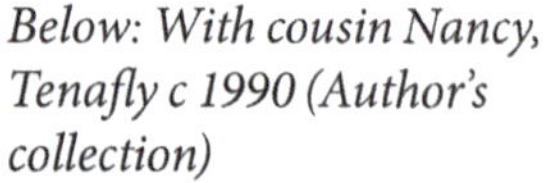

Below: With cousin Nancy, Tenafly c 1990 (Author's collection)

Three generations of Meng women: Bertha, Mei-Mei, Katie
(Author's collection)

CHAPTER 33

BERTHA

After Bertha's success in restoring Ni-Ni's name, she and Paul retired to Sun City West, Arizona. The weather, affordability, slower pace, and desert air were considerable factors to escort them through their senior years. Paul had suffered a stroke and was confined to a wheelchair. Once a gifted orator, singer, and storyteller, Paul could not communicate. Bertha became his voice.

After years of thrifty living in White Plains, Bertha discovered she was suddenly wealthy. It appears that Paul did not disclose much about the family finances until Bertha had to tend to his affairs. Frugal Bertha suddenly appeared at our reunions wearing fur coats, adorned with jewelry, and she began carrying designer bags. On one occasion she kept asking if we noticed anything different about her. Not able to see what was different, she announced, "I just had a facelift!"

She took up synchronized swimming, dressed up for Chinese ribbon dancing classes, played piano, and was an active participant in curating activities for the seniors. As a teacher, she expected organization and efficiency. When she didn't see it, she spoke up vigorously and unabashedly.

Bless her. She finally came into her own, after her fears as a young immigrant college girl alone in Iowa and all the relentless sorrow she endured as an adult.

Bertha convinced Daisy to buy a home in Sun City West and Dad encouraged Mom to buy something there, as well. He believed that when he passed away, Mom could then be close to two of her sisters. Mom agreed and our Sun City West home became an additional place to gather, along with our home in Palm Bay, Florida.

Death took a brief holiday and our family enjoyed what were some of the happiest times for us all. My aunts and uncles moved into their retirement years. My cousins and siblings were deep into their careers in international business (May), education (Nancy), molecular biology (Jesse), law (Bonny), biomedical sciences (Phyllis), business/accounting (Michael), medicine/radiology (Kathy). They had children and a new generation joined the Kwoh siblings, now grandparents and revered elders.

Bertha performing the ribbon dance during her retirement years

Mamie, the eldest, tape recorded our reunions to listen to the sounds of banter and laughter across three generations. We each took turns at the piano and when Mamie's granddaughter, Erica, took up the cello at a young age, we were treated to our own music recital. Mamie surveyed the spread of family gathered in her home, shook her head with happy wonder and kept saying, "You young people bring so much joy into our lives."

The seven Kwoh siblings, now elders, had survived seven decades of wars, political upheaval, discrimination, starvation, persecution, cruel losses, and sorrow. Yet, when they gathered at precious reunions, they relished in the telling and retelling of stories of their youth. They didn't simmer in resentment for the cards they were dealt, they just sang songs from happier times before the soldiers and famine entered their young lives. They cooked, ate, sang around the piano, danced, played cards, and made up for all the lost years of separation. Their gleeful giggles morphing into unabashed laughter were a memorable soundtrack of my youth. Laughter, lots of it. In spite of their hardships, these remarkable Kwohs found their light and passed that glow onto the younger generations.

The seven Kwoh siblings

CHAPTER 34

THE CONTINUATION OF SORROW

The intensity of the laughter started to dissipate in the 1990s when a torment of passings hit our families. Paul Chih-Meng passed away from respiratory failure in 1990 at the age of 90.

In 1993, it was Mamie's turn to experience double sorrow. S.C. died of septic shock on June 6 at the age of 83. A mere four weeks after S.C.'s passing, Mamie's youngest daughter, Nancy succumbed to her long battle with aplastic anemia, a rare blood disease in which the bone marrow does not manufacture enough blood cells. In spite of her illness and the risk, she gave birth to twin boys Alex and Nathan in 1977. Mamie called Nancy a warrior for enduring regular transfusions, pain, surgeries and yet, always managing a smile to put others at ease. She provided a strict and nurturing home for husband David and the boys. Nancy served as the unofficial family historian by preserving and documenting old family photos and creating albums for each hallmark family occasion. Nancy passed away at the age of 45.

As if fate could not be sadistically crueler to Bertha, her youngest son Di-Di died of an aneurysm in 1994 at the age of 39. Among his siblings, Di-Di was the quietest and meekest. It didn't help that he was in the shadow of strong family personalities—namely from the strong Kwoh women—and appeared to get swallowed up within that energetic force field. When he was able to get a word in edgewise, his voice was soft and diminutive, an invitation for others to dominate his conversations.

He found a life partner in Gloria and they moved to Albany, CA, not too far from where I lived, giving me the opportunity to socialize at their home every now and then.

On my birthday I received the news that Di-Di was stricken. I approached the hospital bed and held Di-Di's hand, letting him know I was there. To my surprise, he opened his eyes and said, "Hi, Debbie." I jokingly said there were easier ways to get attention in our family; he responded with a very slight smile before disappearing into his sleep. The following day, January 31st, he suffered a second brain bleed and was put on life support. Di-Di died on Feb 2, 1994, Bertha's 78th birthday.

CHAPTER 35

MAH JONG

THE WEEK THAT CHANGED THE WORLD

A seismic world event occurred during February 21-28, 1972 in the Year of the Mouse. President Richard Nixon embarked on an historic visit to China, at the invitation of Premier Chou-en-Lai, to begin to thaw the frosty relationship between the United States and the People's Republic of China.

China was still isolated from the world. This was the first time that China opened its doors to the West ever since Mao Tse-Tung's Communist party gained control in 1949. For our family, this was a complicated set of mixed blessings, especially for Grace whose father-in-law, Hollington Tong, along with Chiang Kai-shek, took refuge in Taiwan after they fled Mao's Communist takeover of China. President Nixon's visit was referred to by U.S. Ambassador and President Emeritus of the Asia Society, Nicholas Platt, as "the week that changed the world."

Our entire family was glued to the TV set watching every step of this significant trip. The opening banquet was televised from the Great Hall of the People at Tiananmen Square in Beijing. Mom and Dad shook their heads in wonderment to see the flags of the United States and the People's Republic of China displayed side by side. They were witnessing the day when it might be possible to visit China again and to have their relatives who remained in China be allowed to come out.

Among the most notable cultural partnerships that emanated from President Nixon's visit was with the Philadelphia Orchestra. In 1973, The Orchestra, led by Maestro Eugene Ormandy, was asked by President Nixon to represent the United States as the first American symphony to perform in the People's Republic of China.

By 1979, President Jimmy Carter had granted China full diplomatic recognition. Coupled with the enactment of the Immigration and Nationality Act of 1965, which ended the quota system and relaxed border restrictions, Chinese from Communist China began to emigrate to the United States, bringing with them a wave of new Chinese recipes and cuisines, particularly from the Szechuan and Hunan provinces. This led to an influx of chefs opening up new restaurants to offer different types of regional Chinese cuisines unheard of by Americans. By comparison, Cantonese food was now considered bland.

Mah Jong customers began to request that dishes be made extra spicy. Some came in with their own hot sauces and asked to have their dishes specifically seasoned. Dad refused these requests. He did not want to compromise the integrity of the Cantonese dishes for which Mah Jong was famous.

Dietary tastes in the United States were also changing. A wave of fad diets were introduced: the Scarsdale Diet, Keep Slim Diet, the resurrection of the Grapefruit Diet, plus the diet pills Dexatrim and Ayds appetite suppressant candies were promoted as a reminder to reduce caloric and fat intake. Exercise fads such as Jazzercise were a complementary component to the dieting craze. Mah Jong's cooking mantra of "always use the fat" was becoming outdated.

Dad bringing out the kitchen staff, waiters, and servers for a round of applause among the diners

MAH JONG AND THE INEVITABLE

Business at Mah Jong began to wane at this time. The Polynesian troupe underwent a major overhaul. In 1977, Dad abruptly told Leia it was time for a change. He felt her routines had grown stale and he wanted to shake things up to attract new customers. She took the news graciously and said, "Peter, thank you, it's been a wonderful run." She led the Polynesian show for nearly 10 years, introduced the South Seas tropical islands to Mah Jong, and broadened its appeal during its early years. I wasn't home to bear witness to Leia's termination but was saddened to learn that the biggest link between the original troupe and the glory days of the Polynesian floor show was severed.

For the time being, Billy and Johnny remained with the band, along with longtime drummer, Willie. But soon, the band members started to turn over as well. Billy was fired by Dad.

A new emcee joined the troupe in 1978. Frank Scafuri was a local musician, trained at Julliard, and living on Long Island. Frank learned to play Hawaiian music and developed a good enough repertoire to play at luaus in New Jersey. In my 2021 conversation with Frank, he mentioned being hired by bandleader Dick Tucker whose daughter booked cruise trips to Bermuda, where guests stayed at the Inverurie Hotel, known for its Polynesian floor show.

In 1976, Frank had a 10-week gig to play Hawaiian music on the ship and at the hotel. The fire dancer at the Inverurie Hotel was none other than Chief Taofi. Frank and Taofi hit it off immediately. In 1977, Taofi knew Mah Jong was in need of an experienced emcee to replace Leia. Upon

The Mah Jong Polynesian troupe, c 1982.
L-R: Fire dancer Joe Salito, dancers Pua, Lisa Casserly, Cathy Casserly, emcee Frank Scafuri. Back row: drummer Willie, keyboardist, guitarist Mike Brown.

their return from Bermuda, Taofi introduced Frank to Dad and shortly thereafter, Dad called another one of his meetings with the troupe. He brought Frank with him, introduced him to the troupe and announced that Frank was the new front singer. No discussion—it was just the way it was going to be.

Frank Scafuri (singer/emcee), Joe Salito (the sword/fire dancer), sisters Lisa and Cathy Casserly, and Pua (dancers) were the new troupe in 1978. The band members were Willie, Johnny's brother and his friend. What had been an exotic Polynesian troupe from 1968-1975 now became a South Seas floor show comprised of mostly Italian and Irish performers. They coalesced as a troupe but, clientele was dropping. Even though Leia's routine might have been perceived as stale, she had a steady following at Mah Jong and her fans/the regulars ebbed away. I thought Dad's mistakes running Mah Jong were few, but I believe that impulsive decision to terminate Leia was the catalyst for the floor show's decline.

SELLING THE BUSINESS

By now, it was evident that Mah Jong was losing traction. A decision had to be made to sell Gardina or sell Mah Jong. It was a lot easier to sell the restaurant. Dad made the decision to sell it to Alex Chang, who had admired Mah Jong's business and was interested in starting his own restaurant. As conveyed to me in 2020 by Mah Jong organist Johnny Rubino, "Your dad called another meeting and told us that he was going to sell the Mah Jong Restaurant to Alex. Wow, Deb, it was like a death to us all. When your mom and dad owned the Mah Jong Restaurant it had such an awesome atmosphere. When Alex took it over and started to make changes in the luau room he made it look like a cafeteria. He took all the Hawaiian life out of it."[70]

Mom was not told of Dad's intention to sell Mah Jong. She was devastated, disheartened, and worried. She was 37 years old when Mah Jong opened in 1960. She was approaching 60 when Mah Jong was coming to its close. Her worry was financial. She would no longer draw a salary from Mah Jong and her social world—in which she was often the center—would ebb. She felt she had lost her identity.

FRIENDLY

In a spirit of defiance, Mom applied for a job at Friendly, the restaurant next door to Mah Jong. No one could say no since she was the landlord and the building was owned by our Gardina Associates Corporation.

She was hired as a waitress to work the breakfast shift. She rose at 5:00am, did her tai-chi, her rosary prayers, put on her outfit and drove to Friendly to begin her shift at 6:00am. Mom had developed rheumatoid arthritis, causing her finger joints to become swollen, stiff, and painful. The plates at Friendly were large and heavy, so she carried two at a time; one in each hand. For large parties, she made several trips to deliver the food.

When I was home from California on holidays, I awoke to the sound of Mom getting ready for work. She counted her tips from the day before and rolled them up to take them to the bank on her day off. I stopped by for lunch at Friendly. I sat at Mom's station and ordered my usual Clam Boat and Fribble. I felt sad watching her in her waitress role. I could not imagine what she felt like, especially since Mah Jong was within view of Friendly dining room.

Mom with her waitress colleagues in front of Friendly. Note the "New Mah Jong" sign in the background, as established by Mah Jong's new owners. (Author's collection)

At Friendly, she found a new legion of fans among the young waitresses. One was Tracy Fentress, younger sister of my high school classmate Mark. In an email exchange in 2015, Tracy shared memories of her conversations with Mom. She revealed that Mom decided to work at Friendly because she was bored. "How many times can you make a bed?" she asked Tracy.

According to Tracy, "Your mother couldn't stand cheap tippers. She refused to serve them if they came back, which was bad for them since she was the only waitress during breakfast hours. She also knew that Friendly wasn't efficiently run. When Friendly ran a "15-minute-lunch-or-get-a-free-ice-cream" promotion, she'd give the coupon back to the customer before they even ordered, stating that a 15-minute lunch at Friendly would never happen."

Many of the younger waitresses adored her, especially when Mom complained to the Regional Manager about how poorly run Friendly was. Some of the staff came in late, supplies weren't organized for the morning shift, there wasn't enough staff to support the breakfast rush. It was the opposite of Mah Jong's near military precision, and it drove her crazy. Mom's not-so-secret mission was to get Friendly in line. She had frequent phone calls with the District Manager to report problems and she insisted on getting results.

Eventually, the district branch of Friendly awarded her Top Employee in recognition of her seven years of hard work; perhaps to surrender to Mom's relentless barrage of complaints to corporate headquarters.

– PART SIX –

The Sunset Years

The survivors (Author's collection)

CHAPTER 36

THE KWOH ELDERS MOVE ON

Of all of the Kwoh siblings, I had always assumed Daisy would be the first to pass away given her TB and, soon after she retired, a bout with breast cancer. Dad said not to worry, Daisy is as durable as they come and she'll outlive all of us.

It was a healthy and active Bertha who was diagnosed with renal cancer shortly after burying her youngest son. I spent time in Sun City West, visiting with Bertha. Mom had set up her new home just a mile from Bertha.

During the fall of 1994, in preparation for her passing, Bertha asked me to go through her closet and take anything I wanted. She and Mei-Mei had determined what would go to granddaughter Katie, and Bertha wanted me to take some of her jewelry, shoes, jackets, handbags. I couldn't bear the thought of doing so and instead chose a jade necklace, one of her favorites.

I visited Bertha in early February 1995 to celebrate her birthday and mine. Mom joined us in making a birthday dinner at Bertha's home. A Chinese custom is to serve noodles for birthdays. They symbolize longevity: the longer the noodles, the longer the life. Bertha was in evident pain, moving slowly but with determination to make our birthday noodle dinner. We made lots and lots of noodles. As Bertha was lifting her noodles out of her bowl, she raised her chopsticks and weakly said, "Here's to a long life." By then, we knew her condition was terminal.

Towards the end of March 1995, the family was notified that Bertha's death was imminent. The Kwoh siblings, Michael, and I held vigil at her home in Sun City West, joining Mei-Mei and her daughter Katie. Bertha passed away on April 3, 1995.

CHAPTER 37

MOM DIES

I was vacationing in New Zealand during the summer of 1999—in the era before cell phones were widely used. Toward the end of my trip, I had a nagging feeling to call home, but I couldn't figure out how to work the pay phones or calling cards and wasn't able to contact anyone in the States. I was anxiety-ridden and distressed on the 12-hour plane ride back home. When I landed at San Francisco Airport, Michael met me at customs and the first thing he said was, "Mom's sick." She was at our home in Palm Bay, Florida and experiencing symptoms of a racing heart and shortness of breath. Test results from the hospital revealed an out-of-the-blue Stage-4 lung cancer diagnosis. Between her TB, being surrounded by perpetual smoking at Mah Jong, and having only one lung on which to survive—the one that was cancerous—meant that this diagnosis was disastrous.

Michael and I flew to Florida to be with Mom at the hospital and to make plans for her medical options, which were slim. Mom and I had long and loving talks. She kept saying, "I don't want you to see me suffer," or "Don't be sad when I'm gone," or "I'll always look after you." She kept reminding me to, "Always look for a sign - I'll be waving."

We also tended to Dad who seemed shocked that Mom had cancer. He had plans lined up for her to be with her sisters after he passed away. He was going to resolve the Mah Jong finances so she'd be secure, but he could not control this part of our family destiny.

He also could not control his severe coughing spasms at home late into the evening. At first Michael and I thought it was Dad's asthma acting up and that a couple of puffs from his inhaler would calm things down. Dad kept coughing, wheezing, and gasping. Michael said, "that is not asthma; we're going to the hospital." We raced Dad out of the house, Michael and Dad piled into the back seat of the car, I made a beeline to the nearest hospital which was reachable by side streets. I kept hitting red lights and making right-hand turns, then swinging around and dive back onto the main road, wishing a cop would see me and give us a fast escort to Palm Bay Hospital.

Nothing of the sort. Careening right and left while listening to Dad's desperate attempts to breathe were tempered by Michael's deliberate and steady assurances that we were "almost there." *Thank God for Michael,* I thought as I looked at him in the rear-view mirror.

When we got to the hospital, I slowed down to a crawl while Michael got Dad out of the car, held him by the arm and took him into the emergency room. I found a place to park. We met in the waiting room and I cried out to Michael, "What on earth is happening to us?"

We were called into the recovery room where we learned that Dad had a heart attack. He was intubated, his face had an unnatural ashen-brown color to it, his hands were tied to the rails of the bed, and he was fighting to speak. We tried to calm him down, but he was determined to say something and motioned for a pen and piece of paper. When the nurse brought them over, I looked at what he wrote: "Don't tell Mom."

Michael and I were pelted with questions by the doctors: what kinds of medication did he take, did he have any allergic reactions to drugs, what were the drug dosages, and more questions we could not answer. We called Kathy in New Jersey and relayed the questions; she was a doctor and had more familiarity with his pharmaceutical collection, which he kept in a Crown Royal whiskey bag.

"WHAT WAS IN THAT BAG?" I desperately asked Kathy. As she was trying to remember, she thankfully said, "I'll fly down to Florida and join you."

As Dad recovered from his heart attack, Michael and I took turns commuting from Dad's hospital to Mom's hospital across town. When I visited Mom, she asked how Dad was and I said he was fine. She knew something was wrong and asked, "What happened?" I finally told her and then I drove to Dad's hospital to tell him, "Mom knows what's going on."

We moved Dad to Mom's hospital for his recovery. Dad was on one floor and Mom on another. Michael and I were couriers to pass messages back and forth.

During their meals:

Dad: "Take this salad up to Mom."

Debbie delivers salad to Mom.

Mom (eyeing the salad): "What's he having for dinner?"

Me: "Salisbury steak."

Mom: "Bring me some of that."

Debbie races to Dad's room.

Dad (*as I'm cutting up the Salisbury steak*): "What's Mom having for dessert?"

Me: "Peach cobbler!"

Dad: "Peach cobbler? They didn't give me that, bring some of that to me and take this blueberry cheesecake up to her."

Debbie scoots to Mom's room with Salisbury steak and blueberry cheesecake

Mom: "Did he get ice cream?"

Me: "Yes...... I'll get that after I deliver this peach cobbler to him."

And on it went. Three meals a day. Two restaurateurs comparing notes on the food and, sometimes, the inequity of the offerings.

Mom joked around with the hospital staff, giving the impression she would beat her cancer. She refused chemo or radiation. She was scared, upset, confused and distraught that she would die before Dad. I rarely left her hospital bedside. We talked about her life and her concern for her children. She said, "I don't worry about Kathy and Michael; they have good jobs and can take care of themselves. I've always been worried about you the most."

The last time we Chinns were together as a family was at Mom's hospital room in June, 1999. We said goodbye to Dad and Michael, who stayed behind at our Florida home, while Kathy and I flew Mom to New Jersey for medical care at the hospital where Kathy was Director of Medical Education and a radiologist at the Hospital Center of Orange, New Jersey. Mom did not want Dad to come up to New Jersey to be with her. I was the one who had to break that news to him. Mom was livid that she was dying first. I believe the sight of Dad the survivor at her bedside as she declined was too much for her to bear.

When we left the hospital to take Mom to New Jersey, she could not break her old restaurant habits. Sitting in her wheelchair, she directed me to push her towards some of the hospital staff to say goodbye. She had a wad of cash in her hands and tipped everyone on the way out: $5 dollars here, $10 there. I explained that in hospitals, they don't tip the staff. She said it didn't matter, she only tipped the ones who gave her excellent service, especially the orderly who said there was ice cream in the freezer and she could have as much as she wanted. He got $20.

I arranged for first class tickets on Continental Airlines to accommodate Mom's oxygen tank. I provided a car service to drive us from our Palm Bay home to Orlando Airport. As we drove away from home, Mom wistfully remarked, "I'm going out in style." Upon arrival at New Jersey, Mom stayed with Mamie in Tenafly. We rented an apartment in nearby Edgewater; Mom was to stay with Mamie until I could come back and set up the apartment. I left New Jersey and said goodbye to Mom, telling her to hold tight, I'd be back, and we'll have fun living together again when I return. As always, our closing line was, "I love you."

I took a leave of absence from my job at the San Francisco Symphony to move to Edgewater to take care of Mom. I was in denial about the severity of her illness; I had never heard of Stage 4 cancer. Even though Kathy said Mom didn't have much time, I thought Mom would be gutsy enough to win another health battle. I was told that those with Stage-4 cancer can live a long time. I regrettably held on to that optimism.

I prepared to drive cross country—still thinking Mom was going to rebound—and called her before I left San Francisco. Her voice was weak and she couldn't hear me. I wasn't sure if it was a bad connection or if she was fading out. Michael said there was still time to make the trip since she seemed to be fine. I asked my friend, Katie Koch, to drive with me to expedite the move. She planned to fly back to California once I was in NJ. We set out on August 13th and had just passed Reno, Nevada when I had an odd sensation; a wave of nausea and tingling reverberated all over my body. My cell phone rang and Michael asked where I was. I said we had just passed Reno and would be in Utah by nightfall; making excellent time. He asked if I was driving and I said no, I was in the passenger seat. He told me to pull over. At the next off ramp we got off the road and stopped in a parking lot. Michael asked, "Have you stopped the car?" I had no idea what he was getting at until he said, "Mom just died." I couldn't believe it—I thought she was fine and hanging on.

I think after she and I hung up, she just let go; I felt she wanted to spare me the agony of watching her pass away.

While in Nevada, I tried to find flights out of Salt Lake City, Utah. No flights were available and the only option was to turn around and go back to Reno, stay overnight and take an early flight out of Reno International Airport the next morning. Katie would drive my car back to San Francisco and keep it there until further arrangements could be made. While in Reno that night, the allure of the casinos beckoned and I was reminded of the gambling dens of Mah Jong. I was still in shock and denial that Mom was gone. I robotically made my way over to some slot machines, mindlessly dropping in quarters. Without warning, bells and lights went off and quarters came gushing down the chute. I couldn't help but smile and laugh. I knew it was Mom's sign; she was still around and she didn't leave until I had won over $300 in quarters.

My relationship with my mother would be the envy of any child. We loved each other and once we became adults, we learned to get past the discomfort of showing emotions and began to say the words that matter most: "I love you." Sometimes we didn't need to say that; we knew we had a special bond. I called her regularly, to the point where she said I didn't need to call her so much, especially on weekdays at 4:00. That was when she tuned in to watch *Judge Judy* and she didn't like to be interrupted.

She loved crime shows and had an obsession on the life of criminals and the mob, so we celebrated her 70th birthday with a family trip to Alcatraz, aka, "The Rock", a former federal prison located in the San Francisco Bay. It was kismet that on the day of our tour; former prison inmate Nathan Glenn Williams was there as part of his book tour. His book, "From Alcatraz to the White House," documented his life of crime as a kidnapper and bank robber, and eventually his successes in turning his life around, which resulted in a pardon from President Ronald Reagan. When Mom met a real-life ex-convict, she not only bought his book but stayed at his book-signing table to talk, got a photo of him hugging her. She didn't want to leave "The Rock."

We lured her back onto the boat with promises of Alcatraz swag we bought from the gift shop. That Christmas, she received handcuffs, striped prison socks, Alcatraz hat, a prison tin-mug and a library of Alcatraz books about other inmates. She said it was the best birthday ever. I told her that for her 80th birthday, we'd make a return trip so that she could reunite with more of her bad boys. It wasn't meant to be.

On my birthdays I sent flowers to Mom to thank her for giving me life, remembering to remove all traces of carnations to not trigger sad memories of Lowell. We wrote letters frequently and she slipped in money to tide me over in my tough financial moments.

Mom had a hardscrabble life and I felt she wasn't granted a fair break in this sojourn on earth. She grew up with a sliver of time to enjoy a happy childhood. She suffered and endured starvation during the Japanese occupation of China, left her native country at the age of 25 and contracted a recurrence of tuberculosis, inadvertently passing it on to her young son who subsequently died. Her lung removal left her with a deep scar running along the left side of her back scapula. The left side of her rib cage was caved in, giving rise to her feelings of unattractiveness. While in the prime of her life, she learned that Mah Jong had been sold. She became a waitress in an ice cream shop. She was just beginning to enjoy her new role as a grandmother and had just 14 years to enjoy with her grandson. Then her cancer.

When I finally left Reno and arrived at Newark Airport, I was greeted by Teddy and Michael. I burst out sobbing. We arrived at Kathy's home in Maplewood, NJ, the site of all of our Motel 14 family gatherings. Sitting at the dining table were Mamie, Daisy, and Dora. Seeing them and an empty chair where Mom might have sat was just too much to bear. Mamie came over to provide solace, assuring me that Mom went peacefully. She just wanted to leave; it was time. All her life she had not been given much authority to make her own decisions. Dad controlled most of the choices. How ironic that the only event Mom could control in her life in this world was her transition into the next.

CON BRIO

For the memorial service, I put together the music Mom had wanted: *Wind Beneath My Wings* sung by Bette Midler, *Hawaiian Wedding Song*, and of course, *My Way*. The morning of her service, I sat on the deck in Kathy's backyard and looked over all the areas where Mom planted vegetables and flowers. I remembered her telling me to look for a sign that she would be saying hello. I sat on the deck on that quiet August morning and said, "OK, Mom, here I am - show me a sign." I heard a little bird chirping and thought, "Oh! That's you!" Then I heard the neighbor's dog bark and thought it was Mom sending a sign again. Next a telephone rang followed by a car alarm, then another dog barking, punctuated by a police siren. The tempi of Mom's signs were increasing, *con brio*, and I said, "Ma, alright already!" I went inside the house and said to Kathy, "Mom's yelling out there!"

She never got to experience the relief of the financial pressures that caused so much worry for the family. She passed away before the House of Mah Jong came to a close, robbing her of the chance to revel in final goodbyes and accolades for her part in Mah Jong's success. By all rights, she should have been there and for years I was bitter and angry that she was denied that moment of recognition.

Perhaps my biggest sorrow is that she never got to see me evolve into my career to where she would not have to worry about me ever again. She was just beginning to see me find my path as an arts leader. My first job as an arts executive was three months after she died.

CHAPTER 38

MAH JONG FROM 1983-2003

Over these 20 years, The House of Mah Jong was rented to seven different tenants. Two of them were months late with their rent which required Dad to continue borrowing money to cover the mortgage. The fifth tenant, the American chain and pizza restaurant, Bertucci's, was a reliable one. Bertucci's founder, Joey Crugnale, took an instant liking to Dad and did two big favors to help alleviate Dad's financial burdens. Joey paid off all of the notes and the back rent from the previous tenant, Tony Roma's Steakhouse, and offered to rebuild the restaurant from top to bottom in order to increase its value.

As Mah Jong grew, so did Long Island. Syosset was among the desirable towns just off the Long Island Expressway which connected New York City to all points east of the Island. Syosset had its own train station, making it a prime bedroom community within 30+ mile distance from Manhattan. Jericho Turnpike (also known as Route 25), the East-West corridor running through the width of Long Island, was increasingly congested as suburbs were built and more cars were purchased.

The State of New York widened Jericho Turnpike to add more lanes which resulted in damage to the Mah Jong property. Dad's lawyer John Tessier initiated a lawsuit against the State of New York. In late 1999, Mah Jong received a condemnation award from the Transportation Department of the State of New York. After legal fees, the net amount awarded to Mah Jong was just over $437,000, which Dad was advised to use to satisfy the outstanding mortgage; a prudent decision since it would extinguish a debt carrying a 9% interest rate.

But the decision to satisfy the mortgage came with a problem. The receipt of a condemnation award is taxable. All of the cash remaining after paying off the mortgage was earmarked for tax liability.

After paying off the tax obligations, this settlement released Dad of all of his other personal liabilities. At the age of 87, after 47 years running restaurants, he was finally debt-free.

On August 1, 2002, the property located at 140 Jericho Turnpike in Syosset, owned by Gardina Associates Inc., was sold and the corporation resolved to liquidate. At the same time, the House of Mah Jong Corporation, located at 150 Jericho Turnpike in Syosset, began its dissolution.

A small farewell party was arranged for January 2003 to say goodbye to Mah Jong. In a letter to Dad from Arthur Jong, Dad's schoolmate, roommate, and close friend since 1937, dated Dec 20, 2002:

> *Dear Peter,*
> *I am sorry that I cannot be there in Syosset with you this coming January. As you said, 'it's a sentimental thing." Yes, it is. In Mah Jong we have spent half of our business life together from the beginning to retiring. I had the vision as it was conceived that you would lead this business to a successful finish. I want to tell you I was proud to be your partner and share in the success of a business with you. I may add that you and I have come a long way since the day we met at NYU (New York University), perhaps with the longest friendship anyone can boast...."*

The House of Mah Jong officially closed in January, 2003.

CHAPTER 39

DAD DIES

After Mom passed away, Dad lived alone in our Palm Bay home. He had neighbors who checked on him but over time, it was evident that he needed to be closer to family. He kept multiple Crown Royal whiskey bags filled with his medication in each house and at Kathy's house. Sometimes the prescriptions in the Sun City West whiskey bag had expired, sometimes he had an inhaler in Florida but the holder was in the New Jersey whiskey bag. He liked to check himself in to hospitals when he wasn't feeling well because he looked forward to being waited on and having the hospital food. He thought the peach cobbler at Palm Bay Hospital was particularly excellent.

He was extremely hard of hearing by then and kept misplacing his hearing aids. His left hearing aid would be in Palm Bay, the right hearing aid in Sun City West; seldom were the two hearing aids in the same zip code.

The Palm Bay region is prone to hurricanes and during one ferocious storm, we called Dad to see how he was. He reported that he was fine; he had already taken down the bathroom door. When asked why he would do that, he said that in China whenever a major flood comes, it was common to gather the livestock, take down a door and use it as a raft to float to safety. He jokingly added, "Sometimes you take the wife." I had visions of police reports citing an old Chinese man floating on a door along I-95 headed towards Cuba.

Michael moved Dad to an assisted living facility near his home in Concord, California. Dad had his choice of rooms; either a larger room upstairs, or a smaller room near the dining room. As the restaurateur, he chose the one next to the dining room. He hung out and held court with the cooks and servers. He loved to tell stories and the staff were equally eager to hear them.

When Dad got tired of the daily menu offerings, he'd ask to be driven to Kentucky Fried Chicken. The staff weren't allowed to drive the residents without management's permission, but Dad found a way to charm and coax the younger staff members and he'd offer to buy them each a bucket of chicken wings in exchange for abetting his escape. Volunteers lined up to take him to pick up Chinese food or wherever he wanted to go.

On Sept 27, 2005, Dad had breakfast in the dining room and went back to his room where he fell asleep. He died peacefully and, just as he wished for all his Mah Jong customers, he left with a full stomach. He was two weeks shy of his 90th birthday. Michael called me at my office in Berkeley, California and I arrived at the facility before Dad was removed from the room. He looked as if he were taking a nap and I thought how blessed he was to have gone so gently into the next world.

To perk up Dad after Mom's passing, I arranged for this professional photo shoot of the Chinn siblings and my nephew Chris. (Photo: Patti James)

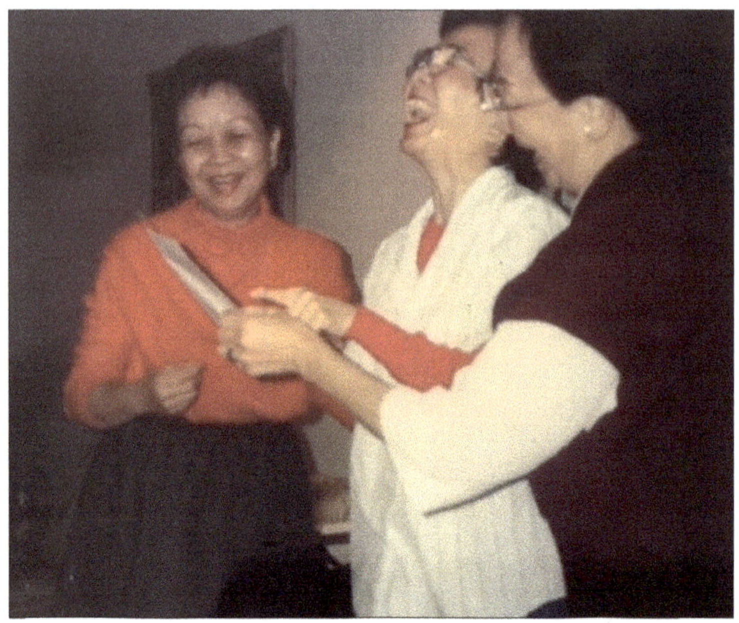

Daisy, Mom, and Mamie singing and laughing

Aunt Daisy, between me and my cousin Phyllis,
the last time we saw Daisy, 2019. (Author's collection)

– EPILOGUE –

Moving Into the Light

Kwoh

詩 Shih (Classics poem)

書 Shu (Books academics Classics)

繼 Chi (promulgates, continues)

世 Shih (Scholars ~~Scholars~~ Earth world, generation century)

鳳 Feng (sphinx colorful Rare, heavenly bird; good omen)

煥 ← Huan (color, fire brilliant flaming bright)

元 Yuan (Very beginning, original The first, head chief, eldest, principle)

(元子 = atom 元年, 元日, 元始 the first)

廣 Kwong (Huge, sprawling, edgeless)

田 Tien 田 (farm)

福 Foo (Blessings)

集 Chi (Accumulates compounds)

家 Chia (Family)

聲 Sheng (Voice Fame Resounding)

傳 Chuan (Spread) 傳

(Diagram drawn by Daisy and Mamie)

THIRTEEN GENERATIONS

The Kwoh family on my mother's side has a list for their generation names. These are similar to poems which describe the desired work and values for the future generations. The list of the names goes back 13 generations to the name of Kwong from the Ching Dynasty (1600s).

Reading down from the top right and continuing down from top left, my ancestors passed along these names and values linking the previous generation to the next one.

Kwong – huge/ edgeless

Tien - farm

Foo – blessings

Chi – compounding of accumulation

Chia – family

Sheng – resounding voices

Chuan – spread/expansion

Shih – classics/poetry

Shu – education, academics, books

Chi – continuation of the Shih and Shu values

Shih – scholars, expansion of knowledge of the world

Feng – colorful, rare, heavenly, sphinx, good omen. This is my maternal grandfather Frank's name, Kwoh Feng Shu.

Huan – fire, brilliance, bright. This is the name of the Kwoh siblings; my mother's Chinese name is Kwoh Huan Ying. Daisy's name is Kwoh Huan Hsing.

Yuan – signifies a reminder of "the very beginning," "origins" and the importance of the "principal, head, elders." This is the name for Jesse and Bonny, children of my Uncle Teddy (Huan Tsing). While none of my other cousins nor I with a last name other than Kwoh inherited this name, we have, nonetheless, embraced our elders throughout our lives.

The translation of my mother's family name Kwoh is "outer wall." It is also spelled "Guo" or "Quo." According to www.mychinaroots.com, "The Guos are believed to be descendants of the Zhou kings. Today, Guo is a multi-ethnic surname, which has been adopted by Muslim Hui, Mongolian, Manchu, and other ethnic groups throughout the centuries."

My elders. And their elders. The original sources of inspiration for this memoir and whose presences still grace my life. How blessed I am to have a family ethos engrained in my DNA that carries forth the importance of perpetual learning, education, family, and self-expression through the arts.

FULL CIRCLE

In 2011, I had the distinct honor of being asked by the Philadelphia Orchestra to serve as a consultant for their China Residency program to commemorate the 40th anniversary of President Nixon's historic 1972 visit to China.

In preparation for the 40th anniversary commemoration scheduled for 2012, the Orchestra signed an historic agreement with China's National Centre for the Performing Arts (NCPA) to develop an innovative partnership honoring the Orchestra's role as a premier cultural ambassador for the United States. This agreement was one of the many results that evolved from the U.S.–China Consultation on People-to-People Exchange, which served to enhance and strengthen ties between American and Chinese citizens in a variety of areas, including culture. Among the leaders of a Global Oversight Committee were Ambassador Nicholas Platt (who accompanied President Nixon during the 1972 trip) and philanthropist Mrs. Nelson "Happy" Rockefeller.

I traveled with a small Philadelphia Orchestra delegation to Beijing, Tianjin, Shenzhen, Shanghai, and Guangzhou (formerly Canton, Dad's birthplace) in 2011 to assist in laying the groundwork for the commemoration ceremonies and the Orchestra's 2013 Residency Program in which Philadelphia Orchestra musicians would travel to various Chinese cities to help develop the next generation of great classical music artists.

It was my first time visiting China. As I walked on the city streets where my family and ancestors once lived, I felt a monumental sense of pride that I was, in some small way, continuing their diplomacy work so central to building cultural, economic, business, political, and educational bridges between the United States, China, and the world throughout the centuries.

THERE AND BACK AGAIN

I had a most unusual childhood for which I am eternally grateful.

I continue to channel my father's values on customer service and hospitality in my role as CEO and on the boards of several arts organizations. I emulate my mother's tough yet compassionate approach when managing staff.

Whenever I'm at a blackjack table, I think of my time in Mah Jong's gambling den and how I learned to read body language and the rhythm of the cards. For better or worse, I can't shake the habit of auditing a restaurant operation while dining. Put me in front of a Hawaiian steel guitar or a slack key guitar player; I'm back "home" in the land of Polynesia.

I have accepted that as a rape survivor, full recovery isn't possible; too many sensory flash points continue to remind me of that summer of 1970. Trigger moments appear and still activate a feeling of dread and overwhelming anxiety. But as long as I live within the core values embodied in me by my ancestors, and center my attention on music, expression, culture, and the arts, I'll be just fine. One of the positive results of my trauma is the manifestation of an empathetic gravitational pull to mentor young girls and women; to provide affirmation, coaching, and encouragement, especially for those who find themselves estranged from hope. This is a guiding principle of my career and one of the greatest joys of my life.

MY UNFINISHED MEMOIR

"Leave a little bit on your plate." This bit of family etiquette demonstrates that we are satisfied but not starving. Daisy said scraping your plate clean is bad manners; it suggests to your host that they didn't feed you enough. It also means your meal is never quite finished and will be continued.

This is my unfinished memoir. As family and self-discoveries are revealed, additional courses are still to be created, prepared, savored, and shared. As I meander the roads of my learning journey, I'll keep a sharp eye and ear for the signs my mother promised to illuminate for the remainder of my life's path: "When you find a coincidence, that is me."

I will follow her light, standing steady in the comforting glow of her memory, nourished by the love she and my father left behind, and anticipate a bounty of insatiable adventures still to come.

Diablo Magazine feature article, "Women In Charge"

*"Debbie Chinn: Champion of the Art"
Cover article, Cypress Magazine,
Pebble Beach, California*

With film legend, Vincent Price who - along with his wife Coral Browne, kindly donated their services for a murder mystery fundraiser that I produced for American Conservatory Theater in San Francisco (Author's collection)

As Executive Director for Opera Parallèle, with three of our most prolific composers: Laura Kaminsky, Philip Glass, and Chris Pratorius Gómez .

With David Gordon, a central figure at the Carmel Bach Festival for 30 years

As Volunteer Council Director for the San Francisco Symphony: preparing for a speech at a docent training meeting.

As an announcer for Baltimore Center Stage's all-day radio marathon fundraiser

I was blessed to have a wonderful 7-year partnership with Artistic Director Jonathan Moscone at California Shakespeare Theatre (2001-2008). In 2019 we reunited at the Bruns Amphitheatre in Orinda, CA with former board member Sharon Simpson on the site where we had originally envisioned a capital campaign 15 years earlier.

Not all of my speaking engagements are serious. Speaking at a scotch-tasting event to support Carmel Bach Festival, aptly called Bach on the Rocks

One of my favorite photos of Maestro Paul Goodwin and me when we were running the Carmel Bach Festival. We're doing a photo shoot at the Monterey Museum of Art where Richard Burton and Elizabeth Taylor stayed while filming "The Sandpiper". It was a private home at the time and this is the tub that they used so... Here we are reenacting Dick and Liz, except fully clothed...and with no suds.

The 7 Kwoh siblings as family elders:
L-R, Front: Daisy, Mamie, Edie, Bertha
Back: Teddy, Mom, Grace

CODA

It is believed that **Mary Hartwell** died in 1920 at the age of 70.

Kate was relocated from New York City to Santa Ana, CA where she lived with Edie and Ang until she passed away peacefully in 1974 at the age of 84.

Dora passed away at her apartment in New York City in 2008 at the age of 85.

The other Kwoh siblings enjoyed a longer span of life than Mom and Bertha who never reached the age of 80.

Mamie, the eldest Kwoh sibling, passed away at the age of 88 on March 12, 2002.

Grace lived to be 90 years old and died on November 2, 2010 in her home in Irvine, CA.

Later that month on November 30th, **Teddy**, who had relocated to Carlsbad, CA to be closer to his son, Jesse, passed away due to complications of diabetes on November 30th. He was 92.

Yang-Hu Tong tended for Grace at their home in Irvine, CA. He passed away peacefully in 2014.

Daisy was relocated, by Edie, to a group home in 2020 just as the COVID-19 pandemic was underway. For the protection of her dignity, few details were shared by Edie and Roy with the rest of the family. During the Christmas holidays of 2021, Daisy spent three weeks back at her home in Irvine. Daisy knew she was home and was even able to play her beloved piano. However, due to staff shortages, Edie could not handle Daisy's care alone and it was agreed that Daisy would move back into the group home where she could get 24-hour care and coverage. Daisy entered hospice care soon after. On February 12, 2022, the day of her 97th birthday, Daisy transitioned into the next world to reunite at long last with Frank, Kate, her siblings, and other members of our family. As my mother's constant companion ever since they were young toddlers, I have no doubt that there is joy, laughter, and dancing in the heavens and that the eternal light of their souls are inextinguishable.

As of this writing, **Edie** is still alive and living in Southern California.

ACKNOWLEDGEMENTS AND DISCOVERIES

Top billing goes to my parents **Nellie Kwoh Chinn and Peter Chinn** who made so many sacrifices and worked tirelessly so their children could be granted extraordinary sets of privileges throughout our lives. I am grateful for the buffet of opportunities they bestowed upon me and for the abundance of experiences that could fill another volume of books. I loved hearing their voices as I encapsulated their stories. They are beloved by so many and even more so by me.

My thanks to those who helped me research the early days of our family's time on Long Island: **Tom Montalbano**, a Long Island historian whose books, *An Early History Of Woodbury, Long Island, NY* and *Syosset*, are published as part of the Images of America series. He read portions of my manuscript and offered excellent improvements to ensure accuracy of citations and facts mentioned.

I thank Huntington Town Historian **Robert Hughes** for his assistance in sending me old articles about Dad and King Wah Restaurant; Architectural Historian and Planner, **Kerri Culhane** for telling me about the life of King Wah's architect Poy Gum Lee and for fact-checking my manuscript drafts in which I mentioned Dad and Poy's partnership.

The earliest support I received was from **Priya Dewan Doty**, my cousin-in-law. When I confessed I was having doubts about where to begin my book-writing, she chimed in with messages of non-judgmental affirmation. Thank you for that precious first boost of encouragement.

I had the great fortune of collaborating with a new colleague who provided wise counsel as this book made its final step towards publication. Much appreciation to my literary lawyer, **Amy Cook**, whose background in culinary education also makes her a kindred spirit.

I am gobsmacked to have discovered that I have a distant cousin connected to me via Jesse Boardman Hartwell, Jr., my great grandmother's father. **Sharon Alford Swonger** is a direct descendent of the Hartwell family line. We have gotten to know each other through the writing of this book and I thank her for sharing information about our mutual Hartwell family members and for fact-checking my excerpts regarding Jesse Boardman Hartwell, Jr.

A wonderful bonus of my research was the chance to reunite with Mah Jong alumni to capture their still-vivid memories which comprise the heart of this book. Musicians **Johnny Rubino** and **Frank Scafuri** provided helpful context on Mah Jong's latter years. Fond aloha to Mah Jong dancers **Olina Brill**, **Mapela Wong**, **Betty Kawamura (Kehau)**, and **Donna Brent Mutryn**, for sharing their stories and for reminding me how lucky we were to have lived in a golden era of dining and nightclub entertainment. The Mah Jong dancers deeply infused my childhood with the music and visual beauty of Polynesia and because of them, my spiritual home is forever enshrined there.

Mahalo to **Pauline De Silva (Pua)** and to **Kat Davis** who sent me precious old photos and articles of Mah Jong from their family archives. Pua and our family's friendship extended long after Mah Jong closed and we are still ohana today.

Thank you to **David Ronis** for his stories from our elementary school days and our shared love of music which grew into a career in the arts for both of us.

All of Mom's beloved cashiers and hostesses, among them **Anna Tumpek Rickert**, **Stacey Krinsky**, **Deb Colton**, and **Lynn Kologi-Youngs** left an indelible impact on Mah Jong. Mom continued to reminisce about them throughout her life, remembering how mature they were beyond their years and how they taught her about Hungarian, Jewish, and American culture. They were Mom's daughters in every sense of the word and I think Mom would be happy to know their memories have been included and that they still remember how tough she was with all of them. Heartfelt appreciation to you all.

I am grateful to **Robert Oxnam** for a rich conversation as he so kindly complimented my Aunt Daisy's contributions as a teacher at Yale University, as his thought partner at the Asia Society, and of my family's historic role in bridging the United States and China via humanitarian and cultural heritage efforts.

I don't read nor write Chinese. Di-Di's wife, **Gloria Meng**, was my lifeline to deciphering Chinese characters from old family correspondence, making sure I used the correct interpretations. Xièxiè!

I invited my cousins **May Tong** and **Phyllis Wang Wise** to share stories of their upbringing and what it was like to grow up as daughters in a family known for our strong matriarchs. Of equal measure, their fathers were influential pioneers. I idolized them growing up and they continue to be a source of inspiration to me today. I thank them for the generosity of their stories.

My sister, **Kathy Chinn Slazak**. What would I do without her? She's been looking out for me ever since I was born. She is a perpetual champion of all my endeavors. Kathy has chronicled major episodes of our family history and her help in putting this book together has been invaluable. I am incomplete without her and thankful for our sibling partnership in life.

I thank my trusted friend, **Marilyn Langbehn**, who reviewed early drafts of my manuscript even though I warned her they were a "hot mess." Undaunted, she scoured through my writing with a big red pen, a fine-tooth comb, and a gentle heart. Thank you for cleaning up after me.

I am indebted to my editor, **Ginna Gordon** and book designer/researcher, **David Gordon**, of Lucky Valley Press, for their loving friendship and guidance. Ginna gently escorted me through the difficult moments of writing about and re-living the memories of the sudden end of my childhood. Her encouragement was a balm. We learned (thank you, Mom, for pointing out another coincidence) that not only did Ginna and my parents live in Akron, Ohio at the same time, Ginna and Mom attended the same church. They didn't know each other. How delightful to know that Mom and Ginna were bonded via Saint Bernard's Church in Akron, Ohio in the 1950s.

One of the many gifts from my partnership with Lucky Valley Press was David's unearthing a surprise fact. Mah Jong singer Leia Kirk was not who she said she was. Leia Kirk was only one of her aliases: others were Leia Blue, Leia B. Carr, Leia Ervin, and Leia Kirk Ervin. It turns out that Leia was not of Hawaiian royalty at all, nor was she born in Hawaii. Her real name was Bertha Irene Blue and she was from Ontario, Canada. She was of English and Irish descent with not a trace of Hawaiian blood in her.

My Hawaiian Ethel Merman was actually Canadian.

My most fervent gratitude goes to **Daisy Kwoh**, my teacher, aunt, and treasured friend, for the learning adventure and discovery of a lifetime. We traversed back in time to honor our family legacy and bring the spirit of our elders forward to memorialize in *Dancing in Their Light*. I am grateful that providence placed us on the same course during this lifetime.

CHAPTER NOTES

PROLOGUE

a. b. Linlin Victoria Lu, China Research Center, *Protestant Christianity in the People's Republic*, January 2016, Vol 15, No 1 https://www.chinacenter.net/author/linlin-victoria-lu/

CHAPTER 1

1. Sharon Alford Swonger
2. U.S. Federal Census Mortality Schedules, 1850-1885
3. Ibid
4. Benjamin Dodman, "The Siege of Tsingtao: How Germany surrendered an empire – and a beer." http://www.france24.com

   Holborn, Hajo. A History of Modern Germany. United Kingdom: Princeton University Press, 1982.

CHAPTER 2

5. Author Iris Chang's book, *The Rape of Nanking: The Forgotten Holocaust of WWII*, chronicles the Japanese atrocities towards Chinese civilians in graphic and horrifying detail.
6. Bernstein, Richard, *China 1945*. Knopf, 2014. Page 62

CHAPTER 3

7. August 10, 2015 https://www.chinafile.com/library/excerpts/what-happened-settlers-japanese-army-abandoned-china
8. Fu Jen Catholic University is a top private university in New Taipei, Taiwan. At the request of Pope Pius XI, it was founded in Beijing as Fu Jen Academy in 1925 by the Benedictines of St. Vincent Archabbey of Latrobe, Pennsylvania. At the request of Pope John XXIII the university was re-established in Taiwan in 1959. "Fu Jen" means benevolence or assistance. The origin of the name is in the *Analects*, the celebrated Chinese classic by Confucius, who wrote, "*I wen hui yu, I yu fu jen*" (A gentleman who makes friends through literature ennobles benevolence). Fu Jen is the oldest Catholic and Jesuit-affiliated university in the Chinese-speaking world. It has been ranked as top 100 in Asia and top 500 in arts and humanities worldwide, and its transnational master's program was ranked 43rd globally by *The Financial Times* in 2017. In China, Fu Jen is the 5th best ranked business school, among the top 8 best colleges in

alumni employment, and the second largest university in the number of students. Sources: www.fiuc.org and www.fju.edu.tw

CHAPTER 4

9. Iris Chang, *The Chinese in America: A Narrative History*. Viking Press, 2003
10. Irene Hsu, *The New Republic:* "The Echoes of Chinese Exclusion" June 28, 2018
11. www.history.com, "Pullman Porters" February 15, 2019, *C.M .Bell Studio Collection/Library of Congress*
12. *The Buffalo News*, Steve Cichon, "Torn-Down Tuesday: In 1940s Chinese of Buffalo Gather at 507 Michigan," July 19, 2018
13. Goodyear Tire and Rubber Company, founded in 1868, manufactured the first set of tires for Henry Ford's Model-T automobile in 1907. By the 1940s Goodyear had expanded into heavy duty aircraft and fighter plane production to support the war efforts.
14. *The Wingfoot Clan,* employee newsletter of The Goodyear Tire & Rubber Company. May 24, 1944, page 3.

CHAPTER 5

15. *Encyclopedia Britannica*, "Chinese-Civil-War" https://www.britannica.com/event/

CHAPTER 6

16. The first American sanatorium for pulmonary tuberculosis, where patients could recuperate in isolation and receive the prescribed treatment of bed rest and fresh air, was established in 1875 by a Bavarian, Joseph Gleitsmann, in Ashville, North Carolina. In 1904, 115 facilities with about 8,000 beds were in operation. By 1923, the number had grown to 656 with more than 66,000 beds. In 1953, 839 institutions with over 136,000 beds were fully functioning.

CHAPTER 8

17. https://www.tc.columbia.edu/newsroom/publications/tc-today/2009/volume-34-no-1/articles/a-legacy-of-firsts/
18. https://www.nursing.columbia.edu/about-us/our-culture/history-timeline
19. *The Electric Washing Machine is Invented* https://greenerpasture.com/Places/ShowNews/32206
    The History of the Sewing Machine https://www.thoughtco.com/stitches-the-history-of-sewing-machines-1992460.

Stoves Through the Ages http://www.homeinspirations.co.za/index.php/kitchen/18606-stoves-through-the-ages

20. Now known as the American Association of Family and Consumer Sciences
21. http://www.chinafound.org.tw/ec99/eshop1387/e_profile.asp
22. Paul Chih Meng served as Director of China Institute for 37 years until retiring in 1967
23. Paul Chih-Meng (the author's Uncle Paul Meng), *A Sixty Year Search.* China Institute in America, 1981. Page 40.
24. ibid, pages 192–193.
25. In 1939, Marian Anderson, at the peak of her career, was denied the opportunity to sing at Constitution Hall, Washington D.C.'s largest classical performing arts venue. The hall was owned by the Daughters of the American Revolution (DAR) and they did not permit African-Americans to perform or attend concerts in the Hall. First Lady Eleanor Roosevelt was among many DAR members who immediately resigned from the organization over the issue. https://www.nps.gov/articles/000/marian-anderson-and-constitution-hall.htm
26. In his book, *A Sixty Year Search*, Paul Chih-Meng argued that Pearl Buck's best-seller *The Good Earth* should be regarded as fiction, not history since its depictions of China-complete with scenes of civil war, famine, and opium addiction validated Japan's argument that China was disintegrating. According to Paul Chih-Meng, a number of people felt that Pearl Buck did China a great disservice with her book.
27. Library of Congress *Catalog of Copyright Entries*, 3rd Series, 1952, p. 119:

    Feng young flower drum song
    A Chinese folk song with English translation by Paul Chih-Meng
    with accompaniment by Huan-Shou Meng.
    Purple Bamboo
    A lullaby song with an English version by Paul Chih-Meng
    and accompaniment by Huan-Shou Meng.
    Wong Ching Long
    Traditional, arrangement for voice and piano by Huan-Shou Meng.

28. www.sigmaxi.org, The Greek letters Sigma and Xi form the organization's motto: *Spoudon Xynones*, which translates as "Companions in Zealous Research"

29. Columbia University Libraries Archival Collection, *American Bureau for Medical Aid to China Records, 1937-2005*

30. Interview with Phyllis M. Wise, *The News Gazette*, "New Chancellor Took Her Own Path," Paul Wood, October 16, 2011.

31. Mamie Wang, R.N. M.A., *A Health Maintenance Service for Critically Ill Patients*, 1969.
Mamie Wang, R.N. M.A. *Assessment of a Cardiovascular Symptom of an Employee Through History Taking*, 1977.
Wang, Mamie Kwoh. "A Textbook for Free China" *The American Journal of Nursing*, vol. 54, no. 10, 1954, pp. 1216–1216. JSTOR, www.jstor.org/stable/3460832

32. "Shih-Chun Wang, Leading Specialist On Brain, Dies at 83" *New York Times*, June 8, 1993.

33. "Teahouse by the Pool," *The Architectural Forum*, May 1970, p 51-52

34. *Emily Hahn: The American Writer Who Shocked '30s Shanghai,* Ned Kelly, January 28, 2020. https://www.thatsmags.com/china/post/28822/emily-hahn-the-american-writer-who-shocked-30s-shanghai

35. Mark McWilliams, *Food and Communication Proceedings of the Oxford Symposium on Food 2015*, Prospect Books, July 7, 2016

36. United States Patent Office, July 29, 1969, Patent Number 3457852, inventor Emily T. Y. Kwoh

37. Defense Language Institute Foreign Language Center, *History of the Presidio of Monterey, Army Language School.* https://www.dliflc.edu/about/command-history/online-exhibit-history-of-the-presidio-of-monterey/

38. ABC-TV News interview with Robert B. Oxnam, "A Fractured Mind", October 13, 2005

CHAPTER 9

39. *The People History*. (n.d.). Retrieved from www.thepeoplehistory.com

40. Robert C. Hughes, "Cuisine from Around the World".
January 19, 2013. https://huntingtonhistory.com/2013/01/19/cuisine-from-around-the-world/

41. Kerri Culhane, Main Curator "Chinese Style: Rediscovering the Architecture of Poy Gum Lee, 1903-1968," Essay accompanying the exhibit at the Museum of Chinese in America, 2015.

42. *The Long Islander*, August 1, 1957, "Former Marine Captain Who Probed Secrets of Jap Ammo Supplies Now Busy with Recipes for Patrons"

CHAPTER 10

41. Arthur Jong's brother, Allan, would soon marry novelist Erica Jong in 1966. Erica's novel, *Fear of Flying* has since sold 20 million copies worldwide.
42. During WWII, Grumman Corporation was among the top companies specializing in wartime military aircraft production. After the War, they were the chief contractor for the Apollo Lunar Module that would eventually send Neil Armstrong, Buzz Aldrin, and Michael Collins to the moon as part of the Apollo 11 space mission in 1969. The Grumman plant in Syosset was where one part of the Lunar Module was assembled. (Kennedy, 1984)
43. Mah Jong had a rotary dial phone as did most offices/homes. Telephone numbers began with two letters or an "exchange"; the exchange for Syosset was Walnut, or WA for short. To convey Mah Jong's phone number: "Walnut One, oh five hundred"
44. Eventually in the 1980s, Dr. Chin established a very successful restaurant in Queens, which our family frequented.

CHAPTER 11

45. http://historiccensus.longislandindexmaps.org/
46. https://projects.newsday.com/long-island/segregation-real-estate-history/

CHAPTER 13

47. http://lostnewyorkcity.blogspot.com/2009/07/remembering-steak-row.html
48. Belmont Stakes, one of the three Triple Crown events in horse racing (the others are the Kentucky Derby and the Baltimore Preakness) is also the oldest; its first race was in 1867. In 1973, Secretariat made history by not only winning the Belmont Stakes but by finishing by 31 lengths, setting the record for the fastest race on dirt. He won the 1½ mile race in just 2 minutes and 24 seconds.
49. The NY Mets were the first and fastest expansion team to win a division title, the pennant, and the World Series in one year. The record was later broken in 1997 by the Florida Marlins.

CHAPTER 15

50. Limestone lettuce was developed by John Bibb 1865 and is a special variety of butter lettuce grown in Kentucky's alkaline rich, red earthen clay soil where limestone is inherently found. As the variety was grown, the

local townspeople began favoring it for its sweet flavor. In the 1920s the lettuce received national recognition by word of mouth and reached peak popularity around the 1960s. Though its namesake is due to the soil of the Kentucky region, Limestone lettuce has been adopted outside of Kentucky in similar soil types in temperate regions within North America. Today Limestone lettuce can be found in home gardens, local farmers markets, and specialty grocers in North America. (www.specialtyproduce.com, 1996-2009)

CHAPTER 16

51. Michael's firm was responsible for numerous design and architectural projects on Long Island. In 1985, *Newsday Magazine* cited Michael as "the man who is changing the face of Long Island." Today, Spector Group is run by Michael's son Scott and their projects are represented world-wide. Included in their commemorative publication of Spector Group's prestigious design projects over the past 55 years is Michael's artist rendering of Mah Jong Restaurant.

CHAPTER 18

52. The word "Oriental" was not considered offensive during this period.
53. This is a collection of basic sheet music with chords, melody, and lyrics without arrangements/notations. Musicians would use these to "fake" their own styles and techniques.
54. In 1933, Harry Owens became the Music Director of the Royal Hawaiian Hotel Orchestra in Waikiki. Among his compositions were *Sweet Leilani* which he wrote for his newborn daughter, and *To You Sweetheart, Aloha.*
55. In speaking with Mapela in 2019—for the first time in 50 years—the first thing she said: "*I still have the dining set and rugs! That was the best deal ever!*"

CHAPTER 19

56. Homeofpoi.com, *History of Maori Poi in New Zealand*, April 30, 2013

CHAPTER 20

57. https://www.jewishvirtuallibrary.org/kaifeng
58. https://chinesejews.com/kaifeng-jews
59. Dan Dietz, *The Complete Book of 1960s Broadway Musicals.* Rowman & Littlefield, 2014. Page 423

CHAPTER 21

60. Written in 1860 by Prince Leleiohoku as a love song and modified in

English by composer Johnny Noble who, in 1935, was the first Hawaiian composer inducted into the American Society of Composers, Authors, and Publishers (ASCAP).

61. Tinikling is the traditional Philippine folk dance which was featured as part of the show's "Polynesian Tour Around the World"

CHAPTER 24

62. Andrzej Miotk, *The historical significance of Thomas Tien Keng-hsin SVD – the first Cardinal of China*, NURT SVD 1 (2018) s. 167-187

63. National Catholic Register, *Taiwan's Catholic Church: Quest for National Identity*, December 19, 2017

64. *See* Chapter 3, Note 8.

65. https://www.longislandpress.com/2018/06/25/elizabeth-taylor-and-richard-burton-long-islands-romance-of-the-century/

CHAPTER 25

66. Cheongsam is translated in Cantonese as "long dress," worn by girls and women. The boy/male version of this attire is called a changshun, which is translated as "long robe."

67. https://ztevetevans.wordpress.com/2016/11/16/chinese-mythology-the-eight-immortals/

68. The beginning of the Chinese ribbon dance is believed to have originated during the Han Dynasty (206 BCE) and honors the unsuccessful assassination attempt on a Han Emperor by someone who blocked the sword with a piece of silk from his sleeve. https://ourpastimes.com/the-history-of-the-chinese-ribbon-dance-12302901.html

CHAPTER 28

69. November 21, 1978. ©*The New York Times*

CHAPTER 35

70. June 27, 2020 email from Johnny Rubino.

ABOUT THE AUTHOR

The proud daughter of immigrants, Debbie Chinn is first-generation Chinese, born and raised on Long Island, New York. While other children participated in sleep-overs, summer camps, and sports activities, Debbie's childhood was spent at The House of Mah Jong, her family's Chinese restaurant where she entered the workforce at the age of three. Her first job was selling cigarettes.

By the age of six, her responsibilities expanded and she spent time on a bar stool inserting umbrellas into cherries and pineapple slices for an assortment of exotic drinks.

As the family business grew in popularity and fame, she was thrust into the land of the South Seas when Mah Jong evolved into a Polynesian nightclub; ubiquitous dining experiences during the 1960s and 1970s. She became an exotic hula and sword dancer performing weekly at nights when not a middle and high school student during the day.

In their quest to assimilate in the United States, her parents abided by the values of strong work ethics, fanatical hospitality, relationship-building, supporting organizations doing good work in our communities, and always taking care of others.

It was a family ethos that is known today as philanthropy.

It is no wonder that Debbie eventually established a distinguished 30-year career as an arts activist, a non-profit consultant, and CEO—leading some of the country's most renowned cultural institutions and their programs—a career inspired by her Mah Jong upbringing. She began championing diversity, equity, and inclusion—a business philosophy instilled in her by her parents—long before it had a DEI acronym.

Debbie is a fervent life-long learner with an insatiable appetite to make sense of these convoluted times by forging bridges via the arts, humanities, and cultural heritage. In this, she carries forth the legacy of her ancestors and elders who contributed to this world's economic growth and reputation in the fields of science, engineering, medicine, aerospace, cultural diplomacy, academia, and culinary hospitality.

She has many passions—too many to mention here, but wine tasting/collecting is high on that list.

Debbie currently serves on a variety of non-profit boards providing advice on governance, finance, fundraising, marketing, strategic planning, artistiic programming, and board/staff relations.

She lives in Northern California with her two cats, Kona and Leilani, surrounded by her collection of 100+ bottles of wine.

WWW.DEBBIECHINN.COM

Photo: Ben Krantz Studios

INDEX

www.ingramcontent.com/pod-product-compliance
Lightning Source LLC
LaVergne TN
LVHW021126160826
845679LV00015B/1665

* 9 7 8 0 5 7 8 3 5 5 9 9 3 *